Lacee,
Look forward [...]
Choose to make a diff[...]
our world. Thanks in advance!
Best, Bob

Lacee,
Look fwd to keeping in
close touch — keep up the
awesome work! Abgs, Hm K[...]

Nov 2018

COUNTERING HATE

How bias, hate and extremism form...
and how we can stop it, together.

BOB PEARSON & HAROON K. ULLAH
with Dan Zehr

BOB PEARSON

PreCommerce

Storytizing

HAROON K. ULLAH

Vying for Allah's Vote

The Bargain from the Bazaar

Digital World War

COUNTERING HATE

Bob Pearson and Haroon K. Ullah

ISBN: 978-0-9996623-0-4

Cover by Paulo Simas
Layout by Monica Thomas for TLC Book Design, *TLCBookDesign.com*

Printed in the United States of America.

To my great uncle, Alexander Didur, thank you for your service to our country and the inspiration you have provided to battle the same hate and extremism that led to your capture and death as a POW in the Korean War.

To my younger brother Muneer (1980–2015) who taught me how to love and learn. To my parents, Dr. Kalimullah and Zarfshan who planted a seed for learning and inspired me to always reach for the stars. And to my wife, Dr. Naba Sharif, who knows me so well, allows my creativity to flourish and is a true life partner. She is always looking for ways to provide support and intellectual encouragement —and always throws me the best surprises!

TABLE OF CONTENTS

INTRODUCTION

"Human greatness does not lie in wealth or power, but in character and goodness. People are just people, and all people have faults and shortcomings, but all of us are born with a basic goodness."
— ANNE FRANK

W e all start out the same. Whether born in Damascus or Detroit, human beings begin life with similar DNA, common instincts for survival and a basic desire to learn and explore.

Inside our bodies, where we don't think about skin color or gender or religion, we are remarkably similar. The same four chemical bases comprise everyone's DNA — adenine, guanine, cytosine and thymine — and they combine to form about 3 billion base pairs, of which an estimated 99 percent are similar in everyone across the world. Even our brains are similar. Everyone's prefrontal cortex, which plays a major role in how we think, act and plan, has a consistent molecular structure. We know some people will be exposed to more diseases due to genetic mutation, and we will battle the myriad disorders that cause our brains and bodies to form differently, but Day One is generally a pretty good day for humanity.

In fact, about 300,000 new people join us every 24 hours. They become one addition to the 7.5 billion of us who already live here, work here and navigate the communities in which we live. Most of us choose to pursue a reasonably fulfilling life, rewarding to us and most of those around us. But a small cohort goes in a different direction; they become filled with hate, even to the point of selfishly single-minded extremism. We don't pretend to know how many young men and women have gone down this path, nor how many will take that journey in the future — but we do know we want to do what we can to decrease that number.

We all can agree we have too much bias, hate and extremism in our world. We have too many people who seek to disrupt our view of normal and force us to pay attention to their world view. They change lives. They far too often end lives. And they never stop trying to find the next young recruit to help them do the same thing again tomorrow.

We, as a team, need to get more focused on Countering Hate.

Focusing on a cause like this, and writing a book about it, becomes a deeply personal pursuit. Bob grew up hearing his mom tell stories about her favorite uncle, Alexander Didur, who fought in the Korean War. A captain in the First Cavalry, 8th Division, he was captured and detained as a prisoner of war for three years before he died. Didur was 35 years old when he passed away on August 31, 1951; he has rested in Arlington Cemetery since. In December 1996, Bob was in Paris and ran point for his company's communications team when a tragic terrorism attack killed the wife of a colleague on the Paris Metro. A few years later, on September 11, 2001, Bob was working in New York City and became part of a larger group of friends who grieved the loss of childhood buddies like Tommy Clark and Richard Madden from Millburn, N.J. Both were the younger brothers of Bob's good friends. Those types of violent deaths never leave you, and the list of them is far longer than we ever would care to count.

| ▌ ▌ ▌ |

About ten years ago, two smart and forward-thinking executives, Ed Tazzia and Kip Knight, suggested a new program to U.S. State Department officials. The new program, called The Marketing College, would add to the knowledge of State Department officials in public affairs around the world. Each class would include up to 50 leaders from locations as diverse as Libya, Kazakhstan, Brazil or Belgium. They'd learn about how to create a story, share it and analyze it to understand why it succeeded or failed in shaping behavior. Bob joined Ed, Kip and the larger faculty as a volunteer several years ago, helping to expand the curriculum. Meanwhile, Haroon participated in The Marketing College as an official at the State Department, where he prepared U.S. thinking on counter terrorism initiatives around the world. Haroon has served as the global planning leader for Secretary of State John Kerry, current Secretary Rex Tillerson and now as Chief Strategy Officer for the Broadcasting Board of Governors in support of CEO John F. Lansing.

Through our combined interactions with colleagues at the State Department and the private sector, we recognized a critical urgency for people and organizations to share the best thinking about how we can counter hate. Otherwise, we realized, our efforts will never move fast enough. In our current form, we can't analyze data, coordinate research expertise and disseminate best practices to all private-sector companies, government officials, NGOs and global citizens battling extremism around the world. We realized that it was time to write a book together, but not just any book. We decided to co-author it so we could do a mash-up of our combined expertise — years of countering terrorism with years of shaping behavior for the world's top brands. Our goal is to think different and to inspire you to join us in countering hate in your own way.

| ▌ ▉ ▌ |

The math works in our favor. This planet is home to about 7.5 billion people, and more than 7.4 billion of them believe in doing the right thing. We can change our world if we choose to do it together. The problem is we often don't move much further than our personal rhetoric and the boundaries of our own couches. We complain about extremists, we might even protest now and then against hate, but we usually don't think about how we can directly contribute to generational change. Instead, we all too often contribute to bias and hate through our silence or in ways that escape us.

Change requires an open mind and a desire to learn what true transformation entails. Unfortunately, we tend to do a pretty good job of polarizing our communities and pitting ourselves against one another. If we were extremists, we'd be thrilled with this behavior. We need to step back and realize how much this activity distracts us, and refocus on the ways we can make a difference in people's lives.

| ▌ ▉ ▌ |

As we set out to write this book, we focused on soft power. Global leaders often seek to quell disturbances with hard power. When it's the only effective choice, it's the choice one needs to make. This is where our military teams come in. We have deep respect for the military, but few of the people reading this book can impact military decisions. We can, however, build soft power that makes a difference. If we work together, we can slow violence over time. It's not as crazy a thought as you may think.

We wrote this book as a wakeup call to the possibilities ahead of us — part call to action and part innovation lab for those who want to counter hate. In each chapter, we set out to share a new way of thinking about a model that you might already know from the past. We want to flip models on their head and ask, "What if we looked at the problem differently? What could we do that would actually change things long term?" To develop answers that can reduce the high-octane extremist machine in our world, we need to think together. We hope this book serves as an accelerator for our growth as a team. But that only goes so far. We realized we also need to provide some potential solutions, or at least pathways we all can follow together to reach effective solutions. Toward the end of the book, we share ideas on how to counter hate.

But we take this one step further, a step that we hope will take you beyond the cover of this book itself. We have created the world's first bias, hate and extremism dataset community on data.world, an open-source organization that's becoming the premier search engine for publicly available data. We will ask every NGO or related party to share their datasets on bias, hate and extremism in data.world, creating a special section dedicated to countering hate. Each participant can benefit from the other's contributions, conversations can occur within the community, data scientists can analyze patterns more quickly, developers can create new algorithms and software, and teams of aligned parties can launch efforts to help us gain a clearer understanding of what is happening in our world and how we can more effectively combat the spread of extremism.

But we also realized we need a place to share next practices with each other, so we can more quickly learn from what works and what fails. We need to think like a technology incubator that cares only about creating ideas that will work. To do this, we have developed a website that features the book, connects with key partners and shares a trove of research supportive of each chapter. We also posted key chapters from *PreCommerce* and *Storytizing*, Bob's previous books on communication and marketing techniques for our digital world. But most importantly, we plan to make it a fertile seed bed for specific insights on how to counter hate — so you and the rest of our countering hate alliance will be able to submit content, share ideas and help further the education of your peers at www.counteringhate.com or in our Facebook Group.

We want the group fighting gang extremism in Chicago to learn from a team in Brussels that prevents youth from entering *religious extremism*. And who knows, maybe that team in Brussels learned how to build a successful media campaign from a few colleagues in Tunisia. We're all in it together, and we want everyone to join.

From there, we'll all innovate together, preparing ourselves to take the lead and gather those who can help us make a difference, one step at a time. Please join us and learn together. We'll do our best to provide some initial insights throughout this book, but we'll also be counting on you to teach us and the rest of our global community as well.

Let's get moving. We don't have time to waste.

BOB PEARSON | HAROON K. ULLAH

March 15, 2018

CHAPTER 1

THE EMERGENCE OF HATE

*"Disruption is a process, not an event, and innovations
can only be disruptive relative to something else."*
—CLAYTON M. CHRISTENSEN, author of "The Innovator's Dilemma"

S alman Taseer had just finished lunch with a friend in the Kohsar market district of Islamabad when a member of his own security team stepped forward and fired a machine gun at him from 10 feet away. Taseer, the governor of Punjab, Pakistan's most populous province, took at least 26 bullets and died on the spot. After he fell, his assassin, a young ex-military man named Malik Mumtaz Hussain Qadri, set down the gun, raised his hands and asked his colleagues to arrest him. The others in Taseer's security force obliged; none had fired a single shot in defense of the man they were hired to protect.

At the time, back in January 2011, Kohsar was a safe, middle-class neighborhood filled with cafes and stores, a popular destination in Pakistan's capital city for locals and expatriates alike. But a change had come over the country in the years leading to Taseer's death. Tragic assassinations and suicide bombings made more local headlines. The Pakistani government's long-held dominance waned as more residents drifted toward hardline views. And in the country's emerging political atmosphere, the motives behind Taseer's murder seemed all too common. A prominent politician, a supporter of Pakistan's democratization campaign, and a trusted adviser to Benazir Bhutto during her two terms as prime minister, Taseer never shied away from stating his beliefs that democracy and pluralism are inseparable and that all religious minorities should be allowed to vote in general elections — opinions antithetical to the positions of hardline Islamic fundamentalists. In more recent months, Taseer outraged his detractors by criticizing Pakistan's strict new blasphemy laws, calling them unjust and indefensible and arguing minorities should not supplant the laws of the state.

Taseer was no stranger to the fact that his beliefs and views put him in danger, most notably from Al-Qaeda and the Taliban. He received numerous death threats over the years, even served time in prison. At the time of his death, extremists held his son hostage in a Pakistani camp. Yet, he remained defiant, and publicly so. Just hours before his assassination, Taseer tweeted a line from Shakeel Badayuni, the Indian Urdu poet, that translated said: "My resolve is so strong that I do not fear the flames from without. I fear only the radiance of the flowers, that it might burn my garden down."

The same social networks Taseer favored already had altered the political terrain in fundamental ways. Non-state actors used them to launch new offensives on the government, deploying a different set of ammunition, insurgency and tactics — a digital war on a digital battlefield. Long before his gruesome murder, and perhaps in ways he never recognized, Taseer became enmeshed in an online battle across various social media platforms, his avatar targeted with cyber weapons. Foes took short audio clips of his speeches out of context, cutting and packaging them for shares by key extremist influencers on Facebook and Twitter. Websites and blogs dedicated themselves to smearing him and others who the authors deemed to have "crossed the line." Geolocation software tracked his movements in real time. Some non-state entities employed bots to retweet inflammatory content against him. And, in a few cases, TV networks carried some of the coverage and reported it online as "breaking news."

The digital war for hearts and minds didn't end with Taseer's death, either. As shocking as the assassination was, the aftermath might have exceeded it. When Qadri, a member of the moderate Sufi organization Ahl-Sunnah Wa Jamaat, entered a courtroom days after gunning down Taseer, huge crowds cheered him and showered him with flowers.

Fanboys hailed Qadri as a hero on websites and blogs, helping push him to the top of the Twitter trend rankings in the region. In the following weeks, Islamic confessional parties used social media to mobilize marches of up to 40,000 people, honoring Qadri's "heroic" action and celebrating Taseer's death. Even more disconcerting, moderate political leaders remained silent, issuing bland statements acknowledging Taseer's passing and choosing not to speak out against the mass rallies in support of vigilante Islamism, lest their comments go viral and their families face the threats of the extremist mass. Indeed, the provincial court judge who found Qadri guilty of murder was forced to flee the country after his home address was posted online, and extremist groups successfully pressured the government to suspend the case against Qadri indefinitely.

Finally, after years of delays, a Pakistani court convicted Mumtaz Qadri of murder. He was hanged in February 2016, but he remains a hero and martyr to many. The tepid response of moderates and Taseer supporters could not stem the tide of extremist sentiment that washed across Pakistani social networks. Multiple videos of the speech that reportedly spurred Qadri to action remain on YouTube, collectively garnering hundreds of thousands of views as of October 2017.

The extremists already had gathered here, in the digital world, long before Qadri struck Taseer in that well-to-do Islamabad neighborhood. They stoked the fires, plotted their actions, and gathered their followers. They had already planned for a virtual beheading.

They're still there today, celebrating their successes.

HATE IS A PROCESS

The bad news keeps coming. The fall of the World Trade Center buildings in New York City. Concert goers gunned down in Paris. A suicide bombing at a religious shrine in India. A gunman raining bullets on a country music festival in Las Vegas. We too often see the results of extreme hate in action. We live in a world filled with hate and bias. And while we, as a society, put on a strong show of outrage when confronted by it, we do a poor job of understanding how to identify and ameliorate hate before it reaches a violent conclusion.

As a result, we've spent years pondering the battle against extremism and violence, engaging it anew with every post-9/11 anthrax letter and each attack in London, Tel Aviv, Mumbai and beyond. Anger feels good as a first reaction; it might even provide a little comfort in the short-term. But we know full well it does little to offset the slow-burn of hate that coalesces over the long span of months and years. So we're left with plenty of questions and not nearly enough answers. Why does this continue to occur? Who would feel so aggrieved that they would send a lethal white powder in an envelope or pack a box with nails and explosives? Who would decide to hate another group of people they never met, simply because they pray to a god of a different name? Who would knowingly recruit people to a cause with the hope that they would kill another human being?

After years of asking ourselves these same questions, we finally awakened to an incontrovertible reality: These questions, on their own, were far too shallow and vague to generate any truly useful answers. We needed a new way of thinking about hate and how to counter it. We needed a new model — in fact, a collection of models — that could help us find the roots of how hate develops and intervene before it bears its horrific fruit. So, we scoured our years of experience in international affairs, data analysis and crisis management. We pulled what we learned from leading diplomats, NGOs and experts who've grappled with the complex dynamics of hate and bias — from ISIS to Russian disinformation campaigns, from Sarajevo to Bamako. For many of these individual analysts and diplomats, the challenge felt unique and overwhelming. But emerging work in algorithmic analysis and data science, including W2O's research in more than 20 languages worldwide, reveals far more commonality and similarity than any single perspective can show. The sophisticated models that analyze how we act online, what we search for to educate ourselves, or how we consume various forms of content all point to the fact that humans, across the globe, are far more similar and predictable than we like to believe.

For us, it suddenly became all to obvious: Hate does not form randomly. It builds through an accumulation of grievances, issues and life experiences. *It's a process — one we all brush up against at some point in our lives. It can be identified. It can be understood. It can be disrupted.*

REACHING EVERYONE AT AN INDIVIDUAL LEVEL

Marketers love to segment groups of people. Whether isolating Baby Boomers from Gen X and Millennials, or zeroing in on a more precise target demographic, they relentlessly seek the largest audience of interest in their brand or message. Of course, most of them try to develop new, more effective ways of framing their customer base. For its part, W2O routinely creates new models to overhaul existing communications, marketing and digital practices, but it bases its approach to disruption on a proven model:

- *Status quo:* Study how the status quo works. What do we do today?
- *Unmet needs:* Identify the unmet needs which exist that aren't being addressed
- *Pain points:* What are people trying to do but can't accomplish? What does our audience view as a pain point and why?
- *Model:* What model can consistently identify those unmet needs and pain points, and then develop solutions that will work on a local level?
- *Scalability:* Is the model usable anywhere in the world?
- *Simplicity:* Is the model so simple that we think, "that's obvious," but for some reason never did it?

The framework itself seems simple enough, but simplicity underlies the success of some of the world's most successful brands. (Steve Jobs' exhortation to "do one thing well" comes to mind.) True to form, the models of today deliver powerful insights into the myriad markets W2O analyzes. But when applied to the concept of hate and how it develops, it revealed some major flaws in the methods we typically use to target an audience and influence their behavior. First, these strategies focus on a relatively short term, seeking to move people for a day, a week or a year. If you're selling beer or laundry detergent, it's perfect: focus on a finite period and increase sales. Second, current approaches too easily label people and groups, often in ways that are larger and more diverse than we realize. This is what we call the *Gen du Jour* approach, since there's always another segmentation, and another after that, and so on. Third, because we rely on messaging and storytelling to reach people who already made up their minds, we have trouble breaking through and changing their narrative.

These approaches miss the central point of how we guide other people toward a lifetime of shared humanity. No company says: "We'd like to reach our customers 20 years before they buy our product. We want to build a great relationship and know how to meet each other's needs from the time they are born to the time of their first experience with us." Yet, when attempting to counter hate, that's exactly what we try to do. We need a set of models that feature a long-term scope, reach everyone on an individual level, and deliver a story of hope long before they latch tightly on a message of hate.

VULNERABILITY AND THE FOUR STAGES OF HUMAN DEVELOPMENT

Nancy Zwiers paced the room, the fifty public affairs leaders from NATO and various State Department posts listening intently — and, perhaps, a little quizzically. One could excuse their skepticism. After all, when they gathered that day at the U.S. Marketing College at the George P. Shultz National Foreign Affairs Training Center in Arlington, Virginia, they probably didn't expect to learn about how kids played with Barbie dolls.

Zwiers, one of the world's leading marketing minds, trained at Procter & Gamble before moving into multiple executive positions at Mattel, where she led worldwide marketing for the company's $2 billion Barbie doll brand. She now serves as CMO at Spin Master, where she works on products ranging from Air Hogs to Hedbanz. Few people on the planet know as much as Zwiers' does about the role of play in a child's development. By analyzing huge amounts of data and research, she developed her theory of "core play patterns." These patterns, consistent across time, geography and culture, come from the inside out. They represent a biological drive — and if you tap into it, you have a much better chance of engaging kids.

As Zwiers walked around the room, she began by laying out the concept of a child's original play pattern, called "exploration and discovery." This innate behavior begins at birth and drives infants to explore the environment around them. As kids grow older, she explained, the pattern expands, fueled by curiosity and the thrill of each new discovery. It starts stretching beyond the physical environment, flowing into everything from verbal interaction to reading—skills not necessary for survival, but certainly beneficial. But at every step of exploration and discovery, the patterns are inherent in virtually every human child. It is consistent across cultures, an instinctive behavior that flows from the inside out.

Entertainment, a key facet of the next stage, flows in the opposite direction. During this phase of development, called "challenge and mastery," children start to seek things outside their comfort zone and core environment. They begin to expand their knowledge and skills through external experiences, such as sports and game play. And as entertainment becomes more interactive, Zwiers explained, the lines between entertainment and play begin to blur. Children soon begin to imitate the characters or role models they admire ("imitation role play"), and soon enough they begin to imagine themselves similarly empowered ("empowerment fantasies"). [See Box 1.1]

BOX 1.1   **THE FOUR PHASES OF HUMAN DEVELOPMENT**

The early stages of development occur from birth to 2 years old, and then progress through more sophisticated learning techniques from childhood to adolescence and into adulthood.

- **Exploration and discovery**—We love surprises, anticipating what's next and engaging in self-discovery.
- **Challenge and mastery**—We play games, compete as teams or as individuals, and start experiencing emotions related to our experience.
- **Imitation role play**—We learn by watching and imitating. This includes what we see in our community, movies or social media, all of which influence role playing.
- **Empowerment Fantasies**—Starting around 3 years old and gaining sophistication as we grow, this drives most play among children and is fundamental to gender identity.

These development patterns linger into our adolescence and formative teenage years, albeit in a somewhat more sophisticated form. What we begin to see, Zwiers told the assembled public affairs specialists, is a set of cares common to teenagers of all stripes. They prefer to hear stories, with a strong preference toward humor, even when broaching serious topics. They feel an affinity for celebrities or other high-profile members of the culture, paying attention to what they say. Even as they struggle through awkwardness and interact socially, they recognize authenticity and are drawn toward it. Images and music resonate more than words. And throughout all this development, turmoil tugs at the exploding teenage mind. Impulse control really means more impulse than control. Peer recognition and acceptance is critical to self-esteem. Emotion overwhelms logic, and risk-taking doesn't feel all that risky. We begin to gain greater independence and individuality at a time when we're least equipped to handle it.

These patterns are so universal because they're grounded in natural neurological development. Our brains are more or less developed by 25 years old, according to most neurological experts. Prior to that, however, our own gray matter plays a nefarious role in the turbulent years of adolescence. The rational thinking of an adult is driven by the prefrontal cortex of our brain, but that region of the brain is still in development during our teens, leaving us to rely on the amygdala to help form decisions. Unfortunately, the amygdala is the bad angel on your shoulder, manifesting itself emotionally, aggressively and impulsively. Of course, most people survive their amygdala-inspired foolishness and develop the neurological capacity to handle complex planning, risk assessment and decision-making. Until then, though, the whole crazy cocktail of emotion, identity-formation and neurological development opens up the ideal opportunity to recruit someone to your cause. This is the time when we are most susceptible to a message of profound hate.

Indeed, it's no coincidence that Mumtaz Qadri was 25 years old when he gunned down Salman Taseer.

THE GEN-NOW MODEL

Clayton Christensen, a professor at the Harvard Business School, has spent decades studying the fine art of innovation and disruption. "Disruption is a process, not an event," he once said, "and innovations can only be disruptive relative to something else." The development of extreme hate is not an event; it builds across the course of weeks, months or years, typically in the formative development stages before we turn 25 years old. As Christensen notes, any innovation for countering is only disruptive within the context of the environment people grow up in today. If we can impact the lives of those most likely to encounter bias, hate and extremism during these pivotal years, we have the greatest chance for disruption.

We call this approach the *Gen-Now Model*. In this model, our target demographic is always 0 to 25 years old — every day of every year. We don't package, stereotype or label this as any sort of generation or audience in perpetuity. We reach children effectively from the time they first get into exploration mode, and keep at it until their 25th birthday. We ask ourselves if communities can improve their ability to play, explore and learn at an earlier stage. We determine how the people we want to reach play and learn on a daily basis, not occasionally via outreach or a seminar. We empower parents with new tools, techniques and outlets to enrich their children's experiences earlier in their lives.

By employing the *Gen-Now Model*, we take the long view about maintaining relevance in young people's lives through whatever means we can muster. We teach, train and supply communities with the tools they need to succeed. And we use marketing and media where appropriate, because it's powerful and it works well at the right time and place. If we are going to make generational change, it's about helping the brains of our brothers and sisters form with as much equality as possible. So, we counter hate by understanding the concept of the "reminiscence bump" (Chapter 2). We use big data and sophisticated tools to analyze sentiment and identify the Pre-Hate journey much the same way companies research PreCommerce behavior (Chapter 6). We learn to seek out and counteract the dangerous connections between grievances, ideologies and influencers (Chapter 10). And we debunk the myths that make it far too easy to dismiss extremism without engaging it (Chapter 12).

Ultimately, we accept it as our mission to make life more fun, more meaningful and more relevant for young people exposed to environments that lead to hateful action. Whether in a gang-controlled urban neighborhood or a hot zone of religion-fueled extremism, we make a difference through our choices of content, our campaigns and our commitment to a shared humanity across the longest term possible.

AN OUNCE OF PREVENTION

BY DENISE CAMPBELL BAUER
Former U.S. Ambassador to the Kingdom of Belgium,
former journalist and longtime civic leader

It was my privilege to serve as United States Ambassador to the Kingdom of Belgium from 2013 to 2017. Until just a few years ago, this charming and historically important country in the heart of Europe was best known as home to NATO and the European Union, World War I and II battlefields, great beer and chocolate, top-notch universities, and beautiful medieval town squares, castles, and churches. Sadly, in recent years, Belgium has also gained notoriety as a European hub for terrorism, due to the role terrorist cells within Belgium played in deadly attacks in Brussels, Paris and beyond.

How did this happen? While the specific attacks themselves came as a surprise to me and to our multi-agency embassy team, the risk of such events was well-known to us. For more than a decade, the dedicated and highly skilled team at the U.S. Embassy in Brussels has worked on issues related to countering violent extremism through a wide range of programs and outreach efforts and has had strong collaboration with the Belgian government.

The causes of extremism are complex, and many have been covered widely in the media. For the purposes of this discussion on countering hate, I would like to share one aspect that I think offers useful and transferable lessons: early childhood education.

This issue was originally brought to my attention by a respected Belgian statesman, Minister of State and Former Speaker of the House, Herman De Croo, who early in his career, served as Minister of Education. As he explained, while most Belgian children start school at 2½ or 3 years old, the children and grandchildren of immigrants often stay home until they are 5 or 6 years old for cultural reasons. In many cases, they are in homes where the language spoken and the primary or sole media sources, thanks to technology, are from their family's country of origin. When these children finally start school, in addition to being behind academically, some will have had little exposure to any of Belgium's three official languages—French, Flemish, and German—or to the broader culture, making success in school much more challenging.

These students may be held back several times, drop out early, or eventually leave school at 18 years old without a diploma or many marketable skills. Youth unemployment is around 25 percent in Belgium, with disproportionately high numbers in immigrant communities. It is not difficult to see how these circumstances could leave persons susceptible to radicalization in their neighborhood, in prison, online, or elsewhere.

The bad news is that this pattern can be deeply engrained. The good news is that there are leaders in Belgium of diverse backgrounds who are well-aware of the challenge and are actively working on solutions. Investment in early childhood education is important for any society; it may be vital in preventing violent extremism.

THE NEW VIRTUAL BATTLEFIELD

Hezbollah might lack the kind of coordinated force enjoyed by ISIS, but the organization has developed a robust e-militia for the new virtual battlefield. Its 'round the clock dedicated team of 25 to 30 online operators produce, generate and repost content that promotes the group's ideology. They work from Hezbollah's social media headquarters, a room filled with computers, servers and large-screen TVs—a command center for cyber warfare, though their operations are primarily geared towards recruitment. Lacking the kind of coordinated force enjoyed by the Muslim Brotherhood, Hezbollah's team tactically befriends susceptible groups, seeing in them potential members for the organization. Much like their organization's supporters offline, the e-militia first establishes trust and then begins to spread their message. But social media gives Hezbollah a much broader audience of potential friends, and its tactics are working. The group's Twitter handle, @almanarnews, had 8,000 followers in 2012. By late 2017, it had more than 100,000.

Like Hezbollah, other groups such as al-Shabaab and Boko Haram rely on "fanboys" to amplify, repost and retweet content. Between 200 and 300 loyal grassroots supporters are tasked with spreading content organically within two to four hours of an initial posting on YouTube. Tactics include manipulating the number of views, reposting, tagging, linking and generating chatter on other platforms. In Lebanon, Hamas, which has a sophisticated social media team, often posts the URL of their YouTube videos on a variety of Arabic-language blogs, daily newspaper comments sections, the American University of Beirut student pages, and a variety of user-generated chat rooms and web forums. It is a laborious task, but a necessary one. Their Islamist propaganda typically violates established platforms' terms of service, so flooding sites not only increases penetration, it helps evade removal.

It has taken little more than a decade for social media to become the indispensable tool for legions of activists, both within the Islamist political establishment and beyond. It is no less important for the tens of millions of disaffected people across the Muslim world, who may or may not have a religious or political agenda. Access to social media technologies provides an open channel for virtually anyone to express their opinion. However, it also provides an open channel for others to shape and sway those opinions. Islamists and Extremists were among the first to recognize this, and they have become increasingly sophisticated and adept at employing the new information weapons to full — and sometimes lethal — effect.

This is not merely a case of spreading propaganda (the "classic" definition of the weaponization of information). Rather, the various ways in which information is disseminated are themselves part of the war. And if social media is a smoking gun, Islamists and extremists are proving to be the most expert at loading the bullets. Forced underground for years, they now use the various digital platforms to wage war on the information battlefield. For the more pragmatic Islamists, the aim is to bolster their mass-market appeal. For the extremists, the goal is to capture a niche audience and stoke fear of the infidel. Different social media platforms are like different weapons, each with pros and cons, some more suited to one group than another, but all are wielded with pinpoint accuracy and deployed with acute force.

The weapons of the virtual battlefield couldn't work better for extremist groups. The foreign recruits who used to make their way cautiously to an ISIS training camp in the Middle East now head in the other direction, seeking to avoid the physical battlefield and return to their home countries, from where they can develop local networks and launch attacks. The target audience is no longer a group, but the individual. Their increasing use of encrypted technologies and the dark web limits the breadth of their exposure, but it allows recruiters to target individuals at a deeper, more personal dimension. They might not reach as many but, absent strong countermeasures, they convert at a higher rate.

COUNTERING HATE

The good news is we understand all this — the process of hate's growth; the audience most susceptible to it; and the tactics that extremist groups use to recruit disaffected youth. But each of these factors represent a necessary component for effective counteroffensives, so our strategy requires expertise from multiple fields. So, with this book, we brought together decades of work in the diplomatic and corporate marketing worlds. The diplomatic perspective gives us insight into these radical organizations, helping us understand how the process of hate develops and how they deploy virtual and real weapons to amplify it. The corporate marketing view provides insight into the sophisticated strategies and tactics brands deploy to sway people, tracking and subtly reaching potential customers long before they're ready to buy. By joining these different perspectives — and adding the expertise of a wide field of corporate and diplomatic officials you'll find throughout these pages — we hope to provide an effective strategic framework for countering hate.

In the chapters to come, we will take a deeper look at how hate develops and spreads. With this as a foundation, we then turn our attention to the virtual battleground, from social media networks to the dark corners of the Web. There, we'll discover the increasingly sophisticated strategies and tactics extremist groups use to spread their views and recruit vulnerable youth. And finally, with all this in hand, we lay out the counteroffensive, a series of our own strategies and tactics at our disposal to counter hate and stem the tide of extremism.

CHAPTER 2

UNLOCKING THE POWER OF MEMORY

"Yesterday is but today's memory,
and tomorrow is today's dream."
— KHALIL GIBRAN, Lebanese-American artist, poet and writer

M ore than 50,000 people packed Luzhniki Stadium in Moscow on August 12, 1998, to hear the Rolling Stones, a band they had listened to, illicitly, for years. The Russian government had banned the import of rock 'n' roll music from many of the world's most popular bands during the Cold War, hoping to shield its citizens from Western influence. Despite the attempt — in fact, because of it — a generation of young Russians discovered underground avenues to hot new albums, traded bootlegs, committed lyrics to memory and covertly jammed guitar riffs in their basements or garages. Like they had for millions of youth in the U.S. and Europe, bands like the Stones became the epitome of freedom for young Russians, despite the prohibitions. So, on that cold, rainy and outright joyous night in August 1998, it seemed only fitting that Mick Jagger would strut onto the stage and begin the Stones' first live show in Russia with *Satisfaction* — everyone reveling in the irony of that song for that occasion.

Of course, by 1998, some 33 years after the initial release of *Satisfaction*, those diehard Rolling Stones fans weren't so young anymore, but that didn't make them any less enthusiastic. There they were, thousands strong, belting out every word to every song, rocking away with Mick,

Keith and the boys. Like their fellow classic rock fans around the world, a live show brought a reconnection with the vim and vigor of youth, however brief and fleeting. Yet the energy gathered in Luzhniki Stadium that night was electrified by memories of the days when albums "were traded like illicit treasure in Moscow's subway tunnels and dark courtyards, out of the sight of the Soviet police," as a *New York Times* reporter wrote the day after the concert. Smuggling around prohibited cassette tapes, secretly discovering a new band and just finding a way to beat the damn system — those recollections sent a white-hot charge through the night.

Human memory packs a tremendous influence on present experience and decision-making, yet few memories carry as much freight, joy, pain, inspiration and thrill as the ones we form in our youth. Not only do these memories help form an enduring foundation for who we become as adults, they're sharpened by the hyper-stimulated state of our developing minds, bodies and souls. As we wind our way through teenage and young adult years, we remember and store events in a way that creates a "reminiscence bump" — one that matches the pattern of human brain development.

Virtually every one of the Stones fans gathered that night in Moscow could've told you about the power of the reminiscence bump. The aggregation of these memories and experiences has tremendous power, but that power only ratchets higher when the bump is built up in an environment of deprivation, authoritarianism, extremism or violence. If a mostly ineffective prohibition against rock 'n' roll records and the lingering effects of life in Cold War Russia could fire a stadium crowd to ecstasy, what might an environment of true deprivation, unadulterated hate or the ruins of war do on the formative reminiscence bump of a young man or woman? And what does this tell us about the potential for countering hate?

THE LIFE SPAN RETRIEVAL CURVE

In the late 1980s, Peter Martin and Michael Smyer gathered a pool of middle-aged and older adults and asked them to reflect on their lives. Among other things, the two researchers — Martin at the University of Georgia and Smyer at Penn State University — hoped to identify the key moments adults remembered from throughout their lives. They interviewed 78 people, almost all of whom recalled events from their 20s and early 30s as the most impactful of their lives. Their 1990 study launched a series of similar research in the decades since, and essentially, they've found that the events of our teens and early 20s form a disproportionate share of the autobiographical memories we can recall throughout the rest of our lives.

This period of identify formation correlates directly with the graph of the reminiscence bump. And no wonder; just think about what we do in this time-frame, even beyond all the physical and emotional development. We fall in love for the first time, perhaps with our partner for life. We begin to determine the interests that will define our lives and careers. We dedicate ourselves to a faith or, if we opt out, develop a belief system about right and wrong. We find out who we can rely on in times of true trouble. And, these days, we learn how and where we can express ourselves via social media or mobile apps.

The reminiscence bump created by these formative moments comprises one piece of what some researchers call the Life Span Retrieval Curve. This curve charts memory retention and aggregation over the course of our lives. We start storing memories around five years old, our storage peaks roughly around 20 years old, and then our ability to store memories for life declines rapidly for 15 years or so. Our ability to recall and store memories reemerges around 35 years old and increases steadily through the remainder of our lives. [See Graph 2.1] When you look at this graph, it explains why we all have so much trouble remembering what we did before kindergarten. In fact, it's rare that we remember much of anything. It also might explain why it's so hard to convince older people that their choices in life might not be as wise as they assume. To some extent, we are hard-wired in our beliefs by the time people try to reach us. Our file cabinets are filled up. Our biases have been formed. If we hate, we have a rationale for it. And if we have moved to extremism, it has a logically charted pathway in our minds, as part of our evolution as a human being.

The concept provides an interesting subtheme to "Inception," Christopher Nolan's surreal 2010 blockbuster. In the film, a group led by Leonardo di Caprio induces a deep sleep in themselves and their target, the new head of a major family conglomerate. They then enter the executive's subconscious mind, seeking to go deeper and deeper until they reach a point at which they can plant the seed of an idea. In their target's mind, that

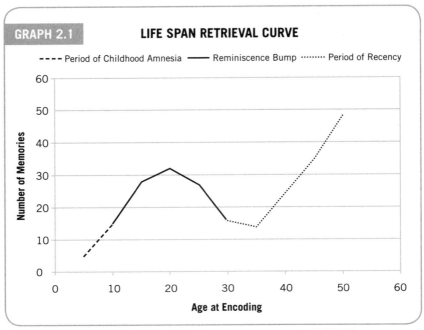

GRAPH 2.1 — LIFE SPAN RETRIEVAL CURVE

- - - - Period of Childhood Amnesia   ——— Reminiscence Bump   ········· Period of Recency

Y-axis: Number of Memories (0–60); X-axis: Age at Encoding (0–60)

Public Domain, https://en.wikipedia.org/w/index.php?curid=31253407

memory blooms into a formative notion that then guides a key business decision. It's a fantastical mind-bender, and it provides a curious allegory for the key role our autobiographical memory can play in our lives.

Impacting someone's life during this critical period, as key memories are formed, can have a disproportionate impact throughout their lives. While a single campaign, a great slogan or a cool message might make us feel good, it rarely breaks through the decades of reminiscence bump memory formation. So, if we intend to counter hate before it calcifies into a hardline mindset, we need to find a way to reach susceptible people in a way that sticks throughout their lives. We need to find ways to resonate with them during the reminiscence bump.

A MUSICAL NOTION OF HOW WE MAKE MEMORIES

Music holds a powerful sway over people throughout the world, in part because we connect with it in so many different ways. The lyrics of a Rolling Stones hit might reach in and shake a young man's soul in Colorado, but the nature of music's non-verbal expression lets the same chorus stir a young Russian who barely knows English. Tempo, volume, key and various other musical elements can stir happiness, sadness, fear and joy. Music has a consistency across cultures, much like the sound of laughter or a baby crying. We react to the beat, whether a guitar rhythm, a piano nocturne or a drum solo. Our brains and bodies dig it, because it so often stimulates the release of dopamine, serotonin and oxytocin, giving us feelings of pleasure.

When the first chord of your favorite song rings out at a live concert, you know the feeling. The neurochemicals that make us feel good flood our brains, heightening awareness and helping us remember those special moments. Sure, music can spark a rich set of emotionally-based reactions that help us forge bonds with certain bands, styles and people, but at its best it also delivers a sort of biochemical high — one that in some cases can help boost long-term memory.

This process is by no means confined to music, nor does it explain any more than one contributing factor to the reminiscence bump. But because of their effects, music and other digital and streaming media could become extremely powerful tools in our efforts to combat extremism. We're entering a time in our world where everyone aspires to have a smart phone, giving them the ability to download or stream music, video and social content. As prices drop and networks expand, more and more of the nearly four billion people with online access will join us. YouTube already reaches more than 1.5 billion people, who consume local, regional or global content. Facebook can reach more than two billion people with its live features. Regional services like Anghani in the Middle East, Saavn in India and China's Tencent have prospered and, in some cases, could dwarf similar services in the U.S. The idea of music so deeply impacting lives might seem trivial, but we already have dozens of channels through which to distribute it to a global audience. And, when it reaches all those end users, like the Rolling Stones fans exchanging illicit bootlegs in Moscow's shadows, music can *imprint* memories in a powerful way.

Evolutionary biologists used this term, "imprinting," to explain the time when a young animal, often immediately after birth, learns what to do by watching and mimicking an adult. In that case, it's a fundamental survival instinct: If we don't watch what mom or dad does and learn to repeat it, we might not make it very far. The same instinct drives us throughout the early years of our lives—until, of course, we hit our teenage years, when it seems we're determined to do the exact opposite of what our parents prefer. We adore mom and dad when they're crucial to our survival. We begin to break from them when forming our own identity becomes paramount. And then we return to seek their wisdom after we've established ourselves as individuals. Mark Twain said it best: "When I was a boy of 14, my father was so ignorant I could hardly stand to have the old man around. But when I got to be 21, I was astonished at how much the old man had learned in seven years."

AN INTERVENTION FOR YOUNG MINDS

While people tend to collect an outsized share of our autobiographical memories during the reminiscence bump of our teens and early 20s, any effort to positively influence thoughts and minds must consider the variables that play into the imprinting of fundamental behaviors and attitudes. Family, friends and neighbors play a critical role in pre-teen years, so what can we do to help a community make a positive difference in the lives of its children? Teens and young adults form their world views based partly on outside social media, mobile communications and other digital sources that reach well beyond their hometown, so how have they learned to interact with peers at home and abroad? As youth build a framework to distinguish right and wrong, how do they have fun and generate the positive memories that make life worth living to the fullest?

The imprinting process can influence attitudes as much as behaviors. After all, we not only learn how to eat and drink like adults, we absorb our parents' hopes and beliefs, as well. In the hot zones around the world, a child's initial adult role models imprint just as deeply as anywhere. Societal variables in the earliest phases of our lives, especially a lack of choices or unwanted choices that are being made for us, seed the field for what we become. No matter who makes the choice or how scarce the resources are, our brains will still complete their journey, imprint what they can and shape our personal narrative for the rest of our lives. We will follow who is in front of us. Our brains will form no matter what they are exposed to in their critical years.

MUSIC REMINDS US HOW SIMILAR WE ALL ARE

BY CHUCK LEAVELL
Author, co-founder of Mother Nature Network,
environmentalist and keyboardist for The Rolling Stones

As a young musician growing up in Alabama in the 1960s, I was certainly aware of the conflict all around me concerning the Civil Rights movement. I was 11 years old and living in Tuscaloosa, Ala., when George Wallace stood in the schoolhouse door in the summer of 1963 to deny entrance to the University of Alabama to two black students, Vivian Malone and James Hood. It was an incredibly turbulent time and there was tension going on all around Alabama and throughout the south. At the same time, I was learning to play the piano and the guitar and listening to a lot of music that was on the radio. My older sister, Judy, was working at a record store, so we both had an interest in this, and we would sometimes pool our money to buy records by artists that caught our attention. The British Invasion was huge at the time—The Beatles, The Rolling Stones, The Dave Clark Five and other artists from "across the pond" were gaining fans at an exponential rate. There was also great indigenous music that we heard and loved, especially the rhythm and blues and soul music by artists like Aretha Franklin, Wilson Pickett, Sam and Dave, and all the great Motown music coming out of Detroit. As time went on, around 1967 I formed my first band, The Misfitz. We had a standing job playing at the YMCA every Friday night, and even were eventually hired by the first TV station to come to Tuscaloosa to be the band for a Saturday morning program called "Tuscaloosa Bandstand," modeled after Dick Clark's "American Bandstand."

Tuscaloosa is the home of a wonderful historically black liberal arts institution called Stillman College. At the time, in 1967–68, a group of singers that were enrolled in Stillman formed a band called The Jades. They were really talented guys, five of them, that sort of modeled themselves after groups like The Temptations and The Four Tops. They had great dance moves and beautiful harmonies. One of them was also a musician, a guy named Freddie, who played keyboards. I eventually got to know them and loved watching them perform. At one point, I think in '68, Freddie, who was delegated to stand behind a keyboard during their shows, came to me and said: "Hey man, would you be interested in playing the keys on some shows with us so that I can get out front with the other guys? I can show you some things that might help you be a better player." Well, I jumped at the opportunity and became the only white face for a time with this all black band.

Now, you can imagine some of the flack and comments I got playing with those guys. But I was having a fantastic time, and was learning some great chords and playing music that I loved. Some of my friends shunned me, and made fun of me and called me some pretty nasty names. But the guys in The Jades were really good to me, really took me on as a "little brother" and we had some wonderful times.

As the '60s were coming to an end, music had become a huge part of the social scene all over America. The Peace Movement had come into play and the civil rights movement had grown and the world was changing pretty fast. At least in part, prejudices were declining and the gap between black and white was shrinking—becoming grayer—and music had played a huge role in bringing people together. There were still some people that harbored ill feelings between the races, but there had been a significant shift and folks were blending together in a way that had rarely existed before. Music had played a huge role in this, and still does. Music brings us together, diminishes our differences, emphasizes our similarities and allows us to get beyond ethnicities, beyond the color of our skin and beyond which side of the tracks we were born. Yes, some music contains angst and even harbors prejudiced feelings, but even that can provide a vehicle to vent frustrations and sometimes prevent violent acts. For the most part music counters hate and promotes love, and we have all seen the healing power that it has. I am grateful beyond words for the career that I have had as a musician, and even more grateful for the way that music has shown me that we are all much more similar than we are different.

Yet, few intervention or relief initiatives think first and foremost about the critical dual roles of the imprinting process and the reminiscence bump. We naturally respond faster and more fully to situations we can see or sense, such as famine, disease and war. Agencies and NGOs spring to action when a country lacks food or water. Foundations and governments battle malaria and other diseases and work hard to get treatments to those in need. International agencies seek to aid refuges and find ways to resettle them. These are critically important interventions, and organizations are doing incredible work in these and other fields, but mental and emotional health issues rarely get the same degree of attention — even though the brains of our youth are arguably the most important natural resource we have on the planet.

Most humans come into the world with similar brains and survival instincts. What happens afterward shapes us for life. Whether through action or inaction, we all play a role in that development. If we hope to sway the most vulnerable youth toward a peaceful path, we need to ensure that their memories serve as a protective shield.

A VIRTUAL SHIELD

We rarely come into direct contact with the impressionable young men and women immersed in environments of hate. However, we live in a world where we can stream news, entertainment and other content around the world via digital and social media. The music and video we consume through mobile phones and other devices exert an influence from cultures a country or hemisphere away. This rich connectivity provides extremists with powerful new weapons, but it also provides us a new and equally potent "virtual shield" to use against their bias and hate.

The concept of a virtual shield implies a virtual battlefield, of course. We have colleagues who are experts in countering hate around the world. Many of them advocate peace on the ground, scattered in some of the most difficult environments to work city by city or issue by issue. We don't see them every day, if we see them at all. These efforts are indispensable for the future of our countries and the globe. We can help them — *if we can marshal the increasingly fragmented landscape of digital and social media influence.*

We know bad actors want to stay in power and spread their influence, so they condition and imprint their values on their youngest constituents, whether through interpersonal interaction or now, with increasing sophistication, via social media channels. Yet, the people they target have the same fundamental wants and needs as anyone. They want to build a positive life. So how do we combat the negative voices and decrease their influence on an individual, community, regional or global level? How do we create the most positively impactful memories for three billion young people around the world? How do we forge a virtual shield?

Despite the positive potential of the digital technologies and content we've created, we are not winning on the virtual battlefield. To date, we haven't directed the full array of our arsenal at a common goal, largely because we don't have the mechanisms in place to succeed. We know the status quo is not sufficient. We know the unmet need and the pain points. But we lack a model to coordinate and align our initiatives. The current model is fragmented and won't scale, so we need to take a new approach to the virtual battlefield.

We need to look in the mirror and realize that we're the ones who need to improve — to realize we're the ones who can unlock the power of memory and experience and form the best minds on the planet.

HARNESSING OPEN-SOURCE AND EXPERT-DRIVEN PLATFORMS TO COMBAT HATE

It's hard to imagine now, but many IT industry leaders scoffed at the idea of open source software. The idea of open, publicly developed software sounded fine in theory, but it would never work as an operating system for PCs or mobile phones. Now, of course, Android is the most popular operating system on the planet, running almost three-quarters of all smart phones as of late 2017. Even some of the smartest people underestimate the collective influence of the crowd. If we want to create a virtual shield for billions of vulnerable youth and young adults, we have no choice but to empower the entire world to learn, share and create its own institutional memory. We'll never move fast enough as a single group or individual, but we can get there if we embrace each other, crowd-source ideas and knowledge and build the sorts of memories and experiences that mitigate bias and extremism.

We're working with an Austin, Texas, startup to create the world's first open-source data hub for countering hate. data.world, co-founded by Brett Hurt, Bryon Jacob, Matt Laessig, and Jon Loyens, is creating a global community that collects statistical sets related to specific topics. They've set out to create a comprehensive search engine of sorts, one that we can use to harness all forms of data — from spreadsheets, to public files on hate crimes, to lists of groups working to combat extremism across the globe. To put the scope of their task in perspective, Google launched in 1998 with access to 2.4 million websites to crawl. data.world started in 2015 with access to 18 million public (open) datasets to crawl and encourage the data.world community to upload. The folks at data.world are developing a platform that individuals and organizations can use to share their data while maintaining control of it. The initiative will help break down the silos that we unintentionally built as we pursued separate, but related goals. As such, the entire world can help analyze and contemplate existing data sets to highlight areas of need or opportunity, craft data-centric strategies to address those points, and then measure effectiveness of those initiatives. We've launched the "Countering Hate" community within data.world, where it's available for anyone and everyone to see and use.

Like the many proprietary apps that run on Android and other open-source platforms, we realized that any effective anti-extremism platform also must have an area of focused, expert-led development. So, we also have created a private community of groups already engaged in battling bias and hate. Here, these organizations and individuals can gather to share best practices, critique and ask advice of peers, and share their knowledge in a safely gated environment. Housed in Facebook, this invitation-only community is modeled after the ways companies successfully shared best practices for years on social media. One of the most successful is www.socialmedia.org, which founder Andy Sernovitz launched with the idea that normally competitive companies would embrace lessons about innovation together. Now, more than 400 companies, including many sets of archrivals, share their ideas and learn from each other, all behind the scenes.

Harnessing both the open-source and private, expert-driven platforms will help give governments, NGOs, think tanks and other leaders the necessary tools and knowledge to build a global, institutional memory that moves the world toward peace. It will accelerate the sharing of insights, ideas and campaigns, and it will provide a forum to collectively deal with the problems that keep us from truly reaching the youth of this world. Tapping into the collective insight of the crowd will help us identify new wrinkles on the evolving virtual battle, and thus help us improve the virtual shields we deploy. Although the actual ideas that will come out of these initiatives remain to be seen, the world of software and mobile phones provides a good allegory for what happens when the world takes ownership for how we innovate.

We don't get many chances to impact an individual's life. With these initiatives, we hope to improve our chances by unlocking data and ideas, using them to build a positive institutional memory for the vulnerable youth of the world and, ultimately, swaying their lives toward peace and prosperity.

CHAPTER 3

THE 5,000 DAY HABIT

"ISIS leaders: We urgently call upon every Muslim to join the fight,
especially those in the land of the two shrines (Saudi Arabia), rise."
— @iyad, verified Twitter account of Iyad el-Baghdadi,
an Arab Spring activist, Islamic libertarian and fellow at Civita.
Based in Oslo, Norway, with 107,000 Twitter followers.

The race is over, and has been for years now. The *New York Times* web
sites landed about 85.1 million unique visitors in June 2017, according
to comScore, which tracks online traffic for the top 50 U.S. digital media
properties. Meanwhile, Facebook drew 203.9 million unique visitors and,
according to CEO Mark Zuckerberg, its virtual community topped 2 billion
that very same month. While the newsgathering operations of the world's
most-respected media outlets still exert a tremendous influence on global
events, none come close to the sheer geographical and popular reach of
Facebook, Google and other social media titans. These social media sites
have opened new avenues for governments, organizations and individuals
to disseminate their own content, in some cases making individuals more
powerful than the traditional news sources ever could be. No wonder they
continue to grow as rapidly as they do.

Countries, companies and individuals now see social media as an
increasingly powerful network they can easily and cheaply deploy to broadcast their views to millions of people. In Saudi Arabia, Mohamad al-Arefe
(@MohamadAlarefe), a Muslim scholar from King Saud University, has
18 million followers on Twitter. Indian Prime Minister Narendra Modi
has 42 million followers. Amr Khaled, an Egyptian activist was dubbed

"the world's most famous and influential Muslim television preacher" by the *New York Times Magazine*. His Twitter account, @Amrkhaled, reaches almost 9 million people with messages meant to be uplifting and positive. Jawwal, the first mobile network operator in Palestine and the territories' largest private-sector employer, has 11 million Twitter followers.

But this new global reach extends well past 140- or even 280-character tweets. More and more countries now produce their version of network news, putting an official spin on the events of the day. The third largest YouTube channel in Libya is called Libya's Channel, a national news production that reaches 3.5 million subscribers. In Iran, the three largest Facebook pages are Al-Alam news (6.1 million likes), Press TV (3.5 million likes) and Manoto TV (3.2 million likes). Al-Alam is a state-owned, Arabic-language news channel based in Tehran, from where it reaches more than 300 million people worldwide, including neighboring Iraq. Press TV features a 24-hour, English-language broadcast affiliated with the Islamic Republic of Iran Broadcasting. To most of their millions of viewers, these channels serve as a viable alternative to biased Western media. And it's not just a one-way or news-centric phenomenon. One of Iran's most popular singers, Arash, had 322,000 subscribers and 173 million views on YouTube as of late 2017. You'll find the same trends around the world, both in countries we consider hotspots or just emerging economies, in general. In Afghanistan, VOA Pashto is the No. 2 Facebook page with about 3.2 million likes. The "Cricket on Facebook" page has 19 million likes in cricket-mad Pakistan.

The world's new network is social, and it's in the hands of any individual or organization with a smart phone or computer. Rather than vague ratings and surveys, this network furnishes precise information about the size of our audience and its reaction to published content. If that content isn't compelling, the traffic and audience numbers will reflect as much. The volume of shares, retweets, likes and comments will wane. We don't have a real-time, precise equivalent for mainstream media. The new social media network has it all built in, and those metrics reveal a key trend: many of the most forward-looking new uses of social media have emerged at media outlets and organizations in the Middle East and Asia, rather than the U.S. and Europe. As the Western world continues to talk to itself, a new generation of world leaders is interacting with a massive audience every day via social media channels.

THE 5,000 DAY HABIT

New Year's resolutions come and go, but few ever stick beyond a few weeks. The gyms fill up in January, but the crowds dwindle as February stretches into March. Surveys suggest as many as nine of every 10 resolutions end in relapse. The failure rate is remarkably high, partly because people don't always take their self-improvement plans all that seriously, but also because people probably take too long a view. The goal shouldn't be your new beach-ready body months down the road, but a commitment to make it through the first three to nine weeks. Research suggests that a new habit can form in anywhere from 21 to 66 days, depending on the study. People who dedicate or lose themselves to a repeated activity for this finite period tend to see the new behaviors stick long term, for better or for worse.

Typically, we think of the habits we form as physical endeavors (e.g. smoking, jogging or dieting) or passive activities we can measure in one way or another (e.g. hours in front of the TV or on our smart phones each night). Understanding the net benefits and risks of these behaviors can help us improve our lives. However, in many cases we don't truly know the outcomes of many powerful new habits that emerge, including the way consumption of content via social media has started to dominate the behavior of young people around the world. And whatever we eventually come to find about this activity, make no mistake: our younger generations are spending an unprecedented amount of time dedicated to this single activity.

If we assume a young person begins to regularly interact with a smart phone when they turn 10 years old, that leaves 15 years — or 5,475 days — before they turn 25 years old and their attitudes and mindsets tend to solidify. For the sake of argument, let's say this young man or woman accesses social media an average of three hours per day over that span. (Published estimates put typical social media usage at two to nine hours a day.) That equals 16,425 hours of social media content consumption during the key years of brain and behavioral formation. Even if you move that up two years, to the first meaningful access at 12 years old, you still have nearly 5,000 days for the habit to form, settle in and become almost inescapable.

This is what we call the 5,000 Day Habit. The youth of our world engage in a daily routine, during which they immerse themselves in entertainment, educational material and information about their world via Twitter, Facebook, Tencent, YouTube and other social media channels. They might consume quality information; they might consume complete dreck. But they're always consuming:

- We "pick up a newspaper and read it." It just happens to be our phone, and we look at it to see what information is relevant and being shared by people we trust.

- We build our own personal media network, so we don't need a formal brand. Our network follows key people and key groups on a handful of channels we view daily.

- Our phone is an appendage. We look at every update. Those who share constantly get more of our mindshare.

- We don't really trust big organizations. They don't reach us with an authentic voice. The individuals we follow teach us or speak to us conversationally.

- We do relax and take time to watch video; we just do it more often on our phone and via social media channels. That's our version of television.

- We get curious about what to explore, and then use search to find out more information.

- We like to listen to ideas from people or organizations from which our elders try to dissuade us. We're teenagers, after all.

- We cannot imagine a day without our phone and its updates.

Let's not pretend this is some radical new behavior confined to those incomprehensible Millennials. Transport youthful Baby Boomers into modern times, and they also would listen to the music they wanted, learn from the people they thought made sense and rarely let adults convince them otherwise. We would gain respect for the people who are there for us every day, appearing on our phones, even if — perhaps especially if — their ideas are risky or we intuitively know they're wrong. Already moving through a period when decision-making, logic and risk-taking collide, we simply would add our personally curated miasma of content to the digital cocktail — and then drink it in for the next 5,000-plus days.

AN AUDITION IN SECONDS
What It Takes to Deliver Your Message Today

BY GARY BRIGGS
Chief Marketing Officer, Facebook

To reach the audiences we deeply care about, we need to focus as much on how and where we deliver the message as we do on the story itself. This is how we can cut through all the noise and distractions that people face every day.

We live in a world today where we make decisions based on what content we'll choose in a matter of seconds. In fact, the time it takes to read this sentence is longer than the time we take to decide if we will watch the next video.

Thus, when the habits of our audience change, so should we. Here are a few learnings that I believe are important for individuals and organizations looking to counter hate, bias and extremism.

- *Our attention span has decreased*—When you are receiving hundreds of emails, messages, texts and news updates all day long, you learn how to make decisions quickly. It's the only way to navigate the river of content rushing at us. This makes our ability to gain attention more important than ever.

- *We need to learn how to visualize our stories*—More and more, people are coming to Facebook to watch video. As a result, it is important that we improve how we visualize our thoughts, concepts and important aspects of our life. If it is not interesting to us, why would it be interesting to others?

- *Thinking without sound is a sound strategy*—About 50 percent of videos on Facebook are viewed without sound. What words or symbols will subtly narrate your video as we watch it?

- *Everyone contributes to the world's story*—More than 1.3 billion of us go on Facebook every day to learn what is happening. Our phones have cameras and we use them constantly to report on what we are learning. Whether we realize it or not, we are all playing a role in deciding what is important in our world.

- *We love live content*—We like watching live sports, we thrive on instant messaging and we like to follow our friends as close to real-time as possible. What does our audience want to see live?

- *Messaging is our main way to communicate*—Messaging is competing with calling, texting and emailing via your phone. What kind of a messaging network have we built to reach our audience?

Inside Facebook, we live by five core values that can apply here as well. Be bold. Focus on impact. Move fast. Be open. Build social value.

Now it's your turn.

MAKING CONNECTIONS WHEREVER YOUTH GO, EVEN IF IT'S BETWEEN TWO FERNS

Most organizations of any size naturally protect the status quo. People are naturally disinclined to change, and the inertia of existing routine makes it extremely difficult to effect change. Knowing just how hard this can be, we often celebrate the rare companies that break the paradigm and do it all differently. This usually requires a charismatic leader who makes it their mission to disrupt a static state, but we can see it in thoughtfully crafted processes and strategies, as well. We just don't see it often enough.

For example, an organization 15 to 20 years ago would build a full-scale press relations department to share its story, create content that television could use, and do everything in its power to influence the popularly shared narrative about its brand. Today, too many organizations try to do the same thing, reaching out to a media network that is decreasing in significance daily. They look at the ratings war update: *"In primetime, the network logged 2.4 million viewers, 483,000 of whom fell into our key news demographic of 25 to 54 years old."* One need look no further than the target demographic to see how far this particular arrow misses the bullseye. Sure, adults in the prime of their careers have more disposable income, and that's worth pursuing. But doing so in the traditional manner completely misses the formative years of youth and young adults, who've all but abandoned these traditional channels. Meanwhile, @MohamadAlarefe sends out a string of tweets to 18 million followers, or Jawwal shares new mobile content to 11 million people. If governments, companies and other organizations intend to be relevant in the social media dominant world that's coming, they need to ask themselves who they really think they're reaching today.

Consider President Barack Obama's outreach while still in office. At one point, as he was looking to increase awareness and enrollment in the U.S. healthcare plan, he did an interview with Zach Galifianakis on a show called "Between Two Ferns," a parody talk show produced by the comedic website *Funny or Die*. Nothing about the decision followed a mainstream media plan, yet the interview was considered pivotal in reaching younger people who didn't tune into cable or network TV or read newspapers and magazines. By entering their world, as it were, President Obama made a direct hit. By late 2017, the video had recorded more than 21.5 million views on YouTube.

LEAPFROGS AND LEGACY NETWORKS

In the United States, Katy Perry and Justin Bieber lead Twitter with 100 and 97 million followers, respectively. In the United Kingdom, the BBC has 33 million followers, followed by One Direction (31 million) and Harry Styles (30 million). Mesut Ozil, a German soccer player for Arsenal, leads all his countrymen with 15.7 million followers. David Guetta, a French DJ and record producer, has 21.7 million followers to lead France. It's not hard to see why most people consider social media as little more than entertainment for youth.

This popular use of social media in the West often clouds our thinking about its role in the lives of youth around the world. We view these virtual communities through the lens of our own cultures, generally dismissing them as little more than the cotton candy of pop culture, and then we extrapolate that view across the worldwide virtual battlefield. This can be a critical mistake. China's top English-language outlet is Xinhua News with 9.6 million Twitter followers. Only one person has more followers in Pakistan than Imran Khan, the politician and chairman of Tehreek-e-Insaf (the Pakistan Movement of Justice). In Afghanistan, ToloTV, a 24-hour news channel, has 135,000 subscribers. Turkish Prime Minister Recep

---

BOX 3.1   **THE DIFFERENT WAYS WE ABSORB CONTENT TODAY**

Video without sound—More than 50 percent of all Facebook videos are viewed without sound. Users regularly watch video on their phone, often in public spaces or with other people around. So, content needs to reach people visually. Most of our audience will never listen to the words we so carefully wrote to follow the lyrics and the scenery of our well-crafted production.

Everyone is a reporter—Our phones have cameras and we use them constantly. Analysts estimate that viewers watch more than five billion YouTube videos every day, and more than eight billion on Facebook. More and more of these are self-created videos shot with increasingly sophisticated smartphone cameras. About 80 percent of YouTube's views come from outside the U.S. In 2014, according to Mary Meeker's annual Internet Trends report, people uploaded an average of 1.8 billion digital images each day.

We share our lives visually—We love seeing things live. Viewers continue to watch Facebook Live videos three-times longer than regular videos. Collectively, we watch more than 100 million hours of video on Facebook each day.

Tayyip Erdogan ranks second in his country with 10.5 million Twitter followers. Most countries in the Middle East, Southeast Asia and other emerging parts of our world have embraced social media as their primary way to not just entertain, but to share news and learn.

These leapfrogging countries and individuals treat social media like an innovative news network, while many in the West are still trying to break ties to legacy platforms. Emerging public leaders, whether elected or annointed, have become increasingly visible on these platforms. They're the ones reaching the world's youth, who have 5,000 days to establish a habit of gleaning all their content needs from the small device they carry in their pocket every moment of every waking day. Today's youth might never pick up a newspaper or buy a magazine. And, as time passes, it becomes less and less likely they'll see much of anything said on television, unless it also shows up on the digital channels they follow. Whose message will they find as they forge their 5,000 Day Habit?

JOIN THE NETWORK

When social media first came of age, consultants and marketing experts urged businesses to "join the conversation." Companies needed to figure out how to remain relevant in the changing media lives of their customers, and to do so they had to participate in the digital discussion. Today, organizations need to consider a different, but related, approach. They need to "join the network." Now, rather than just joining the conversation, companies must build a full digital and social media platform that can reach and hold the attention of its audience for years to come.

Like the legacy outreach networks, this new system comes replete with a ratings system (e.g., likes, follows, shares) and direct audience feedback (e.g., comments and the creation of related content). Companies need only listen to the audience, discuss the topics it cares about, and connect with influencers it respects on the channels it follows. It's a rather straightforward model, but one that requires that organizations deprioritize traditional networks. When it comes to a global audience, that means rethinking the notion of networking. To reach people who speak Russian, one might consider a partnership with Moscow's Ivan Urgant, a Russian television star who hosts the Urgant Show. To reach a sympathetic audience throughout the Middle East and North Africa, a company might seek to engage with Wadah Khanfar (@khanfarw), the president and co-founder of Al Sharq Forum, the chairman of Common Action Forum and former Director-General of the Al Jazeera Network. Khanfar has 2.4 million Twitter followers.

Western governments, NGOs and companies also might start to consider a variety of media outlets that they could help transform into significant global voices across vast social media networks. What if Voice of America, which only has 1.3 million followers on its @voanews Twitter feed, built an audience of 10 million followers? Could the American Forces Network Europe, which has about 1,000 subscribers, get off the ground in any meaningful way to reach broader audiences? Who might want to help Africa Independent Television, based in Lagos, Nigeria, expand beyond its 25,000 likes on Facebook? Who might find synergy in enhancing audiences both for Abu Dhabi TV, which has more than 100,000 subscribers on YouTube, and Israel-based i24News, which has slightly less than 30,000 subscribers?

We need to get much more serious about who we want to be educating, informing and entertaining the youth of our world. Organizations, often run by people older and more dismissive of social media, have grudgingly OK'd the creation of a website, multimedia content or social channels, but they never embraced the fact that the digital technologies were re-creating the world's media network. Yet, Gen-Now will learn about their world through this new network. Its content will imprint upon their memories and build the influential memories of their reminiscence bump. They will view as influential the people, organizations and topics they consume on Facebook, Twitter, YouTube and Instagram — and, perhaps, the news channels progressive enough to "join the network."

The rest of the world will stammer, stutter and point fingers at technology, big data, artificial intelligence, cat videos or whatever convenient excuse they can find. Gen-Now won't care what they think. They're already deep into their 5,000 day habit.

CHAPTER 4

LIFTING OUR MENTAL FOG

"Darkness cannot drive out darkness; only light can do that.
Hate cannot drive out hate; only love can do that."
— MARTIN LUTHER KING, JR.

The fog settles in deep and thick over the San Francisco Bay the night before the conference in Mill Valley. Driving across the Golden Gate Bridge at 2 a.m., drivers can see virtually nothing ahead of them. Slow down. Just stay in your lane, foot poised over the brake, ready to jump on the pedal at the first sight of taillights ahead. The windows fog up, and clumsy-tired fingers fumble for the defrost in the rental car. The crossing takes three or four times as long as it normally would, and by the time the car starts climbing the first hills of Marin, every last bit of energy drains away. Stubbornly ignoring the conditions that could lead to injury, refusing to acknowledge the danger blanketing the windshield — once on the bridge, there's no way to turn back. No choice now; push on, white-knuckled, despite the risk and uncertainty.

Each day, we're blessed with a series of opportunities to decide the direction of our lives and how we hope to influence the people we touch, whether in-person or through virtual channels. When we face important decisions, we typically think more clearly and deliberately. But as we go about the daily machinations of life, we often sink back into a fog of biases. Sometimes we get trapped in our own personal biases. Other times, the fog arises from the influence of other people. Some of these biases are deeply ingrained in our lives. Some are ever-changing, like the subconscious push of a sympathetic story we heard that morning. Regardless, our habits exert the most influence on our behavior when we're crawling through a fog of bias.

When we're young or starting out in a new job or environment, the people surrounding us serve up bias in the form of advice. Hopefully, it helps enhance our lives and successes, but it always shapes people, sometimes permanently. An older African-American man refuses to look at a 19-year-old white college kid, working a part-time job at the North Carolina furniture show back in 1981. The kid asks a colleague why Shorty never looks him in the eye, and is heartbroken to hear: "Hey, that's just the way it is." More often than not, the people in our lives believe they're doing the right thing, but even the best-intentioned mentor might give exceptionally poor counsel. After all, they're stumbling through their own fog of bias, too.

To be sure, many of our biases are essentially harmless, and in many cases thoughtful people understand their tendencies and try to account for them. But place two opposed perspectives in a heated environment, and the friction can push us quickly toward combustion. Consider, for example, the perspective of Israeli Prime Minister Benjamin Netanyahu, in a 2016 speech he delivered to the United Nations' 71st General Assembly:

"I want you to imagine a day in the life of a 13-year-old Palestinian boy, I'll call him Ali. Ali wakes up before school, he goes to practice with a soccer team named after Dalal Mughrabi, a Palestinian terrorist responsible for the murder of a busload of 37 Israelis. At school, Ali attends an event sponsored by the Palestinian Ministry of Education honoring Baha Alyan, who last year murdered three Israeli civilians. On his walk home, Ali looks up at a towering statue erected just a few weeks ago by the Palestinian Authority to honor Abu Sukar, who detonated a bomb in the center of Jerusalem, killing 15 Israelis. When Ali gets home, he turns on the TV and sees an interview with a senior Palestinian official, Jibril Rajoub, who says that if he had a nuclear bomb, he'd detonate it over Israel that very day. Ali then turns on the radio and he hears President Abbas's adviser, Sultan Abu al-Einein, urging Palestinians, here's a quote, "to slit the throats of Israelis wherever you find them." Ali checks his Facebook and he sees a recent

post by President Abbas's Fatah Party calling the massacre of 11 Israeli athletes at the Munich Olympics a "heroic act." On YouTube, Ali watches a clip of President Abbas himself saying, "We welcome every drop of blood spilled in Jerusalem." Direct quote. Over dinner, Ali asks his mother what would happen if he killed a Jew and went to an Israeli prison? Here's what she tells him. She tells him he'd be paid thousands of dollars each month by the Palestinian Authority. In fact, she tells him, the more Jews he would kill, the more money he'd get. Oh, and when he gets out of prison, Ali would be guaranteed a job with the Palestinian Authority. Ladies and gentlemen, all this is real. It happens every day, all the time."

While Netanyahu's perspective is one shared by many Israelis and supporters around the world, we know others come to the same situation from a different perspective. Palestinians and Muslims also see bias and injustice in the Middle East and beyond. In the year leading up to Netanyahu's address, a woman wearing a headscarf was physically assaulted in Austria, while in Germany an elderly Sikh man is mistaken for a Muslim and attacked. A Canadian mosque was set ablaze, while a Belgian mosque was desecrated with severed pig heads. In virtually every Western country, one can find examples of both anti-Semitic and anti-Muslim bias — and, far too often, it becomes violent. What might start as "ignorant" bias can escalate to "kids being kids" vandalism. Soon enough, we say it has become a real problem, but in our fog of bias we rarely realize that, for the victim, it reached that threshold long ago.

This failure to recognize a problem from another's perspective — to empathize — lies at the root of bias. We can do this knowingly or unknowingly, but either way we've locked ourselves into a monochromatic view and closed off our minds. Statisticians refer to certain biases as systematic error, because the sampling is unfair. And in some cases, systematic error and data bias produce results that confirm a researcher's expectations going into the analysis — thus, we see confirmation bias, which only serves to deepen pre-conditioned beliefs. One bias magnifies the next.

People do the same when they fail to test their beliefs and hold onto a one-dimensional view for long periods of time. They enter a filter bubble, seeking information and outlets that support their views. They hang out with people like them, and lose their appreciation for diversity. They cast their lives narrowly so as not to face reconsideration of what's become a core belief. Over time, some people reach a point of anger and frustration. People begin to protest from a state of anger, rather than a state of justice or betterment for all their fellow citizens. In short, they move into hate. And if they continue to narrowcast information as their anger heightens, they move toward more extreme measures — often aligning political, religious or other dogmatic causes.

In short, their personal fog of bias keeps getting thicker and thicker. But unlike the tired, late-night driver on the Golden Gate Bridge, who at least has the good sense to recognize the danger, they drift toward active recklessness, myopic hate and outright violence.

A POTENT COMBINATION:
THE MERE-EXPOSURE AND FALSE-CONSENSUS EFFECTS

Dr. Victoria Romero walked up to address the class with an easy smile that belies her day job as Chief Scientist at IST Research*, a firm that develops information technology to protect us. An expert in social science and neuroscience, Romero is also principal investigator with the Defense Advanced Research Projects Agency (DARPA) Memex program, which analyzes activity on the deep and dark web to identify and track illicit activity. An expert in ISIS counter-messaging, she takes a very pragmatic, research-based view of how others influence us.

"The more often we're exposed to something, the more we accept it, trust it and like it," Romero told the June 2017 class of representatives from 45 NGOs in Washington. It's called the 'mere-exposure effect'. In a nutshell, people develop a greater preference for topics, people or things with which they're more familiar. This happens with words, language, paintings, faces, sounds and much more. If you see a person frequently, they become more pleasing and likable as you become more familiar with their appearance.

The mere-exposure effect can exert a powerful influence across social media channels. An outsider might check out an extremist site on a few occasions and write it off as egregious, but someone listening every day begins to develop an appreciation for the message and even begins to build

---

* Now Chief Scientist at Next Century

trust with the person or group at the other end — even if they're publishing from halfway around the world. And if you see 5 million or 10 million people following that person or feed, well, chances are the mere-exposure effect has helped grow that audience.

Just as confirmation bias can ratchet up a systematic error in statistics, a sense of shared agreement can build upon the mere-exposure effect. Familiarity and alignment heighten into the "false consensus effect," Romero told the NGO representatives. Participants begin to overestimate their beliefs and values, viewing them as typical and perceiving a broad consensus that, often, doesn't exist. Human beings have such a keen desire to join groups and to believe their views align with their fellow adherents. It heightens confidence. Even for extremists who know most of the world opposes their hateful beliefs, the potent combination of mere-exposure effect and false consensus effect leads them to overestimate their support:

- They have built-in mechanisms to protect against those who suggest they're wrong.
- They imagine that more people are on their side than truly are.
- When presented with evidence that proves they're wrong, they believe the person providing the update is misleading them or is injecting bias.
- If they track an issue intensely, they make decisions based on scant information, projecting their biased selves into a situation to come up with an answer.

THE TWO ROUTES TO PERSUASION

Human beings always figure out ways to rationalize their behavior. Understanding this is critical to understanding how we begin to positively influence people who hate. Because our own rationalizations seem rational to us, we tend to think of persuasion as a direct route, one based on evidence and logic. This is the central route shown in Figure 4.1, which is based on the "Elaboration Likelihood Model" developed by Richard E. Petty and John Cacioppo in 1986. However, persuasion works more frequently through a peripheral route — mainly because most people don't listen well, don't think critically about what they're hearing, and respond more readily to cues from charismatic figures.

FIGURE 4.1 — THE ROUTES OF PERSUASION

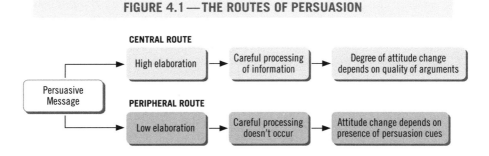

Graphic courtesy of Dr. Victoria Romero

The divergent responses to each of these routes become more stark in situations of extremism, when the persuasive messages don't conform to deeply held biases. In many of these cases, the audience might see an earnest entreaty as a dire threat, and it sparks the expected response. To the class of NGO officials in Washington, Romero explained this through the lens of the Terror Management Theory, which was developed by Jeff Greenberg, Sheldon Solomon and Tom Pyszcynski. In the face of perceived threats to our safety or our way of life, humans rely on a handful of predictable reactions to cope:

- We cling more tightly to our worldviews to deal with the perceived threat
- The fear of death or harm moves us to a more extreme position
- We prepare to defend our views
- We see the world in black and white and eschew subtlety
- And we heighten any existing preference for stronger, iconic leaders

Essentially, our brains naturally prepare us to align to fight for what we believe in. It works effectively when one nation-state rallies to battle another. It works equally effectively when an ideologically driven group is motivating its "troops" to fight a war on its own terms.

SACRED VALUES AND NORMAL VALUES

The central and peripheral routes of persuasion can help guide delivery and tone, but we need to think carefully about the core values we embed in a message. Emphasize or attack the wrong set of beliefs, and the effort will push its audience deeper into extremism and hate. We can categorize these beliefs as "sacred values" and "normal values." As the label suggests, sacred values are those we hold most dear, the values we refuse to relinquish for any amount of money, influence or other enticements. They're off-limits. We see this play out in American politics on a regular basis. Pro-choice and pro-life factions will not change their views. It remains remarkable when someone changes their stance on second amendment gun rights, and it typically happens only in reaction to exceptional events or circumstances.

The same entrenchment applies in nationalist, religious and extremist contexts. Here, our understanding requires a careful consideration of which issues are too sensitive to broach (the sacred values) versus the issues on which one might change his or her mind (normal values). Yet, we rarely do this. We too often lead with our chin, a bad habit that's regularly modeled by political campaigns. Someone running for office whips up his or her support base by focusing on sacred values and how they're under attack by the "other" side. It works remarkably well for fund raising and mobilizing supporters. This rarely changes anyone's mind; it merely reinforces existing polarization and motivates existing proponents to action. This is what extremist groups do to rally their own base.

So, how do we sway the more-impressionable members toward peace and positivity?

To do that, we need to identify a set of "normal values" and create a message that can nudge people toward a a reconsideration of them. Fortunately, we all have beliefs we profess to hold much more deeply than we actually do, and we process these differently in our brains. These non-sacred values activate the parts of the brain associated with reward and logical cost-benefit analysis (i.e., the reward circuit and prefrontal cortex). Sacred values activate brain areas associated with rules (the tempero-parietal junction) and fear and disgust (the amygdala).

Speaking to her class of NGO leaders, Romero outlined four steps to consider when navigating sacred and normal values:

- Study the audience's local sacred values
- Parse your message to make sure it doesn't conflict with sacred values

- Do not offer material incentives for changing or contradicting sacred values

- If possible, attach your message to a sacred value; supporting a sacred value can be beneficial

UNDERSTANDING THE LOCAL MASTER NARRATIVE

And here, Romero switched gears, to something that sounds easy enough but represents the most difficult pivot to make. Effective persuasion, she said, requires an understanding of the "local master narrative" that informs how people think. (In business, we call this walking in the shoes of the customer.) In many cultures, for example, the local master narrative suggests that underdogs will remain mired in their struggle, and only in the rarest circumstances will they overcome adversity. Compare this with the U.S., where the American Dream suggests that anyone, from any background, can rise to the top with hard work and a couple of breaks. Or look at England, where class identity is an ingrained, accepted part of British culture.

But we also need to understand our own master narratives and how they compare with and contrast to the narratives of our audience. Western readers of this book probably believe in the power of evidence and a logic trail to support a point of view, and they often assume that most of the world develops their perspectives in a similar manner. In reality, emotions tend to prove more effective and persuasive than facts, and the facts are bent to support the emotional state. So, despite little chance of success, we identify a group we view as hateful or extremist and try to reach them with rational, fact-based arguments. But what plays well in the conference room doesn't translate to the family room.

It might even make things worse. As young people form the memories, identities and habits that will shape the rest of their lives, they build those on a framework of what they see, hear, read and feel every day. They know what "normal" feels like. So when a person or organization injects a new set of facts — whether through social media, a sponsored Web ad or more traditional channels — it feels alien and wrong. Usually, it's ignored. Often, it's actively and passionately rejected.

Effective messaging aligns with the habits, the memory formation, the social channels, the devices, the values and the local master narrative of those we want to reach. But beliefs rarely change overnight. We have to practice extreme patience if we intend to build the depth of trust needed to accommodate an appeal based on both fact and emotion. And during that slow, agonizing process, Romero noted, we need to keep things simple. After all, she explained, research shows that we prefer to pass along the types of information that elicit happiness, fear or disgust, rather than a deep dive into details. At work, light banter or gossip is easier than a practical discussion of line items on the budget. Virtually no one reads a controversial piece of legislation or analyzes the methodology of a GAO report. When discussing the latest hit movie, most of us talk about plotlines and performances rather than lighting and cinematography.

We naturally prefer to skate across the surface when we converse, and we readily consume the same sort of surface-level communications from the communities with which we align. We come to trust the people in front of us every day, on our favorite channels, and we absorb what they think is important. Critical thinking about an argument — especially one we're already inclined to believe — goes out the window. We forget the source and remember the information. We recall as facts things that might be fictional or distorted by highly biased sources. If something feels true in our guts, it becomes true in our minds. Someone or something needs to push us deeper.

TRANSPORTING OTHERS THROUGH STORYTELLING

Through her work with DARPA, Romero worked with the agency's Narrative Networks project, collaborating with Eric Schumacher and Matt Bezdek of Georgia Tech and Richard Gerring at Stony Brook University to see how critical thinking defenses can be deactivated and how sensory and emotional processing can be enhanced. They hope to find ways to make our messages more readily accepted by reticent audiences. And a key part of that, Romero told the class in June, is the idea of "transportation" — how we immerse ourselves in the world of those we hope to reach, a concept originated by Gerring.

What she and her colleagues have found, she said, is that by immersing ourselves in the world of those we're trying to influence, we can adapt our messages to their perspectives and behaviors. Furthermore, by using that local insight to craft a story and think more like the characters in it, we can begin to forge a tighter bond between our message and their emotions and values, increasing the likelihood that the audience will embrace it. This use of stories can sustain attention, influence identification and social learning, and normalize controversial and unfamiliar ideas and behaviors. [See Box 4.1] Plus, by becoming a more naturally received part of the audience's content flow, we can influence them in a relevant and entertaining way.

BOX 4.1   **PIXAR'S 22 TIPS FOR EFFECTIVE STORYTELLING**

In 2012, director and Pixar storyboard artist Emma Coats tweeted these storytelling tips:

- You admire a character for trying more than for their successes.
- You gotta keep in mind what's interesting to you as an audience, not what's fun to do as a writer. They can be very different.
- Trying for theme is important, but you won't see what the story is actually about til you're at the end of it. Now rewrite.
- Once upon a time there was ___. Every day, ___. One day ___. Because of that, ___. Because of that, ___. Until finally ___.
- Simplify. Focus. Combine characters. Hop over detours. You'll feel like you're losing valuable stuff but it sets you free.
- What is your character good at, comfortable with? Throw the polar opposite at them. Challenge them. How do they deal?
- Come up with your ending before you figure out your middle. Seriously. Endings are hard, get yours working up front.
- Finish your story, let go even if it's not perfect. In an ideal world you have both, but move on. Do better next time.
- When you're stuck, make a list of what WOULDN'T happen next. Lots of times the material to get you unstuck will show up.
- Pull apart the stories you like. What you like in them is a part of you; you've got to recognize it before you can use it.
- Putting it on paper lets you start fixing it. If it stays in your head, a perfect idea, you'll never share it with anyone.
- Discount the 1st thing that comes to mind. And the 2nd, 3rd, 4th, 5th—get the obvious out of the way. Surprise yourself.

- Give your characters opinions. Passive/malleable might seem likable to you as you write, but it's poison to the audience.

- Why must you tell THIS story? What's the belief burning within you that your story feeds off of? That's the heart of it.

- If you were your character, in this situation, how would you feel? Honesty lends credibility to unbelievable situations.

- What are the stakes? Give us reason to root for the character. What happens if they don't succeed? Stack the odds against.

- No work is ever wasted. If it's not working, let go and move on—it'll come back around to be useful later.

- You have to know yourself: the difference between doing your best & fussing. Story is testing, not refining.

- Coincidences to get characters into trouble are great; coincidences to get them out of it are cheating.

- Exercise: take the building blocks of a movie you dislike. How d'you rearrange them into what you DO like?

- You gotta identify with your situation/characters, can't just write 'cool'. What would make YOU act that way?

- What's the essence of your story? Most economical telling of it? If you know that, you can build out from there.

LEARNING YOUR ABCDE'S

Storytelling helps us cut through the fog of bias, both ours and that of our intended audience, but doing this effectively requires the discipline and focus of models that were developed and tempered with decades of global marketing experience. Few companies have as strong a history of building global brands as Procter & Gamble. Ed Tazzia and Kip Knight started their careers at P&G, eventually crafting a straightforward but effective approach to how companies should market their products. The two marketing gurus call it ABCDE—audience, behavior, content, delivery and execution. The model is central to the U.S. State Department's Marketing College curriculum, which Tazzia and Knight helped launch in 2008. Here's a brief explanation:

Audience—Who is your targeted audience? Settle on only one and define it narrowly.

Behavior — What do you want your audience to do? It should be related to an objective you've developed. It should be specific, actionable and measurable. And you should know the benefit of your message.

Content — What tone (what adjectives) of messaging will resonate with your audience? What is the 'reason to believe' for your audience? What specific information is interesting and persuasive to your audience?

Delivery — How will you deliver your message to your audience? Who will deliver it?

Execution — What are different ways to measure short, medium and long-term success? How can you measure the behavior?

The ABCDE model is a simple one that is hard to do. It's a strategic filter, demanding that your plan is on target. Every program or campaign, whether marketing for P&G or trying to sway potential recruits away from an extremist group, needs to be able to answer these questions in detail. If you can fill it out and the answers inspire you, great. If not, you have more work to do.

THE REALITY CHECK

Humanity does not have an especially harmonious track record. We've killed hundreds of millions of our peers over centuries of warfare. We do not treat all people with equal respect, especially women, ethnic minorities and those who follow faiths different from ours. We've figured out ways to enslave others, and to discriminate against peers during an average workday. Our brash proclamations on social media alienate our friends and acquaintances, often without us even realizing our offense. We tune in to hear divisive commentary on cable television, absorbing whatever fits our mindset. We are, inherently, walking fog machines of bias.

Yet, we have a remarkable capacity for peace, understanding and cooperation. Despite our violent history, the vast majority of the 7.5 billion people on the planet seek peace, want to encourage hope and try to enhance their local, regional and global communities. In his book, "Stride Toward Freedom," the Rev. Dr. Martin Luther King Jr. charted out six principles of nonviolence. [See Box 4.2] They served as a guide for people hoping to transform their country and bend it toward racial justice. They

THE KEY LEARNINGS FROM "MARKETING COLLEGE"

BY ED TAZZIA
Principal, Sycamore and Company

Over the thirteen occasions we taught the Marketing Communication College for the U.S. State Department, three things continued to resonate. First, the ABCDE model works. Second, the benefit message has to be a benefit to the audience, not the speaker. Third, the College needs to be taught to the highest levels of the organization to be truly effective.

The model works

The core of the Marketing College has been consistent from the outset: Don't start with execution, start with strategy. Don't get enamored with the latest medium or technology before you understand your audience and your strategy. Because the latest medium or technology might not be the right vehicle to tell your story in an effective way.

The specific ABCDE model—audience, behavior, content, delivery, evaluation—has evolved to this simplified version, which is easy for the non-marketer to understand and take back to their day job. We have observed that too often our students are being asked to work on a project with no understanding of the objectives or strategy. A manager wants a blog or a Twitter feed—often because they have seen others with blogs or Twitter feeds. But these vehicles might not be right for the objectives or strategy, assuming the manager had any objective or a strategy to begin with.

Focus on the target audience

Too often our students and their management believe their job is to "explain and defend" policies, and that's certainly a part of the role in many situations. However, if your objective is to change the way people think and behave, the real job is to "understand, inform and influence." And the only way to influence people is to determine what matters to them, not just tell them what matters to you.

Work the top down

Most of the students we have taught in this course are part of one of the most top-down organizations in the world. And while our students have taken the learnings from this college back to their jobs, we have expressed to their senior managers that the way this model will truly take hold is if they, the people at the top, demand it. Senior leaders must also ask: Who is the audience? What is the desired behavior? What is the content? How will it be delivered? How will it be evaluated? To align with our audience, we also need to align inside our own organization.

remain just as relevant today, in the U.S. and around the world. If we hope to keep charting a path toward hope, and away from the bloodshed, violence and hate that marks humanity's past, we would do well to heed King's principles.

BOX 4.2

THE REV. DR. MARTIN LUTHER KING JR.'S
SIX PRINCIPLES OF NONVIOLENCE

1. *Nonviolence is a way of life for courageous people*—It is active nonviolent resistance to evil. It is aggressive spiritually, mentally and emotionally.

2. *Nonviolence seeks to win friendship and understanding*—The end result of nonviolence is redemption and reconciliation. The purpose of nonviolence is the creation of the Beloved Community.

3. *Nonviolence seeks to defeat injustice not people*—Nonviolence recognizes that evildoers are also victims and are not evil people. The nonviolent resister seeks to defeat evil not people.

4. *Nonviolence holds that suffering can educate and transform*— Nonviolence accepts suffering without retaliation. Unearned suffering is redemptive and has tremendous educational and transforming possibilities.

5. *Nonviolence chooses love instead of hate*—Nonviolence resists violence of the spirit as well as the body. Nonviolent love is spontaneous, unmotivated, unselfish and creative.

6. *Nonviolence believes that the universe is on the side of justice*—The nonviolent resister has deep faith that justice will eventually win. Nonviolence believes that God is a God of justice.

CHAPTER 5

THE URGENCY OF HOPE

"Helplessness induces hopelessness, and history attests that loss of hope and not loss of lives is what decides the issue of war."
— Sir Basil Henry Liddell Hart

The flashbacks return at random times. Walking through an airport. Taking the dog for a walk. Usually times when I (Bob) reflect on life.

I picked up my office phone at Rhone-Poulenc Rorer (now Sanofi), and a business executive from Maryland came through on the other end of the line. He asked if he could come visit us and discuss Rilutek, the drug we were developing to fight ALS, better known as Lou Gehrig's Disease. Sure, I told him, come on by. A week later, unannounced, he arrived at our front desk, and a colleague escorted him back to my office. He immediately launched into a flurry of questions about the Rilutek clinical trials, our commitment to ALS and what we planned to do to help the community. He started out in the typical staccato style of an executive, but eventually started to relax. He looked me in the eye and said: "Bob, I now know you and your company will do what it takes to get this drug approved, and you'll do the right thing for patients and my wife, who's dying of ALS. I feel better now. Thank you." And with that, he left.

It shook me — not his abrupt appearance at our offices or his brusque questioning. What hit me there, and it left me in tears, was the depth of his hope in what was, for all practical purposes, a hopeless situation. One of my proudest moments in my career came a few years later, when my colleagues and I announced the launch of Rilutek, the first drug approved to treat ALS.

I would come across that remarkable hope in the face of urgency again in the years to come. During a board meeting for the Huntington's Disease Society of America, Barry, the one board member who suffered from the neurodegenerative disease, listened intently as his limbs herked and jerked. Barry's presence and the outward manifestation of the disease screamed at us: "Move faster! Raise more money! Make a difference today, not tomorrow!" Yet, Barry supplied a calm and optimism that many of us often lost in the face of the long research road ahead. And in one of our first meetings with ACT-UP, the coalition created to advocate for AIDS patients, the late Jonathan Lax didn't hesitate to interrupt our briefing on the progress we'd made toward a vaccine. "Why don't I brief you instead," he said. "It will be more productive." He excused himself for a minute while he took his medicine, and then updated us with a level of detail on our clinical trials that went well beyond my knowledge. He knew the ins and outs, the issues we were having and he was in direct conversations with our team.

None of these remarkable people had the luxury of time. Everything about their lives was urgent, yet each of them exhibited the same phenomenon about time and reality. People who realize they have little time left, facing death or disability, often evolve into a positive, more hopeful and more focused mindset. Every day counts, and they will make it count. That's what I remember in those times of reflection; working for 30 years with people battling disease opened my eyes to it. Even when timelines are clipped — and often *because* they're clipped — hope still rises.

TWO SIDES OF HOPE: URGENCY AND LIMITATIONS

Chemistry can get awfully complex awfully fast, but the field does provide us with a nice allegory for our understanding of hope — the enantiomer. Without drifting into complexities, enantiomers are molecular structures made up of two compounds that are mirror images of each other. Each "side" shares the same physical properties, but they interact differently with polarized light and certain other molecules. As a result, different enantiomers can have different biological effects. When we formulate a new pharmaceutical, one of the drug's "sides" might create the efficacy we want, but the other could generate adverse side effects. Thalidomide is one such drug. Initially sold as a sedative in the late-1950s, it was withdrawn from the market because the other "side" caused birth defects. Yet, researchers never gave up on this drug due to its activity. They used it for leprosy and to try to counteract HIV-related weight loss. In the 1990s, Celgene realized the drug could fight a blood cancer called multiple myeloma. A derivative of thalidomide called Revlimid was approved in 2005 for one type of blood cancer. By the following year, Revlimid and Thalomid, another derivative, were approved to treat multiple myeloma.

Much like the duality embodied within enantiomers, hope displays two related but different sides — its urgency and its limitations. While urgency can heighten hope, as it did with the many people I met during my tenure with pharmaceutical companies, it also can fade and disappear altogether. The limitation of hope is that it can't last forever. The same timeline that makes hope radiate in its urgency, also erodes and dulls the same hope gone unanswered. Once diminished, hopelessness can spread like a disease, subtly wearing away optimism for the future. Yet in most humans, a yearning remains, and that increases our susceptibility to extremism and hate. When we can't find a hopeful place in our world, we will find the best alternative.

We believe hope plays a vital role in countering hate, so much so that we created the HOPE Index. Inspired by Maslow's Hierarchy of Needs [See Figure 5.1] and applied to the context of extremism, it employs algorithms and data science to help understand whether our efforts create environments that increase hope and empower youth to dream, or allow the degradation of optimism and leave youth seeking alternative solutions. We need an algorithm because measuring these environments and outcomes requires an analysis of hundreds of different, interrelated variables. But we first need the model to guide our evaluation.

FIGURE 5.1 — MASLOW'S HIERARCHY OF NEEDS

Abraham Maslow's famous paper, *A Theory of Human Motivation,* was published in Psychological Review in 1943. Psychologists before him talked about needs theory and related ideas, but Maslow made it simple. Survival comes first for all of us. We cannot think beyond this point until our basic needs are met. Once we feel safe, we care more about what others think about us. Do we have a place in our community? Do we belong? This leads to esteem—we need to feel respect and acceptance from others. Finally, we have an intense desire to belong to something of importance. It makes us feel valuable and it helps us cope with the ups and downs of life. When you are self-actualized, you have become the person you set out to be.

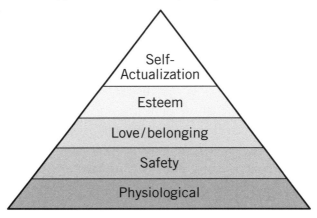

THE HOPE INDEX

We build hope one step at a time, much like the ascending cadence of Maslow's hierarchy. One step makes the next step possible. And, in the spirit of Maslow's famous pyramid, we build our model from the bottom—starting with *environment* and working our way up through *poverty, open minds* and *human rights.*

ENVIRONMENT

We begin building our model and subsequent algorithm with environmental variables. These create the atmosphere of hope or hopelessness that begins to condition the youth within. We categorize these as entry, risk and respect:

- *Environmental Entry* — We already know how to dramatically decrease infant mortality and expand educational activities. How actively are governments, NGOs and other agencies working to drive down infant deaths and provide a primary education? These are some of the earliest signs of a caring environment.

- *Environmental Risk* — How likely is it that a violent crime will occur in the community? How many homicides occur per capita in a year? What exposure do youth have to events of terrorism (e.g. number of incidents, fatalities, injury, property and infrastructure damage)? How many *religious extremists* or other terrorists have emerged from the community? In short, how safe do young people feel on a day-in, day-out basis?

- *Environmental Respect* — What are the rates of human trafficking? Does the community house a large share of disempowered refugees? Do we care about those who are most in need? A government sends a strong message with its investments in the population, particularly through aid for disadvantaged residents and the percentage of GDP dedicated to health and education.

Like Maslow's model, if we can't live in a safe environment — or at least live in a place where the government is working with us to make it safer — it's hard for us to progress further in our quest for hope. The intensity of the environment is less important than the intent. We are looking for locations where a country is trying to improve, and we can see when those efforts matter.

POVERTY

We look at poverty in a slightly different way. We view a lack of job opportunities as a form of professional poverty. A lack of schooling equates to intellectual poverty. Health poverty extends from inadequate resources for care of the population.

- *Professional poverty* — What percentage of the population is under 25 years old, and what is the unemployment rate among those youth old enough to work? How long has the rate of youth unemployment stayed in that range? If unemployment or underemployment remains chronically high for an extended time, a young person's long-term view of the world changes. The prospects and successes of a young adult and his or her peers prior to 25 years old influences their lifelong memories in a critical window of neurodevelopment and formation of the reminiscence bump.

- *Intellectual poverty* — What is the average educational level? What are literacy rates like? In general, someone who raises their education and literacy levels hopes to progress beyond his or her current state.

- *Health poverty* — What is the rate of malnutrition? How adequate is housing, water and sewer infrastructure, health care facilities and access to vaccines and other medicine?

We've seen many cases in which employment and education gains have overcome issues of housing and even food scarcity. In the West, business magazines are filled with stories of executives who overcame homelessness or other disadvantages. They faced many challenges and, to their credit, overcame them. But few in the developed world suffer the same depth of all the alternative forms of poverty that batter youth in developing countries.

OPEN MINDS

We can see and measure the potential impact of new ideas and new ways of thinking. People exposed to more and different beliefs, cultures, religions and societies — those who experience the diversity of humanity on this wonderful planet — more readily envision new approaches to their status quo.

- *Access to technology* — Can I access media from around my country and around the world? What are the penetration rates of smart phones and/or broadband Internet access? How much does censorship limit the flow of information and diverse experience?

- *Access to travel* — Can I leave my country? How often do people leave? How many people have emigrated to other nations? If I decide to relocate, even temporarily, where can I find a strong diaspora to support my transition?

- *Access to education* — Can I leave my country to pursue education? What percentage of people in my community, city or country have college or post-graduate degrees? What opportunities do I have to attend a university with a diverse set of people and viewpoints?

HUMAN RIGHTS

Finally, at the highest order of the HOPE Index lies human rights. This drives directly at the self-actualization atop Maslow's hierarchy — the measure of respect each person deserves so they can pursue their interests in a way that doesn't diminish the equivalent respect they pay their fellow global citizens.

- *Individual rights* — Am I being discriminated against because of who I am? Do my neighbors, governments and communities respect my rights as a woman, a disabled person, or an individual within the LGBT community?

- *Group rights* — Do people dislike me because I am part of an organization, religion or other association? How prevalent is intimidation, ethnic conflicts or other bias/hate crime?

- *Country rights* — Do I have the freedom to make life choices, to trade, to invest? Can I express myself in a way that fulfills me if I'm not infringing on others' rights to do the same?

A note on population and sample size

The algorithms built on the HOPE Index can process myriad data points, but credible measurements rely on an appropriate sample size. As more data sets become available in the months and years to come, we will be able to construct more granular HOPE Index readings. This is a critical next step for the model, because nation-states tend to have a lesser influence on the development of hate than do sub-regions, cities and neighborhoods. Eighty-eight of the 233 countries have 10 million or more people. Once you cross this threshold, the need to focus on a city or sub-region becomes increasingly important. We still want to consider country-level data, but it's important to focus on smaller areas wherever possible.

DELIVERING HOPE

Our work with the HOPE Index provides a deeper understanding of the power of hope, the devastation of hopelessness, and the factors that nudge young people toward one outcome or the other. It also makes clear the urgency of hope — that we have a limited runway to reach young people before they decide where they want to reside on the love-hate spectrum.

THE POWER OF HOPE

BY COL. WILLIAM S. REEDER JR.
Author, *Through the Valley: My Captivity in Vietnam*

Colonel Reeder is a retired U.S. Army officer and highly decorated combat veteran of the Vietnam War. In 2014, he was inducted into the U.S. Army Aviation Hall of Fame. He has received the Silver Star for gallantry, two Distinguished Flying Crosses for heroism, an Air Medal for valor and three Purple Hearts.

I returned to Vietnam for my second combat tour in December 1971. On May 9, 1972, my Cobra attack helicopter was shot down, exploding on impact and leaving me badly wounded. I survived the crash, but was captured after evading the enemy for three days.

In my book *Through the Valley: My Captivity in Vietnam*, I describe what it was like to be held for weeks in jungle cages and then enduring a grueling three-month forced march on the Ho Chi Minh Trail to the notorious prisons of Hanoi. The ordeal cost the lives of seven in my group of 27 POWs. During my captivity, I was abused, starved and denied medical care. I was brutally interrogated and beaten, my shoulders were dislocated, and I was caged with my feet clamped in wooden stocks, all the while suffering from a broken back, infected leg, intestinal parasites, dysentery and three different kinds of malaria.

I'm sometimes asked if I harbor hatred against my captors. My answer is, "No." They were human beings, acting as they'd been raised in their communities, educated (or brainwashed) by their communist government and scarred by war. Had our roles and life's experiences been reversed, I'm sure I would have behaved the same way.

As a prisoner of war, I lived with people who were very different from me. During much of my time in captivity, I was the only American, traveling through the jungle with a small group of South Vietnamese prisoners of war. For several weeks, while separated from them, I traveled only with my guard, moving among groups of North Vietnamese soldiers, my enemy, and encountering members of the civilian population of North Vietnam along the way. This gave me the opportunity to interact with these people as they were, to look beneath the veneer of difference, to able to see much of what we hold in common as human beings.

One lesson that experience taught me is that we are all God's children. We are not born with the cultural bias that we learn in our youth and often carry with us to our graves. Despite the many differences we exhibited, I found we also shared much in common at our core—our basic humanity. Ever since, I have tried to relate to people as individuals, not prejudging anyone because of their appearance or birthplace or religion.

During my captivity, I grabbed hold of hope and never let go. I credit my survival to faith and the power of that positive spirit. So, no, I don't hate. Instead I have tried to replace ignorance with knowledge and reject fear and hatred, seeking to gain greater understanding and new friends instead.

Left untreated, it spreads like a disease, only one that we can't treat with the latest wonder drug. We can't snap our fingers and provide a young man in Syria a fruitful career, a family, stable housing and food, vacations to foreign lands, a top-notch education and the amenities we enjoy in Western countries. But if we start assuming we'll never get there — when young people begin to believe an optimistic, peaceful path will never get them there — then disease sets in.

That's what makes the HOPE Index and its capacity to identify the places and the issues on which we need to focus so critical. This is why data.world's community has become an invaluable place to share data, analyze variables and learn from the results. And it's why the Facebook community is becoming an indispensable library for best practices in countering hate.

We need each other to make a difference, and we don't have time to waste if we want to magnify the urgency of hope before it is diminished. Doctors and scientists realize they need to move with speed every day because their patients are counting on them. Our patients are the youth of this world. They will never ask for our help, but they urgently hope someone can figure out how to make their corner of the world a better place.

CHAPTER 6

THE PRE-HATE JOURNEY

"The paradox of education is precisely this:
that as one begins to become conscious, one begins to examine
the society in which he is being educated."
—JAMES BALDWIN

T he realization struck me when I (Bob) still worked at Dell. By the time I left the company in 2009, the idea started to congeal into the thesis of my first book, *PreCommerce* (2011), which looked at how we buy goods online. My Dell colleagues and I had started to realize that, while we tended to focus nearly all our time and resources on the transaction itself, the moment of sale represented less than one percent of the time our customers spent online in their entire lives, while 99% of their time was spent in the PreCommerce phase, where they are learning, sharing and listening to their peers. We knew all the traditional models of brand aware-ness, advertising and messaging, of course, but now we understood we could directly influence customers during this pivotal time — in the actual moments when they were molding their attitudes toward our products, services and overall brand. I joined W2O shortly after leaving Dell, and I carried this growing idea, which I dubbed PreCommerce, along with me.

Today, any marketing professional worth his or her salt knows that customers already have searched for information and followed a brand for weeks, months or years before they come to our store or site to buy. In 2018, it's a well-established expectation that customer beliefs form well before a transaction. Seven years ago, though, suggesting companies commit far more of their resources to the period before the transaction was a radical notion. But we've seen the power of flipping models on their head, especially with the advent of the Internet. Just look at search: In the typical model, a company shares content online, pays for top-of-screen advertising on Google or Bing, and then examines its results. If it doesn't like the rankings for key queries, it puts out more content and pays for more advertising, trying to ensure that customers see its story first. This all occurs as part of what everyone knows as search engine optimization and search engine marketing.

The new model recognizes that a few smart people in Mountain View and Seattle organize virtually all the content loaded on the Web, making it easier for others to find. If we deconstruct the operation from this perspective, we realize we don't need to do much more than identify the top 100 or so queries that customers use to find out about our product, study the top few screens of search results for each of those queries, and then develop an algorithm to analyze the data. Now, we can rank the top people and organizations that populate the first screens our customers see. We now know exactly who influences the searches that reach 90 percent of our audience. No need to guess anymore — if we choose to advertise we can take a super precise and efficient approach. And, if we do this well enough, we might not need to advertise at all. It's called "search media relations," and it seems obvious enough. But it didn't exist until 2016.

We're not remaking the wheel here. While we might reshape and transform our marketing and business models, we still have the same core motivation: understanding the "customer journey." We want to understand how to reach people, gain their attention and then build their interest in our brand. That might include building out a customer journey map to diagram the exact steps a potential or current customer takes to engage with our products. We analyze the information they seek, where they go online to find it, who they call for more help, and the information they seek to gain from us directly. We analyze these patterns over months and years, continually analyzing and refining our outreach to positively influence them anytime, anywhere and on any media channel they prefer.

We go into amazing detail to successfully reach customers, but we don't always succeed. Sometimes the customer experience falls far short of their standards, especially if we don't respond appropriately to their needs or don't make ourselves available to them when they need us. So, we study this, too, to correct what we're not doing well — and we fix our deficiencies so we can, once again, enhance our customers' lives.

THE PRE-HATE JOURNEY

The idea of "pre-crime" came to popular attention with the movie "Minority Report," in which a trio of psychics called "Pre-Cogs" identify crimes before they're committed. Tom Cruise plays a cop who arrests people before they pull off their dastardly deeds. The idea reemerged in our minds during 2017, when *Wall Street Journal* reporter Holman W. Jenkins, Jr. wrote about the concept shortly after James Hodgkinson opened fire on a Congressional softball game and injured Rep. Steve Scalise (R-LA) and three others before being killed in a shootout with police. Jenkins ruminated on the point at which we, as a society, might accept a pre-crime ear of law enforcement. At what point, he asked, would Americans accept the idea of authorities identifying potential violent suspects with big data, artificial intelligence and cooperation from major social media firms.

Democratic societies with well-established civil liberties tend to reject the idea of a pre-crime environment, in which powerful new technologies allow authorities to track citizens in ever-greater detail. Already, though, the New York, Los Angeles, Chicago and other large metro police departments have widened the scope of their surveillance capabilities via big data and algorithmic analysis. They regularly bump up against competing privacy and security concerns. And while those concerns can inhibit many advances in law enforcement — sometimes for the better, and sometimes for the worse — the underlying notion of understanding the pre-crime journey makes perfect sense. Like companies do in their efforts to understand and influence PreCommerce, law enforcement officials want to gain more insight into the 99 percent of time a potential criminal isn't committing the actual crime.

Similarly, those who hope to counter extremism in their communities and around the world need to develop a deeper understanding of what we call the "Pre-Hate Journey." People too often take the easy, knee-jerk way out. We just presume they hate America, they lack education and don't know any better, or they're just religious fanatics who want to wipe out anyone who doesn't believe as they do. We blame the development of their hatred on a bad website, a vocal person or a radicalized organization. We dismiss others as crazy or backwards, and then go back to our daily lives. Yet, no one becomes hateful overnight. These questions ignore the fact that reaching a point of critical hate requires a journey. It's not one speech or one organization's lure that tips a young man or woman over the edge. It's a process, and one that's difficult to understand — but one that can be disrupted with the right insights, messages and timing. [See Figure 6.1]

The Pre-Hate Journey also has an analog familiar to most corporate marketing professionals — the customer journey. Companies put millions of dollars and thousands of hours into understanding precisely how their customers reach the point of purchase. Unfortunately, we don't do a version of "customer journey mapping" for those who hate. No one harnesses data sets and algorithmic analyses in a way that can illustrate various Pre-Hate Journeys and identify our best options for positive intervention. We have yet to figure out a way to scale our Pre-Hate analysis in the way a *Fortune 500* company would, spending millions of dollars to scale up and find their next one million customers. Instead, we approach hate one country, one NGO and one leader at a time. Given all the information and data at our disposal, it begs the question: Why not?

For one, we haven't yet conducted a thorough examination of the Pre-Hate environment. What are the conditions that form hate? How are we impacting those conditions? What might we do about the current environment while working to improve our future efforts? What variables skew toward more hatred in every part of the world, and what variables exert more negative influence in one community versus another? We can't answer these questions if we don't know what information to gather, so we need to replicate what we did with the concepts of PreCommerce and social media relations. We need to flip the model on its head and ask: "If we wanted to create the best environment to develop hate, how would we do it?" Look at it this way, and it doesn't take long to develop a framework of H.A.T.E. — four factors that facilitate and foster hate and extremism.

- *Hide* — It's easy to be anonymous online, especially on the dark web. It allows people to publicly unload their worst ideas on the world or privately scheme a plan of action.

FIGURE 6.1 — THE HATE INFLUENCE MODEL

The idea of circuit breakers can help us visualize how to counter hate. To prevent young men and women from moving down the path toward extremism, we need to deploy messaging that interrupts the Pre-Hate Journey at key points. These "circuit breakers" offer prime opportunities to channel grievances toward more productive pursuits. The Hate Influence Model, which is based on extensive field work and data analysis, reveals three key circuit breakers along the major stages of the Pre-Hate Journey.

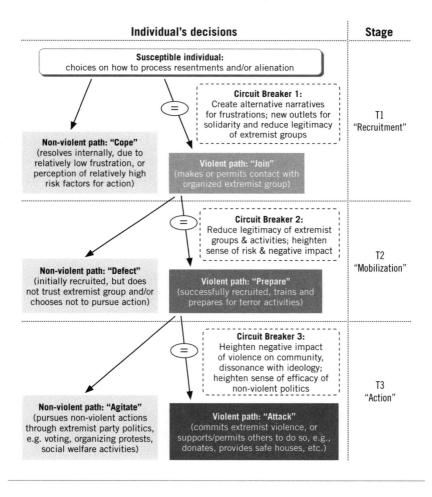

- *Association* — One can find like-minded people, share their biases, learn how others hate, get inspired by their ideas, and teach one another how to be more successful in their extremist quests.

- *Thought Control* — We believe the "world" suppresses our thinking. They don't let us protest, they arrest us, or they take down our online content. This stokes our fire. We have our enemy, and we will prevail.

- *Enforcement* — The outside world's paranoia about their sacred data leads to strict security and privacy rules. That allows us to work uninhibited in an encrypted environment. Authorities can't legally track us or interfere with our activities if we don't engage in direct criminal activities. (And, if we do, they can't find us anyway.)

Think of this as a model designed to breed hate. This makes it easier to hide and associate with fellow haters. It spurs sharp reactions to authority and creates rules to protect others that actually benefit us even more. It's the perfect environment for the entire Pre-Hate journey, and we've created it ourselves. Our best intentions have become our undoing. We need to rethink the strategies, tools and tactics that fall within each of these H.A.T.E. phases, weighing the benefits of freedom and security for us against the risks of promoting hate and extremism in others.

HIDE

The Internet delivered levels of innovation, convenience and connectivity that few people could've imagined 25 years ago, thanks in part to decisions made around that time. When confronted with a choice between regulating more security or allowing e-commerce and network expansion to bloom, U.S. government officials chose the latter. The decision opened the door for the amazing array of websites and social media channels we enjoy today; it also opened the door for an equally amazing depth of anonymity and illicit activity. It doesn't get much deeper than on the dark web.

Sites on the dark web require specialized networks and browsers that use encryption technology to keep a user's identity anonymous. It's not like the Web most of us know, largely because it's all but impossible to ascertain geo-location or track any evidence of activity. It is truly confidential and off the grid — a private computer network to which you have no access. One can buy any illegal or prescription drug. Need some counterfeit cash or a few stolen credit cards? They're available on the dark web. Buy a few terabytes of hacked personal medical data, or hire someone to hack something — for the right price, of course.

Like mushrooms growing in darkness, the dark net is a seedbed for hate and extremism. Whenever someone makes money illicitly, someone else figures out how to deploy technology to make more money. In the 1990s, the pornography industry innovated faster than most *Fortune* 500 companies, leading the way in video-streaming and other digital content technologies. Financial gain drives innovation, and innovation on the dark web helps extremists leverage technology faster than the mainstream. Every day we let the dark net remain in its current form is a day those who hate gain on us. They learn new ways to hide and, like Whack-A-Mole, pop out to recruit and draw others into that black hole of anonymity. They develop new ways to generate income and survive outside of the traditional job market. And they covertly plan and collaborate on economic, corporate and human terrorist attacks.

The dark web has become the R&D department for bad actors, and we currently have no effective countermeasures for it.

BOX 6.1   **THE DARK WEB NEXT DOOR**

If you're trying to hide, what do you worry about? You want to cloak your location and ensure no one can see your messages, personal data or browser history. You also want to ensure no one can follow your trail of activity online. If you use basic encryption techniques, you can hide the contents of your email but you can't hide the source, size and timestamp data. That's a problem if you want to hide. The Tor browser remedies this by sending your information through an extremely complex routing system, making it nearly impossible to see where the data originated, what it is or where it's going. Government authorities will use browsers like this to track public information without tipping off their surveillance. It's one of several ways to remain anonymous and keep information confidential.

Imagine the dark web and all it offers: Want a supply of heroin, an untraceable handgun, and a Platinum Amex card that will last you about three days? With the right software, the right knowledge and the right connections, they'll show up on your doorstep. Because we can't see the dark web, we keep our heads in the sand and pretend it's not happening. It's happening, and it's happening closer to you than you'd ever imagine.

ASSOCIATION

The anonymity of the dark web and, to a lesser extent, the Internet itself facilitates association in ways both beneficial and dangerous. Consider, for example, the many sites dedicated to medical-related communities. Our medical condition is deeply personal, but when faced with a threat to our well-being, many of us seek community for comfort and knowledge. A patient might not want to discuss their disease or disorder without the cloak of privacy. In cases like this, anonymity allows association in a way that adds value for society and the individual. One patient might hear of a treatment, doctor or method that will improve their health, or the health of a loved one.

But the network effects of association also have their downside. Extremist groups can collaborate, recruit and expand from the dark corners of the Internet, with little exposure to those trying to counter their hate. We understand this rationally, but it helps to consider mainstream comparisons we all face to get a more visceral sense for how powerful the influence of veiled associations can become.

Corporate-Oriented Sites—Employees at most organizations know colleagues could target them on intranet sites that allow for anonymous comments. Unfettered by exposure, workers can air grievances, justified or not, against the company or their fellow employees. And if other employees feel similarly, they will find ways to congregate on these sites—and, even more troubling, they often will find ways to gather offline as well. Yet, experts who manage global forums and idea communities with tens of millions of annual interactions know that participants still get very instructive and remain very direct even when they're identified on these sites. The idea that you get better feedback anonymously is a myth.

Grassroots Activism—People often support a controversial political cause or rally against an organization, perhaps even their own employers. But many mask themselves so someone else can't tie their activism to them. While they publicly express their displeasure, they only join the mob because they aren't publicly identified as part of it. This might expand the reach and influence of an activist initiative, but control of the effort usually remains concentrated in just a few hands.

Cyberbullying Lite — We see something we don't like on Facebook, so we rail against it. In so doing, we erode the bonds between friends and acquaintances who might believe differently. In this case, the self-selected anonymity of silence breaks existing associations and, potentially, creates new counterproductive ones. Remember Yik Yak? It allowed college students to share gossip anonymously. The company, which started in 2014, raised $73.5 million and had a valuation of $400 million — and then went out of business. Turns out fostering cyberbullying isn't a great business model.

We are comfortable being anonymous if it allows us to discuss something privately or to go after someone else we don't agree with. But on the next order of the H.A.T.E. model, the ability to hide also allows us to form or break down associations. It facilitates negative connections directly, and in an indirect manner it allows us to inadvertently break down our positive associations through bullying and intimidation.

THOUGHT CONTROL

The development of these associations, which so often grow in anonymity, facilitates the coalescence of power and influence in ways that can suppress free expression and thought. Most of us engage in some form of suppression, whether intentionally or not. The key is understanding what we're doing, changing our behavior and stopping our subtle, yet destructive behaviors — especially when part of a crowd stuck in group-think.

Suppression implies that its victims stop thinking or feeling something because they're told they must, usually by a government, church, family or community. But people typically react like a spring — when pushed, they eventually snap back. Suppression does not tamp down emotion or anger. In fact, the rawest emotions often return with more zeal and vigor, not less. Even the simplest images can gain more longevity when one tries to suppress them.

Dr. Daniel Wegner, an American social psychologist, published research that confirmed as much in 1987. Wegner asked certain study participants to *not* think about a white bear for five minutes, and then think about that white bear for the next five minutes. He found that the thought of the bear came back stronger for those who initially tried to suppress it. Wenger's findings were consistent with similar research over the years, and we can see how it plays out in a variety of settings — often through our own actions. We immediately delete social media accounts that have terrorist leanings. We immediately protest groups with which we don't agree. Particularly in the West, we have grown accustomed to shutting down or shutting out the issues or groups to which we object. Lately, we even protest controversial speakers on college campuses. Every day, people engage in societal suppression in the name of "The Cause." That cause might be what most people would call just or good, but we still need to acknowledge that our actions make it easier for the targets of our scorn to use our objections for gathering momentum, followers and resources. Those we suppress gain energy from the fight.

In 1994, Wegner published a subsequent study in which he found that thought suppression spurs a person's mind to more actively monitor for the topic being stifled. We essentially become more sensitive to the topic at hand, and more aware of its messages. Some research suggests suppression might even trigger our need to move from thought to action. If that is the case, someone on the fence about an extremist group might move closer to alignment with them, perhaps even inspired to actively join the organization because of the overtly suppressive tactics used by its critics.

The antithesis to suppression is recognition, respect and community. In the early days of the HIV/AIDS pandemic, protestors would infiltrate the campuses and workspaces of pharmaceutical and other companies. The firms that tried to stop the incursions failed. Companies that listened to the protesters, invited them in and even broke bread with them ended up building effective relationships. That was hardly an environment of terror and hate, but those who lived through the HIV outbreak can recall just how heated the debates could get. Even in far more extremist environments, more potential alignment exists than we care to admit or seek. Mothers there want the same thing as mothers here. We all want to be recognized and respected for what we do at work, at home or in our communities (both offline and on).

Our needs are simple. So, if we are not getting those needs met at work or at home or online, we will keep looking for the next best place until we do. Just like suppressed thought, suppressed recognition and respect keeps people churning until they find a community that furnishes those values. It could be a private community forum on the dark web or an offline group of like-minded people, but we all seek the self-actualization we find in the communities that accept and respect us.

ENFORCEMENT

Sociologist Robert K. Merton famously coined the term "unintended consequences." Merton laid out a range of catalysts for these unintended consequences — complexity, perverse incentives, human stupidity, self-deception, failure to account for human nature and on and on. There's no shortage of examples, of course. Consider, for example the "Streisand effect." In 2003, Barbra Streisand sued Kenneth Adelman and Pictopia. com for posting a photo of her home. Before the lawsuit, about six people had viewed the photo. That jumped to more than 420,000 when the suit was filed. We can have the best of intentions but end up with the outcome we feared or didn't expect.

In the Pre-Hate environment, privacy and cybersecurity are the two main drivers of unintended consequences. Societies worldwide are very concerned about protecting personal data and ensuring that hackers can't access private financial and medical information. The European Parliament put in place stringent data-protection standards, and California is signing bills to deal with everything from security to surveillance concerns. When it comes to cybersecurity more broadly, experts currently focus on combating ransomware, securing apps on the Internet of Things, countering phishing and whaling attacks and girding our virtual gates for sophisticated artificial intelligence attacks. You could look at all the Top Ten lists of digital privacy and security risks, and you almost certainly won't find the risk that arises if we do not actively counter hate and terrorism. We write rules and pass legislation that protects us, at least when viewed from our perspective of the world. We do far less thinking about the unintended consequences our actions have on others.

As a result, we've created an environment conducive to Pre-Hate. Data protection standards make it harder for companies and governments to track people online. Surveillance standards make it harder for us to view what's happening online or off. Search standards in many European

CROSSING THE FINISH LINE TOGETHER

BY NAIMUL HUQ

Senior Director, Global Brands, W2O Group

Morehead-Cain scholar at the University of North Carolina, Chapel Hill; TEDx speaker

I never imagined that Omaha, Nebraska, would be the bastion of enlightened multiculturalism. My fellow students in school were predominantly white. I was the only brown Muslim kid, but I integrated well. Having been born in the American South and raised in the Midwest, I didn't know any other way. My primary identity was American and I spoke English, but my religious and cultural affiliation was Muslim and Bengali-American. At home, we spoke Bangla until the schoolteachers complained that I was having trouble communicating. After that we spoke it less.

I knew what to expect from my town. From when we moved there in 1987 until I left in 2004 I went through the cycles of bitter, turbulent winter, floral and temperate spring, humid, bright summer and crunchy, colorful autumn. Weather was our most dynamic attribute. I camped year-round with the Boy Scouts, from Cub to Eagle, attending Troop meetings in a Marian Church and joining their prayer through the lens of my own beliefs. I learned a deep spirituality in a household that valued regular worship and scholastic pursuit, and taught us to recognize the Divine in all things. My dad, a university professor, would always invite door-to-door missionaries inside so he could better understand their position and enjoy a debate. We were encouraged to make many friends, whether Christian, Jewish, Muslim, Hindu, Unitarian or Agnostic, and always strive to deepen our own faith.

Omaha's position as a crossroads of railways, commerce, military and medicine produced the unexpected benefit of meeting so many different people. And generally, people were nice. Drivers would pause at intersections to wave us in, gentlemen held doors open for my mom, and my neighbors were as excellent as you could hope—always stocked with borrowable sugar and flour, vigilant in those times I ran out the door as a small child with my bottle clenched between my teeth, dressed in diapers and curly hair. My parents are incredibly social people and I like to think I expanded their network by drawing our neighborhood to our door to return me from my numerous escape attempts. It takes a village to raise a child, especially when he loves to run.

I was running when I had my first encounter with abject racism. I was sixteen, skinny, dressed in red shorts, red and black team jersey and a red bandana that held back a mop of black hair. It was the season's second Junior Varsity 5k Cross Country race on a cool fall morning and I was making good time. The first third of the race was over and I was getting my second wind, powering up a hilly path that ran adjacent to an asphalt road. I was a few steps ahead of another kid who had been trailing me for the past mile. Halfway up the hill a convertible drove up beside me. Four jeering young men turned on me and started screaming:

"Nice headband you Saudi Arabian motherfucker!"

"Go back to your country terrorist!"

"Fuck you!"

And they drove off, laughing.

The attacks on 9/11 had changed the world my sophomore year, just weeks before my own grassy knoll incident while running. I first heard a rumor of the attack as I walked from marching band practice to history class. A student ran down the hall exclaiming, "someone just bombed the World Trade Center!" In class, we started our lesson by turning on the television and listening to speculation that it may have been a wayward prop plane that hit the north tower. And then we watched a second plane hit the south tower and knew this was something else.

Like all Americans that day, I was stunned and upset and scared and angry and saddened by the terrible loss. But it wasn't until that afternoon when my dad called and asked me how I was getting home, and I heard the fear in his voice, that I recognized the danger to my own life. At first, I was incredulous. I had planned to attend practice that afternoon and couldn't imagine this would affect me. But I listened to my parents for once and went straight home. We started to hear stories about attacks against Muslims, Sikhs, and brown-skinned people across America. An FBI report from 2014 showed that in 2000 there were 28 hate crime incidents against Muslims in the US. In 2001 that number spiked to 481.

When the convertible drove off I stopped running. I hadn't had time to respond to them or process what they had said, but it dawned on me that I wasn't as safe as I'd always imagined—and I never would be. I thought about quitting when the kid who had been trailing me jogged up and said, "Just ignore them," before racing on. I started running. It wasn't what the kid said that mattered; I couldn't *ignore* what had happened. But I realized I wasn't alone: someone had seen and heard what they said. Someone spoke up. With just three words, he had given me support and perspective.

Unfortunately, it's the racists in the convertible—not my fellow runner—who provide an analogue to the bigoted vitriol suffusing social media. In confronting the unknown, vocal hatred is often regarded as action. Cloaked in anonymity, violent thoughts are given rostrum and reach through receptive communities. The microcosm of those men in the car is multiplied a thousand-fold, and word travels fast. Everyone can reach anyone, and when they do they breed. Some agree and share. Some respond, expressing their own hate. Others, feeling emboldened, take things further. Dissenters are shouted down and sometimes hounded into silence.

We can't ignore the hatred, but we can try to understand it. The vast scope of the issue represents an opportunity to learn more. We have more context, insight and evidence of hatred than ever before. I can count on one hand the number of racist carpools that have yelled at me in response to the color of my skin. I learned from those experiences, but imagine what I might learn about hate if, god forbid, 10 million drivers, one after another, spewed the same anger at me.

We might never have the answer. But the circumstance of our time is that we can comprehend the dark depths of the human condition through the largest behavioral study in history—the Internet. While we figure this out, consider speaking up. Your words can get someone over the finish line.

countries make it easy for an individual to disassociate from the negatives of their past. As a society, we might rightly believe this is how it should be. But we also must acknowledge that these policies benefit the bad guys, too, and we need to understand precisely how so:

1. *Personal Data* — These protections restrict the ability of authorities to track phone records, use meta-data and track someone simply because they fit a negative profile.

2. *Search Engines* — Policies in Europe and elsewhere make it easier to push not only our miscues off of search results, but other records that might incriminate us as well.

3. *Deleted Social Accounts* — Corporate guidelines for objectionable social media accounts are easily monitored and circumvented, and often push users to the dark web and other encrypted communities.

4. *Ransomware and Hackers* — The focus on combatting the symptoms, rather than the cause, inherently gives bad actors an upper hand. No network is ever 100 percent safe, and the next innovative attack is always coming.

5. *Encryption and Privacy* — While we debate whether Apple should allow more law-enforcement access to its iPhones, hackers and other extremists are devising hacks to bring down companies, financial networks and critical infrastructure systems.

6. *Machine Learning and AI* — Organized extremist and hate groups already are developing machine learning tools to help improve recruiting efforts by gathering data, teaching machines to find susceptible targets and reach out with the right message, at the right time, on the right social media channel.

7. *The Bubble and the Real Conversation* — When most people are distracting themselves with the hot controversy of the day, bad actors are planning their next moves and raising money through illicit markets on the dark web.

8. *The Profiling Debate* — The technology exists to better identify and surveil likely criminals and bad actors. Privacy and civil liberties prevent the use of many such applications in the West, but those prohibitions protect both extremists and law-abiding citizens.

We won't run out of legitimate debates and initiatives on any of these topics, and we should be debating these critical issues. But as we do so, we need to think about how our need for privacy and security has unintended consequences, including some that help bad actors more than they help the general population.

We need to remain cognizant of just how ineffectively we're dealing with the Pre-Hate environment. And we need to realize how little we know about the Pre-Hate Journey that entices too many of our youth from around the world.

CHAPTER 7

THE OTHER BATTLEFIELD

"Among the peoples of the world,
strange new vortices of power will appear unexpectedly."
— MARSHALL MCLUHAN
(media theorist known for coining the phrase "the medium is the message")

W e'd gathered on a late autumn day at the Foreign Commonwealth Office in London to resume discussions about how we might break the ISIS brand and erode its status as a "superpower" of terror. While there, my colleagues and I (Haroon) would help organize the next meetings of the 71-nation Global Coalition to defeat ISIS, an alliance created in September 2014 to coordinate the local, regional and global fight against the Islamic extremist group. Getting countries to pony up cash and combatants to strike at the terrorist group with something stronger than rhetoric was tricky and laborious work, outright dicey at times. So, we also focused on ways we could strengthen civil society voices and disrupt ISIS communications and tarnish their "brand." For the latter initiative, we partnered with technology companies to optimize our counter-ISIS strategies online. The terrorist organization used social media platforms in innovative ways, but our high-tech industry partners knew how to reach similar audiences with different messages. We have our tragedies, but we have our heroes, too.

We ate lunch that day in the House of Lords, where a close colleague and friend, MP Tobias Ellwood, spoke about his recent travels in the Middle East. He and I traded war stories and talked about young people in the Middle East, many of whom find themselves on the front lines of

89

revolution and extremism. Once we finished lunch, Tobias escorted me around the back of the picturesque building to a beautiful monument facing St. James's Park. The monument features the names of 202 British citizens who died in the 2002 Bali bombings carried out by Al-Qaeda and affiliated groups. Tobias gazed at it silently for a few moments, then reached out and caressed one of the names: Jonathon Mark Ellwood, age 37. Tobias' older brother was an academic historian conducting research in Bali, working to expand cross-cultural understanding. His brother sought to teach tolerance and faith in humanity, Tobias said, but he was killed by extremists for whom such understanding and compassion were anathema.

Their hate would emerge again just a short walk from where Tobias and I had contemplated the deeply personal impact terrorism has on its victims' friends and families. On March 22, 2017, in the heart of London, the self-radicalized Khalid Masood's eighty-second rampage across Westminster Bridge and through the gates into New Palace Yard killed four people and injured fifty before authorities shot him dead. Chaos and panic spread like wildfire as Parliament went into lockdown and thousands fled the scene. ISIS later claimed Masood as one of its "soldiers." Many rushed for cover inside the Houses of Parliament and frantically tried to call loved ones. One MP ran in the opposite direction, toward the attack, his prior army training and instincts taking over. He discovered the bloodied PC Keith Palmer on the floor, having been repeatedly stabbed by Masood, and instantly started CPR as others watched. Palmer died from his wounds. The MP who tried to save him was hailed for his quick thinking and courageous efforts. It was my friend, Tobias Ellwood.

The next day, a somber Sunday, Prime Minister Theresa May stood outside 10 Downing Street and spoke to a nation reeling from a string of attacks in the heart of their cherished capital:

"We believe we are experiencing a new trend in the threat we face as terrorism breeds terrorism and perpetrators are inspired to attack, not only on the basis of carefully constructed plots after years of planning and training, and not even as lone attackers radicalized online, but by copying one another and often using the crudest of means of attack. We cannot and must not pretend that things can continue as they are." [1]

May voiced a recognition of precisely what we have diagnosed in this book — online radicalization, new virtual battlefields and the implications of digital guerrilla warfare. As the London attacks demonstrated, violent extremists like ISIS have undermined stability far beyond their physical presence in Iraq, Syria and other conflict-ridden regions. They pose a threat to international peace and security more broadly, and in places as far afield as Europe and Southeast Asia.

We continue to see new twists in ISIS's strategy, the latest being the weaponization of fear, which shows up in ISIS tweets, memes, encrypted postings and other social media channels. The group's communicators around the world spend their days using social media to interact with would-be terrorists, methodically feeding each recruit's deranged desire to develop local networks or carry out attacks in their own countries. ISIS and other hate groups have turned social media into their most effective weapon for turning a recruit into a radicalized attacker, and we've seen the results of their success in London, Nice, Berlin, Orlando, San Bernardino and beyond. No longer does ISIS woo people to fight in Syria and Iraq; they're now recruiting for the "Digital Caliphate."

UNDERSTANDING ISIS 3.0 AND THE NEW VIRTUAL SAFE HAVEN

As ISIS loses more ground on the physical battlefield, it must ensure it can maintain influence in the battlefield of ideas. The call for followers to travel to the "caliphate" in support of ISIS has been markedly reduced, if not made altogether obsolete. This has forced ISIS to alter and accelerate their messaging tactics, enter the digital realm and harbor in a virtual safe haven. The group's messengers now tell supporters to stay where they are and wage war for ISIS wherever they live. Their brand is shifting from that of an ideological organization seeking territory to an umbrella brand for grievances, psychopathy and warped hatred. Instead of recruiting to gain terrain and a bountiful utopia, ISIS is promoting a clandestine, decentralized, international insurgency for marginalized and impressionable youth.

Meanwhile, the foreign terrorist fighters who once made their way to ISIS training camps in the Middle East now head in the other direction, seeking to escape the battlefield and return to their home countries,

THE IMPORTANCE OF WORKING AS ONE GLOBAL TEAM

BY LORD CHADLINGTON (PETER)
Member of the U.K. House of Lords

Recently, near my home in London, a car came off the road and ploughed into 11 people on the pavement. Brave passers-by leapt into action to apprehend the driver and the police reaction was both rapid and heavy. It transpired that this was a tragic accident, but the immediate assumption was that it had been another "lone wolf" attack, like the June 2017 Westminster attack. That we should first respond to an incident of this nature as a terror attack, specifically a suspected Islamist attack, rather than an accident is telling. Such single person attacks are the new face of terrorism—hard to predict and therefore prevent, and with maximum fear impact.

Despite the real and imagined terror, relatively few people have been victim to an attack in the U.K. Statistics published by *The Telegraph* in October 2017 suggest fewer than 50 deaths in 2017, whereas at the height of The Troubles in Northern Ireland there were nearly seven times as many fatalities (353 people were killed in the U.K. in 1972). But the U.K. threat level continues to be at "severe" despite data that shows Europe is one of the safest areas in the world for terrorism related incidents.

I believe we have our special services—GCHQ and MI5 to thank. Five attacks have been foiled in the two months since the Westminster attacks alone. Clearly, Brexit is likely to impact the ability of these services to work with our international neighbors. The director general of Europol, Rob Wainwright, believes Brexit will adversely affect the fight against organized crime, international terrorism and cybercrime. So now is the time for us to up our game in the fight to counter hate.

Islamist extremism is one of the single biggest global threats and defeating this ideology is one of the great challenges of our time. And yet we have a polarization of opinion. Some deny Islamist extremism is connected to Islam, despite terrorists so often self-identifying as Muslim. Some argue it is driven by poverty, but this feels to be only part of the picture since evidence shows many terrorists come from well-off homes. Some say we have brought Islamist terrorism on ourselves as a response to western foreign policy, but the 9/11 attack on New York happened before the Iraq war. These arguments miss the point because they create a justification for extremism and violence.

There are those on the other side of the coin who argue the problem is Islam itself. Clearly, that is not true either; the clash between civilizations is not inevitable. Dividing the world into "us and them" simply isn't productive. This won't defeat extremism, it will breed more extremists. Instead, we must respect and celebrate the Islamic faith, while condemning and taking firm action against Islamic extremism. We must not conflate the two.

Extremism is an exploitative process, it attracts by giving false clarity amid complexity. Mohamed Lahouaiej Bouhlel, the Nice killer, is a recent example of an unstable life given deadly purpose by extremist Islamism. I believe we will discover that the recent New York attack is borne of similar radicalization from a life that lost purpose and direction*.

There is no magic pill but nor is the situation hopeless. We should work tirelessly with Muslim communities to help reclaim Islam from extremist interpretations. Campaigns like the #MyIslamCampaign can bring a sense of belonging to people who feel lost or excluded in our fast-moving world.

Instead of dividing the world into "us and them," we should build trusting relationships within communities to avoid extremism and enable security services to be alerted if something is amiss within the community. We cannot allow extreme Islamist ideology the safe space it needs to breed. We should keep a close watch on social media accounts to disrupt terrorist activity online. We need to saturate the information sphere with counter-messaging and alternative interpretations. And, lastly, we should all work to discredit the ideology embraced by lone wolves.

*The 10/31 NYC attack by Sayfullo Saipov was considered as a terrorist action.

from where they develop local networks and launch attacks. The target audience is no longer the group, but the individual "soldier." Their safe haven on the dark web and encrypted social media platforms still limits their reach, but their noxious call is more personalized, and thus more persuasive, easier to heed. Halting their ability to leverage these private spaces has now become crucial to defeating ISIS.

Currently, the challenges posed by digital anonymity and hidden association make it harder to identify and track the inspired, self-radicalized attacker, as we discovered, in bloody retrospect, in Dhaka, Medina, Kabul, Ansbach and elsewhere. Keeping abreast of the activity in the digital underworld has become critical to the safety of citizens in the U.S. and nations around the world. How to counter these violent extremists' anonymous use of the Internet is a core focus in the fight to defeat ISIS, particularly for law enforcement and the public and private sector experts working on counter-messaging strategies. Washington, the Global Coalition, and private high-tech companies are making it increasingly difficult for ISIS to spread its poisonous ideology to vulnerable audiences. For example, Twitter has suspended more than 635,000 ISIS-related or affiliated accounts that abused the platform in the eighteen months between mid-2015 and the end of 2016. Twitter sped up the process of removing ISIS accounts and their regenerated online handles. Other anti-ISIS coalition members deployed a range of new analytic tools, sharing intel with allies to get ahead of the curve and stymie online recruitment wherever possible. At the same time, the Global Coalition's own Twitter accounts (in Arabic, French and English) continue to build a strong following with messages aimed at counteracting ISIS's online presence.

So far, these and other efforts have shown progress. Counter-ISIS content is now more prevalent online than ever before, and pro-ISIS content is declining in open forum social media channels.[2] Research shows that opponents of ISIS outnumbered ISIS supporters as much as six-to-one on some social media platforms. As a terrorist group, ISIS increasingly struggles in the face of these more organized and sophisticated initiatives, many of them spurred by the Global Coalition.

CAUGHT AT THE DIGITAL CROSSROADS

Many of the young people we interviewed for *Countering Hate* represent the new social media revolution, which has pushed the Islamic world into the eye of the storm. The movements spurred by these youths have shifted the pivots of power, disrupted the production and consumption of information, and even recast the structure of societies. They "took media into their own hands" to create a bottom-up, citizen-driven revolution that supplanted top-down totalitarian regimes.[3] Yet, social networking can't ensure that a resultant political regime will reflect the values of the media messaging that helped to bring it into power. The Islamist regimes that rode digitally driven revolutions and counter-revolutions to power are not transparent, liberal or secular, despite the hazy notion of social media as an essentially democratic force.

In fact, with the emergence of democratically inclined regimes, which are more concerned than ever about public opinion and dissent, Muslim governments have pushed back hard on the open Web. Newly installed Islamist regimes want to quickly assert their independence from — and defiance of — Western hegemony, particularly in the wake of disastrous military interventions in the region. Their ultimate goal remains what it has always been: all Muslim nations partnered under a connection to religious authority. In some cases, this certainly means less freedom, not more, and will bring on a retrograde de-democratization. Some may call this a fatalistic view; others say it's merely realistic.

In one of the most important power shifts in human history, social media empowered millions of people, giving them a voice they didn't have before. Social media consumers represent a new kind of global citizen, one with a fresh take on geopolitical relations, who knows he or she is being heard by an international audience, and who plays to that crowd. In recent years, Islamist political parties and movements — the main opposition to the political establishment in the Middle East and beyond — discovered they could reach the masses through these same public online spaces and engage them in the fight against entrenched power structures. They have assumed power, and sometimes lost it again (e.g., Egypt). But their effective use of social media has changed the fundamental nature of elections and electoral politics already. Core middle-class voters want to see Islamists continuing to kick out the old ways and taking their countries in new directions, while Islamic political power-players exploit the Internet's riches to propagate their conservative sociopolitical and religious messages.

Based on the surveys, interviews and research we've conducted on the ground, we know social media platforms now play *the* pivotal role in getting millions of young people to participate in political activities for the first time. The Islamists are remaking the Muslim world's political order, taking the structures we've known for more than a century and refashioning them as a hybrid form — part Islamic, part secular. These events have significant implications for the West and our alliances with Muslim-majority nations, as well as our war on terror.

LOOKING FORWARD AND BACKWARD

This new reality underscores the need to understand the broader context of history and the motivations underlying the campaigns of Islamists and extremists. Such awareness will vastly improve the ability of foreign policymakers to navigate the ever-changing and often bewildering political terrain that's visible online. Oversimplified and uninformed depictions of Islamist opposition politics — and in particular, misperceptions about the role of social media in Islamist recruitment and mobilization — already has affected international policy in detrimental ways. As a result, we've seen clumsy mismanagement or total neglect of potentially vital relationships. Understanding how Islamic organizations are motivated by both pragmatic/political and religious considerations will help Western governments deal with their political actors, whether allies or antagonists. More specifically, realizing that extremist politics don't always derive from ideological absolutism will open new opportunities for diplomacy.

The lack of official engagement with important groups outside the executive branch is most pronounced when weighing how international governments deal with Islamists, especially regionally important officials or groups. Since 2001 and at various times since, the Islamists have arisen as a potent political force in Egypt, Tunisia, Libya, Lebanon, Syria and Iraq. However, Western governments' contact with these leaders has not only been limited, but in most cases actively avoided. The same "hands off" approach has informed relations with other networked and hierarchical Islamist groups in key areas of strategic importance. More than simply refusing to engage these parties, much of the West's policies toward Islamists aim to suppress, disable or circumvent their hold on power. Founded on the conventional but faulty wisdom that political Islamism is driven by economic disenfranchisement and militaristic zeal, many international governments try to weaken confessional Islamic parties by limiting their engagement and providing few avenues for cooperation and capacity building.

We believe the motivational assumptions underlying these policies are counterproductive for all the parties concerned. Islamists and their social media outreach efforts almost certainly will remain an integral fixture of the political landscape, regardless of third-party efforts to eradicate or stymie them. (In fact, as we learned in the last chapter, attempts to suppress them might spark a stronger backlash.) Though it's critical to understand that Islamic parties can be differentiated from extremist groups, they do have loose ties in some instances. More commonly, they have complex interactions with violent extremists but remain invested in the electoral political process and know they would not gain from a transition to autocratic religious rule. Despite their rhetoric on social media and their depiction in the mainstream press, these parties are important potential allies to Western interests.

Fortunately, some Western policymakers are starting to realize that the historical conduct and core interests of Islamist opposition parties hint that they could be useful partners in limiting the spread of violent extremism — if we can properly incentivize them. While Islamist parties have recently deemed it an electoral advantage to affiliate in varying degrees with militaristic organizations, these affiliations (such as the Jabhat al-Nusra or the Taliban) actively work to destabilize the political system that Islamist parties depend on for their own survival. Rather than pushing Islamic parties further into the arms of extremists through policies of suppression, Western powers could exploit this inherent tension between the two sides and seek points of shared interest with Islamic parties.

WALKING THE DIGITAL WALK

With the information battlefield wide open, this type of outreach will require a major realignment of perspectives. Western nations must interact with political parties seen as moderate within the Arab or Middle Eastern context, not only those seen as moderate by Western norms. To be sure, this shift poses domestic political challenges within the U.S. and allied Western nations. Officials who pursue this progressive approach risk being labeled as cooperative with polarizing groups, especially the organizations that employ heavy anti-Western rhetoric and maintain known connections with extremists. However, Western policymakers would do well to look beyond the speeches and proclamations of Islamic parties, to determine their underlying motivations and create innovative ways to provide support to groups that espouse antiviolence measures.

Social media provides useful insights into their "mass market" strategy, but it also offers us innovative new tools we can use to help them spread a positive and peaceful influence. In public diplomacy and education, we should directly challenge the idea that the West opposes Islam—a tough nut to crack these days. Social media is rife with conspiracy theories and extremists on both sides actively seeking a declared war between Islam and the West. For extremist groups, this is how they target niche audiences. We should send the message that expanding access to quality education is a priority in every corner of the Muslim world, noting also that religious schools can play an important role as they do in the West. Western powers should emphasize that the problem lies not with madrassas but with murderers. We should stress that for the Muslim world, and for the West, a truly effective counter-hate strategy must target the drivers of violent radicalism, not the symptoms. Radicals who seek to kill should be pinpointed, pursued and prosecuted wherever they're based, whether state or non-state actors. *The task on social media is not to endorse or agree with all groups, but to keep the channels of dialogue open and to challenge the wild inaccuracies and misconceptions about Western policy.* Websites like SoulPancake and Reddit offer content that allows young people to discover key answers about extremism. These platforms are also able to highlight core messages regarding the West's long-held respect for religious concerns and traditions, pressing the point that terrorism is the problem, not the righteous tenets of Islam.

Building these sorts of workable relationships with Islamist parties can ensure that international development aid goes toward modern healthcare and education initiatives. As their use of social media makes clear, Islamist parties often strive to provide a positive counter-narrative to violence. Unfortunately, they've been too wary of outside influences and resources, worried those programs could undermine their own patronage structures and usurp their local authority. In some cases, these parties have used social media to take credit for new schools, roads, water systems and clinics that were built with Western money and know-how. In other instances, security concerns halted projects which led to high personnel turnover. Finding ways to make cooperation more palatable for both sides will heighten the effectiveness of incoming aid and education resources.

Of course, there will be certain Islamist political actors or groups with whom direct or even indirect cooperation is impossible. While we argue against viewing all Islamists as ideologically intransigent or wholly opposed to Western interests, we acknowledge that some individuals or local offshoots will be so closely linked to violent extremists that no light can shine between them. Some cases might require targeted efforts to disempower these dangerous political actors. Since Islamist politicians derive much of their power from their mutually reinforcing control over local religious institutions and their messaging, proposals for better Internet governance might offer one of the more promising strategies for undermining those militant extremist groups.

BREAKING THE BRAND

Muslim nations have a long history of imperialism, colonialism, regionalism, feudalism and factionalism, which makes them more likely to foster religio-political power dynamics. The power and resources historically attached to religious leaders stand in tension with a secular and feudal type mode of political power. We see this expressed now in democratic electoral politics. Islamic political parties combine both types of power, but with specific limits. Those who favor religious identity find their access to electoral politics restricted; electoral politics inhibit religious affiliation and identity.

The Islamists' online drive toward a deeper engagement in electoral politics and democratic "branding" appears more strategic than ideological. Today, incentives increasingly encourage electoral participation, rather than religiously derived politics and extra-electoral power grabs. Despite the ruling elites' systematic exclusion of Islamist parties and the inability of these parties to control national parliaments in Muslim countries, they continue to exert significant electoral power at a local level. Thus, they cannot be ignored. Fortunately, they often will respond to persuasion that's not strictly ideological, despite bold anti-Western postures.

Of course, we also must consider voter behavior and aspirations when shaping our international policy for Muslim-majority countries. We must accept the legitimate autonomy of Islamic groups, understand the sharp differences in sect, ethnicity and region, and recognize the uneven distribution of material resources in these countries. These factors can have a major influence on voter behavior. At the national level, for example, more citizens will support Muslim democrats — or even secular parties — that are integrated into state networks because they're predisposed to distribute material benefits and support. But in local races, those same voters favor Islamists who offer both spiritual and material benefits, the nature of which can vary widely.

ATTITUDES AND PRACTICES ON THE GROUND

Few areas of study are more relevant to assisting Western foreign policy than today's communications networks. The advance of Internet technology, social media platforms and the rise of Islamist politics dominates the current political terrain. A wave of books, articles and commissioned reports on how we should communicate with the Muslim world emerged in the aftermath of the 2016 U.S. presidential election. Myriad organizations have launched conferences on strategic communications and messaging. The new U.S. administration entered to a flurry of public diplomacy proposals calling for revised budgets, new input into policy formulation and new diplomatic offices within the government and in partnership with the private sector. The proposals also covered a range of internal efforts and recommendations, such as improving the language skills of U.S. foreign service officers. Yet for all the recommendations, some of which have been implemented, we continue to wrestle with questions about the effectiveness of public diplomacy in Muslim countries.

What's far too often missing in public diplomacy is precisely what provides the foundation of any decent business plan or military strategy — an understanding of the operating environment. Previous studies of the social media phenomenon have downplayed or completely ignored what Muslim populations collectively think or do. These studies have overlooked the explosive nature of social media networks and the symbolism of Islamist politics. Instead, the focus has been on what the West can do unilaterally, not what the West can do vis-à-vis the attitudes and practices found on the ground. An essential part of understanding the public environment in Muslim countries involves examining the political organizations that represent them and how they communicate on the information battlefield. Too much is at stake to ignore it.

1 http://www.dailymail.co.uk/news/article-4570104/Theresa-s-huge-gratitude-emergency-services.html

2 Examining ISIS Support and Opposition Networks on Twitter, Rand Study (2016), Bodine-Baron, Helmus, Magnuson, Winkelman.

3 Schmidt & Cohen, 2013, p. 23.

CHAPTER 8

HEZBOLLAH, GREENPEACE AND AARP: FORMING POWERFUL GROUPS

"That is the paradox of the epidemic: that in order to create one contagious movement, you often have to create many small movements first."
— MALCOLM GLADWELL

K halid G. was a baby-faced 15-year-old kid from Beirut. His father ran a fruit stand near the Najmeh Square clock tower; his mother earned a few extra Lebanese pounds sewing crafts. Though not dirt poor, the family of eight barely scraped by, and Khalid had to fend for himself at an early age. He couldn't afford much, but he loved computers and software ever since someone took him to an Internet café when he was eight years old. When he visited the cafes now, coding came easy and he picked up new skills like a natural. By the time he turned 12, he had a prolific social media presence. He earned extra money as a waiter at the local coffee and hookah house, but any income was secondary to his ability to build a digital community, something he lacked in his neighborhood.

Khalid also liked going to the local Hezbollah madrasa, where classes in religious history and scripture preceded simple but filling meals, chess classes and organized soccer teams. He was smart, athletic, made friends easily and took the religious instruction seriously. After attending the school for several years, he started to think of the leaders at the madrasa as more like family than his own, and one day a senior imam took Khalid aside and talked to him about people who didn't respect the Lebanese.

After his passionate admonition, the imam held Khalid's hands: "Let us pray together."

The next day, Khalid and several other boys piled onto a bus that took them to a large suburban house. There, a Hizb warrior showed video tapes of civilians killed by drone attacks and photos of Syrian soldiers urinating on the corpses of fallen freedom-fighters. "The Syrians do not care about our people, our women and children," the man told the boys. "They don't even consider us human." The powerful presentation left the teenagers filled with hatred, eager to fight and kill the despised Syrian invaders.

Things progressed quickly from there. Later that same week, Khalid and several other young men took part in a secret ceremonial proceeding that incorporated them as members in the Hizb e-militia's team. The recruiter praised the boys: "You have the honor of pledging your lives to the glorious cause of peace and harmony in a world united under a new battlefield." And with that, they were sent to a social media training center, where new recruits work on coding and programming. As Khalid stood in line waiting for a work station number, the teenager swelled with pride. He was one of the chosen few.

In barely more than a decade, social media has become an indispensable tool for legions of activists like Khalid, both inside and outside the Islamist political establishment. The same channels have become equally important for the tens of millions of generally disaffected people across the Muslim world, people who might or might not have a religious or political agenda. Access to social media platforms gives anyone the means to express their opinions, but it also opens the door to any number of influencers to shape and sway those beliefs. Islamists and extremists were among the first to recognize this, and few people or organizations employ these new information weapons as well as they do.

This goes well beyond the classic definition "weaponized information," which implies little more than propaganda. In today's social and interconnected virtual world, the ways in which organizations and people disseminate information is itself a part of the war. If social media is a smoking gun, no one has better aim than Islamists and extremists. Forced underground for years, they now can use a wide range of platforms to wage war on the information battlefield. While more pragmatic Islamists seek to bolster their mass-market appeal, extremists target a niche audience and stoke their fears of the infidel. The different social media platforms they use work like different weapons — each with pros and cons, some more suited to one group than another — but extremist groups wield them all with pinpoint accuracy and deploy them with acute force.

The Hezbollah e-militia that Khalid had joined is a dedicated, 24/7 team of roughly 30 online operators who produce, generate and repost content that promotes the organization's campaign ideas. Its social media headquarters looks like a high-tech control room at some Western company, filled with computers, servers and large-screen TVs, all monitoring data. It's a command center for cyber warfare, with their operations geared primarily toward recruitment. Lacking the kind of coordinated force enjoyed by the Muslim Brotherhood, Hezbollah's team moves more tactically to befriend susceptible groups, seeing in them potential new members for the organization. Much like their offline tactics, they establish trust before interjecting the organization's message. Social media simply gives them a broader audience of potential friends and recruits. And the tactics are working: the group's Twitter handle, @almanarnews, had 8,000 followers in 2012. By 2017, it had more than 100,000.

The larger and better-established social media channels often clamp down on extremist messages and recruiting efforts, so many Islamist organizations operate across multiple social media platforms concurrently. They're also moving further toward the margins of the web, using decentralized and less-popular social media networks such as Diaspora and Friendica to spread propaganda. These sorts of sites, functioning with open-source software and existing on private servers, are a double-edged sword: While they make third-party oversight more difficult, they don't deliver as large an audience. So extremist groups such as ISIS tend to use them as jumping-off boards, developing content before repurposing it elsewhere. Either way, their variety of approaches contributes to the overall impression of determined and concerted campaigning.

The groups that stick to the mainstream social media channels hit them all hard. While some sites obviously appeal more to certain audience segments than others — Ask.fm and Facebook are used to reach a younger audience, for instance — an across-the-board bombardment seeks to grab and retain the attention of social media users on whatever channel they might choose. ISIS's multipronged approach using Twitter, Facebook and Instagram increases the likelihood of someone seeing their material, whether searched for or just stumbled upon. But it also creates a feedback loop that can ensnare social media users, giving adherents even more incentive to remain active online. And the content keeps coming 24 hours a day—often documenting in real time what occurred in the past 24 hours and what might be in store for *mujahideen* fighters in the 24 hours to come. The series "Mujatweets," popularized with the Twitter hashtag #mujatweets, was launched in 2014 by ISIS's al-Hayat Media Center.

IT'S CATCHING

Like Western companies seeking that word-of-mouth brand buzz, the golden ticket for Islamist and extremist groups is to go viral online. In their book "Going Viral," Karine Nahon and Jeff Hemsley define the phenomenon "where many people simultaneously forward a specific information item, over a short period of time, within their own social networks, and where the message spreads … to different, often distant networks," until the content reaches a widespread audience and no longer spreads. There is, then, no explicit threshold that defines viral content. "Going viral" is more a process than it is a particular moment. Yet, we often discount the intensity of those moments, because we tell ourselves a group is small, there's not much it can do or it doesn't have a lot of influence. *But the groups that represent the largest movements in our history all started with a singular moment of intensity that evolved into an organized force over time.* They started in places we never visited with people we never heard of and with resources we overlooked.

ISIS realized long ago that they have more luck catalyzing the actions of lone wolves or new groups if they pump out content that resonates with disaffected young men and women. They know someone, somewhere will rise to the challenge and create the next cell, faction or group. And why shouldn't they know this? Organizations from Greenpeace to AARP to Hezbollah have already shown the way. All three started out of an incident or an unmet need, tied that need to a broad vision and developed that passion and mission into globally relevant institutions.

INNOVATION IN UNLIKELY PLACES

BY TIM RECEVEUR
PeaceTech Lab

PeaceTech Lab works to reduce violent conflict using technology, media and data to accelerate and scale peacebuilding efforts.

Amidst dire headlines, a new wave of entrepreneurs are using increased access to exciting technologies, media and data tools to spark a wave of innovation for social good, enhancing lives in conflict zones from Afghanistan and Pakistan to Iraq and South Sudan.

These innovators include Nawres Arif, a Basra-based pharmacist turned technologist who decided to build a makerspace to provide inspiration to his local community. Through a crowdfunding campaign, he launched Science Camp in his backyard, providing a space for young innovators and entrepreneurs to collaborate and experiment with many of the latest technologies, such as 3D printing, robotics and graphic design. The space will provide students with marketable skills in a country wracked by high unemployment.

Nawres is just one of the 250 technologists in the PeaceTech Lab's worldwide network. These bright minds come together with local civil society, governments and technology experts to explore the use of cost-effective and readily available technologies like data analysis, mapping and online security tools to address complex drivers of conflict. Nawres joined us in Basra as a trainer at our PeaceTech Exchange (PTX) workshop to help these groups tackle corruption through better accountability, transparency and citizen engagement.

Jorge Luis Sierra also falls into this category. A Mexican journalist by background, Jorge Luis has participated in PTX workshops in Iraq and Turkey and coordinated with the Iraqi Journalist Rights Defense Association (IJRDA) to launch a nationwide project to track attacks against Iraqi bloggers and journalists. In addition, Jorge Luis and the PeaceTech Lab partnered to pilot the Salama app, a personalized risk-assessment service for journalists. The app determines the level of vulnerability when covering high risk stories, and it highlights the areas in the journalist's security protocols that need improvement.

In addition to issues like corruption and journalist security, PeaceTech Lab uses technology to accelerate solutions to challenges like hate speech, countering violent extremism, gender-based violence and more. In all, we have trained nearly 1,000 organizations and 150 government officials in nine countries. We've learned many key lessons from that experience, including these three:

- *Build for local adoption:* Use tools that will work in the right environment, including translation into local languages when possible.

- *Don't underestimate the transformative role that technology can play in resolving conflict:* Smart phones and mobile networks are spreading and improving by the day. For example, we've seen significant drops in election violence, gains that can be linked to better tracking of sentiment on social media and rapid responses facilitated by instantaneous communications.

- *Don't overestimate the role of technology:* Always keep in mind that technology is only a tool and it's only as good as the people using it—people need to be at least as well-versed in the conflict dynamics as they are in the technology.

To scale up innovative technology ideas to resolve conflict, PeaceTech Lab also started the world's first PeaceTech Accelerator in 2017 in a partnership that includes C5 Capital, Amazon Web Services (AWS) and SAP NS2. To learn more, visit www.peacetechlab.org.

Greenpeace

In the 1960s, the threat of an underground nuclear weapon test on the island of Amchitka, Alaska, spurred a group to form in protest. The members of the Sierra Club Canada quickly became disenchanted with the tepid response of their group, so they set out on their own to sail to Amchitka and continue their protest. They named their boat The Greenpeace. They sailed out to face a U.S. Coast Guard ship but turned back due to weather. Little did they know that the mere intention of standing up to the government would unlock the door to an organization that now has 2.8 million supporters.

They merely set out to bear witness in a style of non-violent protest that so many people around the world find admirable. Over the years, Greenpeace has widened its scope to include climate change, forests, oceans, food, water, refugees and many related topics. What started as a small group angry with a government's decision to test a nuclear weapon has developed into an organization with the ability to shape the behavior and views of both private and public sector officials worldwide — and all of that emerged within the last 50 years.

AARP

A retired educator, Ethel Percy Andrus, formed AARP in 1958 as a successor to her precursor group, the National Retired Teachers Association (NRTA). Andrus wanted to help people age in a healthier and more productive way, but she initially worried about health insurance for retired teachers. So, she partnered with Leonard Davis, an insurance executive. Together, Andrus and Davis began to build the organization we now know as AARP, with more than 38 million members over 50 years old. It has become one of the most powerful lobbying groups in the United States.

As an important aside, it's worth noting that AARP generates most of its own income, so it doesn't depend on the government or any single large philanthropist or influencer to ensure its future. Many of the most influential groups have this in common, including most extremist and terrorist groups. The ability to self-fund can provide tremendous freedom, flexibility and power.

Hezbollah

In 1982, members of the Abu Nidal organization, a PLO splinter group, wounded the Israeli ambassador in London in an assassination attempt. Israel countered by launching an offensive against the PLO in Lebanon. The casualty count was severe: 344 Israeli soldiers, hundreds of Syrian soldiers and more than 1,000 Palestinians were killed; thousands more were injured on all sides, according to the 1988 *Country Studies/Area Handbook* on Israel, published by the U.S. government. But Lebanon took the brunt of the destruction: almost 18,000 Lebanese killed and more than 30,000 wounded.

Hezbollah formed amidst the rubble and broken bodies of the war. A group of Lebanese Shi'ite clerics, determined to drive Israel from Lebanon and form an Islamic state in Lebanon, continued the fight long after the war ended. Backed by Iran, the group evolved into a leading political force, and it remains one of the more influential organizations in the Middle East today.

A PERCEIVED NEED, A CONCEIVED VISION

Regardless of how we view these groups, each of them started from the same kernel—a perceived need for which they would advocate, protest, lobby or fight to the death to preserve. Greenpeace believes it can non-violently protest to achieve its goals. AARP will always throw its considerable political weight behind the issues it believes are critical for the health and wellness of older citizens. And Hezbollah believes it is protecting its right to protect Muslim communities and spread an Islamic revolution.

Each group also expressed a broader vision that resonated with a far larger group, and that's what led to its growth. Vision might not produce efficient operations, financial acumen or the other factors critical to the long-term success of a startup company. But it does draw people to its cause, and from that the operational strengths can emerge.

ISIS, Al-Qaeda and other extremist movements know this as well as anyone, which explains why they place such a high value on endlessly pumping out their story. Some version of their story will inspire new leaders. Those new leaders will arrive with the skills the organization needs to thrive, and then they'll incrementally innovate those same stories to tell it

SPORTS IS THE GREAT UNIFIER

BY AHMAD NASSAR

President, NFL Players, Inc. (the licensing and marketing arm of the NFL Players Association, representing nearly 2,000 NFL players)

Pope Francis believes that sports are the great unifier. More than music, more than art, more than religion, in fact.

As President of the NFL Players Association, I had the ability to go to the Vatican to talk with the Pope about empowering communities all over the world. The Pope, who I admire greatly, brought civic organizations, community leaders, private sector and governments from around the world to talk about unity and empowerment. And I truly believe sports can play that role in countering hate of all forms.

As President of the NFLPA, I have negotiated licensing agreements with top companies like Nike, Topps and Panini, YouTube and Fanatics. But what really gets me even more energized is being able to work with local communities and NFL players on grassroots work to empower youth.

I've seen first-hand how sports give a platform for young people to learn about teamwork, perseverance, competition and honesty—all critical values to combat any form of hate or bias. And the key to that empowerment is storytelling, offering an alternative narrative that is authentic and compelling. That is why I enjoy connecting players with local communities, because they are able to foster a bond, provide mentorship and have conversations with young people that they may never otherwise have.

their way — and their way will spawn new movements and sub-groups in support of the overall cause.

A Silicon Valley venture capital firm might give a company $5 million and say good luck. The same firm will give $5 million to nine other firms and hope one or two of them make it big. A 20 percent success rate is pretty good in the venture capital world. In the world of hate and extremism, content and a strong storyline replace hard currency, but those organizations still approach their "business" like venture capitalists — they don't care if most of what they say fails to resonate. If their story resonates with just enough potential new leaders, they'll spin off new cells, sub-groups and movements. And if that goes unchecked for long enough, that collective movement will make a difference in our lives, for better or worse.

When we hear a single person or a small group talk, and when we realize they've started to resonate with a wider audience, we best take them seriously. That leading voice on a small social media channel today might become the leader of a group that hacks your company's database, engineers a bombing in a major Western city or organizes a tense protest in your hometown. Tomorrow's leaders are giving us a public audition today. We need to pay attention.

CHAPTER 9

A NEW MODEL

"Content is fire, social media is gasoline."
— RYAN KAHN

T he video is mesmerizing. As the screen hops with upbeat pop music, a handsome, Middle Eastern teenager sits in his room, pondering what he wants out of life. Nice clothes, cool friends, a hipster lifestyle — things might seem far from the chaos and turmoil in the Middle East, but as the video makes clear, there's more to true happiness than what happens in the physical world. There's a spiritual side, with or without religious overtones, that guides you on the path to self-fulfillment. And you, dear viewer, can find this within yourself, within your community. This slick, unremittingly positive video encourages viewers to foster peace and goodwill toward people in all walks of life, and it offers the promise of a better future for the young than their fathers have known. It runs just seventy seconds, but it presents a powerful narrative of hope and positive thinking.

Within days of its release, the video went viral across the Middle East. Within weeks, it had grabbed 14 million views, making YouTube stars of its actors. Immediately, young people across the region reposted the video and various versions of it on social media. They edited their own versions on the Snap app. They created and uploaded GIFs on Telegram, WhatsApp, Signal and scores of other messaging apps. They collectively produced a massive counterblast to the vast sea of extremist video proliferating online. As one young man in Cairo said on a Facebook post of the video. "This is why ISIS, al-Qa'ida and Taliban should be afraid. The Resistance strikes back!"

It didn't take long for others to notice the video and use it to promote their own ends. In Amman, a group of Jordanian college students formed an online group inspired by the video, making copies of it with their own branding inserted. In Fez, Morocco, a group of students put together a 60-second film festival to encourage the production of videos along the theme of tolerance and unity. In Cairo, the video and its knock-offs were used by community coalitions and civil society groups — including those affiliated with the ousted Muslim Brotherhood — to rally more recruits and raise funds. By distributing these videos with a new name and logo inserted at the beginning and end, the groups thumbed their nose at the establishment. On the Telegram app, several channels remain devoted to new ideas for media productions based on that same viral video.

But where did the original video come from? Who was reaching out and communicating a message of hope to millions of impressionable young people?

Researching this video led me (Haroon) to Jeddah, Saudi Arabia, where I stumbled upon what someone in Silicon Valley might dub a "social media incubator." The U-Turn Organization, tucked away in a small, nondescript office building on the outskirts of the city, produced the video and a wave of other media content that created a huge buzz across the region. Though young Saudis and Gulf youth in general were among the earliest and savviest of digital consumers — some data suggests they constitute the largest viewership of YouTube videos per capita, with more than 5.5 hours a day — I still found it hard to believe that many of the enormous ripple effects across the digital landscape emanated from this unassuming studio in Jeddah.

As I visited with UTurn's chief executive officer, a young man named Kaswara, he pulled back the curtain of his hidden empire. He showed me around the facility and its "green rooms," where highly creative tech artists developed unique content. The whole place bustled with laptop-wielding young men and women in loose flowing thobes. The U-Turn staff views itself as a grassroots resistance team working against militant jihadist groups and caliphate wannabes. Kaswara explained that they maintained a 24/7 eye on terror groups with a sophisticated monitoring dashboard — some of the best big data counter-extremist analytical tools I've seen anywhere.

Kaswara and a senior associate showed me a gruesome, frame-by-frame breakdown of the infamous ISIS video of the downed Jordanian fighter pilot being burnt to death in a steel cage. The clip was meant to scare and terrorize, which it certainly did, sending shivers of horror across the globe as it went viral. ISIS released the video in multiple versions, one three minutes long and a lengthier, movie-like version scarcely watchable for its visceral ghastliness.

U-Turn distributed the frightful video — not for clicks or mere shock value, but to show the young and the righteous the level of evil they were up against. They reached out to their network to basically crowd-source responses and to get the young, creative community involved in countering this gruesome propaganda. By so doing, they empowered anyone with a mobile phone to take part in the movement for a better world. Nothing illustrates this battle for superiority on the digital battlefield more than the work and activity at U-Turn.

BLURRING THE LINE BETWEEN PHYSICAL AND DIGITAL WARFARE

Digital technology's advances have sparked seismic rebellions across the Muslim world. They've underpinned uprisings led by Islamists, used social media and associated networking technologies to harass and defeat secular and/or corrupt regimes. These tools gave digital rebels the capacity to wage guerrilla warfare on their own terms and without the need for massive budgets — essentially weaponizing information. From recruitment, mobilization and organization to fundraising, censorship evasion, image protection and the formation of unlikely alliances between governments and private-sector conglomerates, the ability to exploit social media has been a game-changer in Muslim-majority countries.

It should come as no surprise, then, that leaders and officials in those countries display a conspicuous distrust of the Internet. Muslim governments claim that social media "causes unrest." Turkey's ruler has called Twitter "a menace." He's right. If enough citizens are unhappy, Twitter and other social media technologies present a significant threat to power. Even in heavily censored countries, the Big Brother dynamic has flipped; these days, Little Brother does the watching, and leaders are left to worry. As of this writing in late 2017, more than 125 million of the 381 million people living in the Middle East and North Africa (MENA) had Internet access. About 60 percent of the MENA population was less than 30 years old, and more than 53 million people were actively engaged with social media and recognized its power to hound the establishment. As clearly shown by the peer-to-peer organization of the Arab Spring revolts from 2010 to 2012, young citizens empowered by digital connections could challenge the old guard and, in many Muslim countries, push it to the brink. As one message on social networks during the 2011 Egypt revolution said: "If your government shuts down your Internet, it's time to shut down your government."

Governments fought back with a combination of digital and brute physical force, but the fight for hearts, minds and power continues to rage across the virtual battlefield. Of course, the establishment and the opposition always took advantage of new communications technologies to spread propaganda and incite fear of the enemy. The 19th century wars demonstrated the earliest practical usage of telegrams for relaying commands and coordinating movement between battalions in real-time. In World War II, the use of radio allowed effective coordination between air and land forces, but it also delivered messages designed to inspire allied citizens or sow fear and panic in enemy countries. The overall sophistication of the means improves dramatically, but the ends remain essentially the same.

ISIS and other extremist groups employ the same tactics through increasingly powerful digital channels. They use the dark web to plan and execute devastating attacks in Paris, Brussels, Hanover, Dhaka and Orlando, and then magnify the psychological power of the assaults through social media channels. They have become "the first terrorist group to hold both physical and digital territory," said Jared Cohen, the CEO of Jigsaw and an adjunct senior fellow at the Council on Foreign Relations. On the ground, ISIS troops murder, pillage and oppress. On the Web, their "digital warriors" post gory content intended to glorify the organization as an unassailable and righteous caliphate, sending warnings of what lies in store for those who'd choose to oppose them.

In fact, the recent conflicts in the Middle East offer a stark reminder of how the lines between physical and digital warfare have blurred. Extremist groups have spread fear and panic across the globe. They've created or hijacked hashtags for use as digital weapons, exaggerating news of small-scale ambushes or highlighting heinous crimes against helpless individuals as massive victories on the battlefield. But their primary source of strength doesn't reside in the strategic prowess of their leaders or the barbarism of their soldiers. Rather, it manifests in their ability to harness the power of social media and use it to strengthen their control on both physical and digital terrain. As a result, social media transformed a ragtag militia with substandard weapons and an uncanny taste for violence into a global force that threatens the combined military might of some of the most sophisticated armies in the modern world. ISIS and its army of digital warriors used Twitter, Facebook and Instagram to both establish control locally and spread disinformation and fear globally.

The digital world provides a façade, a level of abstraction that obscures their true, ugly motives. Thus, in the hands of an ISIS digital warrior, all the hashtags, buzzwords and memes become doubly effective, rendering enemies weaker but also rallying supporters and susceptible youth behind the flag of the Caliphate. As a result, thousands of Muslim youth from Europe and the US have fled their countries to join the ISIS ranks, either as infantry or even as wives for their soldiers. In the digital world, many Muslim youth saw evidence of ISIS and its righteous struggle, its actions justified by the terminology and institutions held sacred by most Muslims. In the real world, ISIS pillaged, murdered and raped innocent men, women and children in full disregard for the fundamental teachings of Islam. The abstraction afforded by digital technologies let ISIS disguise its terrorist activities under the garb of *religious extremism* and the *caliphate* — misinforming impressionable youth in Muslim-majority countries, and propagating the troubling association between Islam and terrorism in the West.

The extremist's online recruitment and engagement strategy mimics the digital presence fostered by a multinational firm's public relations department. Blogs, comments, videos and pictures posted on social media and other online forums are produced with professional precision and choreography to increase their appeal and authenticity, especially for young audiences. ISIS has recruited professional cameramen, choreographers and marketing experts, who spend a considerable amount of effort and time to ensure that the organization's images, videos and messages contain all the necessary ingredients for engaging, compelling and authentic content. The organization supplements its professionally crafted content with the large number of personal accounts created by ISIS-affiliated fighters, who regularly post pictures and videos of their daily lives, further increasing authenticity and appeal by humanizing ISIS fighters as people with similar interests and characteristics. Potential ISIS sympathizers on Internet forums and social media are promptly identified, targeted and recruited using a subtle strategy that can take months and years to work but lands new converts at a higher rate than one might imagine.

TWO STRATEGIES FOR TAMPING DOWN DISSENT

Social media's empowerment of ordinary, disenfranchised citizens has stoked the embers of freedom, but the fire has not spread uniformly throughout the Muslim-majority countries. While digital technologies helped nurse revolutions out of unorganized grassroots initiatives, the full government upheaval in Tunis was followed, eventually, by the return of a military-backed government in Cairo. In the meantime, groups like ISIS and Al-Nusra established a deep foothold using the very same tactics. Rather than needing deep pockets and years of work to organize and mobilize enough bodies to threaten a sitting government, it now takes little more than a few hours and a $20-per-month Internet connection. And the increasingly rich content environment online has itself been emboldening. Clay Shirky, the widely cited new media professor at New York University, noted as much back in a 2011 essay for *Foreign Affairs* magazine: "As the communications landscape gets denser, more complex and more participatory, the networked population is gaining greater access to information, more opportunities to engage in public speech *and an enhanced ability to undertake collective action*." [Our emphasis.]

PUSHING THE BOULDER UP A HILL
Why Are Terror Operations Successful?

BY FRED BURTON
Chief Security Officer, Stratfor

Burton is a former police officer, counterterrorism special agent with the U.S. State Department and New York Times *best-selling author. You can follow him on Twitter: @fred_burton*

Terrorism ebbs and flows, but it never ends. With the latest trend of soft-target attacks, there is brilliance in the simplicity of the terrorist actors, making the job of predicting and preventing attacks almost impossible. Someone needs just a car or truck and a willing actor to kill. There's no need to build a bomb or purchase a gun. Recruits don't need to go to a training camp in Libya or Afghanistan to learn how to kill. All the know-how is there on the Internet and in the media for the taking. Simply put, I'm not optimistic things will ever change. As a former counterterrorism special agent with the U.S. State Department, I've seen the same cycle of violence and response to terror for decades.

On the operational level, once a terror attack starts to unfold, a rapid public safety response is required to neutralize the threat. It primarily focuses on efforts to reduce the body count, with a primary mission to neutralize the threat (i.e., kill or capture the attacker). The challenge for first responders is containment of the attack and rapid mass casualty care. In many cases, the questions and witch-hunt for blame begins even before the first responders have finished their work. "How could this have happened? What did the security services miss? Was the actor known to intelligence services?"

Having the benefit of more than 30 years analyzing terror, I've thought long and hard about why terror operations are successful, all in hopes of unpacking past attacks or thwarting potential new ones. Needless to say, it's a frustrating career choice, and one I don't encourage anyone to make. I've come to the conclusion that successful terror operations boil down to two key failure points on the part of counterterrorism agents and analysts. The first is a failure of human intelligence; the second is a failure of tactical analysis. I speak a lot about this to cops and students of terror so they can learn from our past mistakes.

Human intelligence is key to thwarting attacks ahead of time. In essence, agents need a source with intimate knowledge of the plot, or at least someone close enough to the operation or planned action who can tip off authorities. The source may be a first time walk-in or a cooperating individual working for the intelligence services. For example, the source that tipped us off to the whereabouts of Ramzi Yousef, the mastermind of the first World Trade Center bombing, was a walk-in who didn't want to die carrying a baby doll bomb aboard a commercial aircraft. He also wanted the large cash reward. At the time, we were offering $2 million for Yousef's capture, using an aggressive public service campaign to hunt him down using old school wanted posters, public service announcements hosted by Hollywood actors and matchbooks with Yousef's picture. We were lucky that the source came forward, or I'm convinced Yousef would have continued to kill and bomb passenger aircraft. Luck can play a part in counterterrorism operations, but money can be a powerful motivator, too. In Yousef's case, the successful use of the informant's information made the source a wealthy man.

A second key variable in thwarting terrorist attacks is tactical analysis, or the ability to connect the dots before an attack begins. This is easier said than done. Have you ever noticed, after the attack and after all the dust has settled, that it becomes clear the attacking person or group had been plotting to kill, perhaps even in this specific way? Ferreting out those warnings and indicators *beforehand* is the analytical challenge. Thus, one usually needs human intelligence to help the analysts put the pieces of the puzzle together, before the truck bomb starts rolling towards the target. Once the attack starts to unfold, your chances of thwarting the larger plot are remote. I've also learned that it becomes critical to disrupt the attack cycle in the planning phase or when the attack team is conducting pre-operational surveillance of potential targets. However, making sense of the dots or nuggets of intelligence ahead of time is probably the biggest challenge facing any counterterrorism team. This problem is only getting worse as the flood of information grows more overwhelming, both within classified channels and in the open source.

In the end, the forces that fight terrorism must stay ahead of the curve every single time. The terrorists only need to get lucky once.

Several studies have rightly challenged the notion of a near-exclusive relationship between political revolts and social media. No doubt myriad other factors must exist to foment a full-on revolution, but the accessibility of these constantly evolving platforms has created new outlets for public expression, global communication and political organization. Certainly, revolutions do not occur because of Twitter or Facebook, but their role in providing a meaningful outlet for public disenfranchisement can't be overlooked.

Social media platforms and their ability to help mobilize and escalate citizen-state confrontations increase the possibility of a full-scale upheaval that threatens national sovereignty or, in worst cases, leads to all-out anarchy or civil war. The Arab Spring and the role of social media in amassing people and catalyzing them against their government is but one such example. Governments tend to select one of two options to ensure their citizens don't turn from online government bashing to open protest and civil disobedience — censorship or inciting fears of a common enemy. Censorship requires the disruption of the types of communications that allow sizeable groups of people to coordinate an organized anti-government protest. Authoritarian regimes within Saudi Arabia, Iran and China have adopted this method, putting in place strict online policing and laws that impose harsh penalties on individuals and groups that incite rebellion. Other governments have cooled the rise of negative public sentiment with widespread campaigns designed to intensify nationalistic sentiments, typically by using social media and other mass-communication channels to incite fear of an external enemy. This creates a sense of loyalty between state and its citizens.

Proponents of both approaches can claim successes. Critics of both can find failures. The common bond throughout: a more politically aware and active citizenry, thanks to those digital channels. In fact, analyses conducted in recent years indicate that Muslim social networking has become a major causal factor in the exponential increase of new voters in the Islamic world. Citizens view social media as a kind of "edutainment," a new phenomenon in the political arena that is helping convince young people everywhere that taking part in politics is not just for their parents' generation. These groups' younger cadres took up digital technology with more acuity than the legions of complacent, older government bureaucrats, who failed to perceive the need or muster the capacity for online campaigns that might gain support and reinforce loyalty. This tardiness proved damaging, and many governments are still scrambling to catch up.

In the meantime, the rebels have changed the way millions of people live and choose their leaders.

CHAPTER 10

THE ELEMENTS OF TERRORISM

*"Democracy is necessary to peace and to undermining
the forces of terrorism."*
— BENAZIR BHUTTO

*(the first woman to head a democratic government in a Muslim majority nation;
Prime Minister of Pakistan from 1988 to 1990 and again from 1993 to 1996.)*

W ith the charismatic presence of a Kennedy, the once and future Prime Minister of Pakistan, 54-year-old Benazir Bhutto, addressed the energized crowd of thousands of supporters who had gathered in the garrison city of Rawalpindi. It was early evening on December 27, 2007, and by that point in the race Bhutto was winning in most national polls. She was all but a shoe-in for a third term. An exciting and personable candidate, she was rare in the mean-streets racket of Pakistani politics. Security and terrorism remained a major concern, especially after a thwarted attempt to assassinate her eight weeks earlier, when she returned from years of exile. The bomb blast spared the popular leader, but it killed about 140 supporters and bystanders. So when Bhutto concluded her speech at the rally and the thunderous cheers broke out, her security detail immediately moved in to escort her toward a waiting motorcade. A rock star vibe permeated the whole event.

Bhutto had served as prime minister from 1988 to 1990 and again for three more years in 1993 to 1996. She was the daughter of the ousted and executed Zulfikar Ali Bhutto, who had served in the 1970s as both president and prime minister. After a military coup deposed her father's regime in 1977, the 25-year-old Benazir was thrust into a leadership role in Pakistan's largest opposition party, the Pakistan People's Party (PPP), which her father had founded. She eventually would become the first woman to hold the top political office in any Muslim-majority country — largely because of her popularity with common Pakistanis. So when the motorcade left the noisy rally, it seemed perfectly natural that she would ride in the car with the sunroof, which allowed her to stand and wave greetings to the many thousands who lined the streets. Anyone could see she was loved and adored by the masses, clearly their choice as the right person to lead Pakistan out of its political, economic and social problems.

As she smiled and nodded to the people in her gracious way, a nondescript man armed with a semi-automatic pistol jumped out of the crowd and opened fire on her. He was nervous and the rounds sprayed wildly, so he reached for something in his pocket. Instantly, he was ripped apart by the heavy-duty blast of a bomb strapped to his sides. Bhutto's car was rocked, and she disappeared from view.

Pakistan is no stranger to terrorism, and it provides a rich field for research on extremism. Growing up in small-town America, one hears all the stories about places like Pakistan being the most dangerous place on earth. We see the scary pictures on TV, and our older neighbors talk about how modern Pakistan feels like the Cold War Soviet Union — a dark place with little rhyme or reason. Yet most Westerners who go there find a different reality. The perception that impoverished Pakistanis hate everything American and have little choice but to join extremist groups is washed away. Instead, one realizes that other factors drive the types of extremism that convince young men to strap bombs to their bodies and kill beloved leaders who might otherwise help improve their lives.

GRIEVANCES, IDEOLOGIES AND INFLUENCERS

While no one can point to a single, uniform path to radicalization, we can identify several common factors that guide most extremists in their Pre-Hate Journey. ISIS and other terrorist organizations regularly exploit grievances by offering young recruits a sense of purpose, belonging or adventure. They rally new proponents around a powerful ideology, usually one that plays off religious obligations. And they rely on charismatic influencers who often might fail in most recruitment efforts but know how to identify the best targets and know which messages and channels to use to optimize their chances with them.

Grievances

ISIS and other groups seek to exploit political grievances against governments by citing their policies in the region and by highlighting alienation and discrimination against Muslim communities around the world. In Muslim-majority countries, extremist organizations will stoke the perception that governments repress religious freedoms, violate human rights, restrict political expression and do little to build economic opportunity. In the Arab world, a strong sectarian dimension pervades the ISIS narrative, as the group calls on Muslims to defend Sunni communities against the Shia. And in many other parts of the world, the presence of "push factors" such as poverty, illiteracy and poor education provide a fertile field in which extremism can grow. ISIS and other groups also try to exploit a variety of psychological factors, including issues of identity and spiritual imperfection. Some recruits seek to make up for past indiscretions and engage in "self-cleansing" by embracing the terrorists' vision of Islam. Although ISIS' use of violence is rejected by Muslims generally, their grievance narrative resonates broadly.

Ideology

Terrorists use a warped version of Islam to argue that Muslims may use terrorism to defend their communities around the world, going so far as to manipulate Quranic verses and *hadith*, the sayings and actions of the Prophet Muhammad. As a part of this narrative, they misuse and exploit the concepts of *jihad* and *takfir* (or, the declaration of certain individuals and groups as non-Muslim). In their call to reestablish the Caliphate, ISIS has added an additional element to this message. The group manipulates the historically grounded respect many Muslims hold for the early Islamic caliphs, claiming their small band of fighters, through divine support, will capture territories, fulfill the vision of a truly Islamic state and defend the *ummah* (the Islamic community as a whole). Terrorist groups use these concepts to instill a sense of purpose, empowerment, adventure and religious obligation and reward.

The role of ideology is particularly important because it accentuates all the other factors in the radicalization process. If an individual has a grievance in his or her personal life, extremist recruiters will aim to sway them with twisted ideological ideals that provide a sense of purpose and reward. If the grievance is political in nature, the terrorists tweak their message to emphasize a vision of an authority that empowers them and their allies. Thus, ideology becomes the vehicle, justification or excuse that violent extremists use to act on their grievances.

Influencers

Recruits rarely radicalize on their own. In most cases, a figure in their community or an individual or group acting online seduces them with a powerful blend of grievance and ideology. Research shows that young recruits typically come from middle-class families in urban areas. The geographical concentration of this smaller middle-class cohort helps explain why Islamist parties tend to do better in provincial, regional and local elections than at the national level. In fact, studies show that most recruits join terrorist groups because of identity grievances, not poverty or related environmental factors. Most of these recruits have studied at public universities and are fed up with the corruption and mayhem around them. Extremist groups offer an effective change narrative — a black-and-white answer for how to change society by applying a different set of rules. In the absence of other solutions, the clear-cut answers provided by religious extremists look especially enticing.

The media narratives that pervade TV, radio and social media also play a significant role in swaying susceptible youth. More than 110 million people have access to television programming in Pakistan, tuning in at a rate similar to other countries in the Middle East and South Asia. Between 7 p.m. and 10 p.m. (prime time hours), more than 35 million people will watch one of the 90-plus TV channels available in Pakistan. These media networks help shape ideas about extremism and the multiple bombings and attacks that have become almost commonplace in Pakistan.

After Bhutto's death in 2007, a married couple recounted their shock at a comment their son had made. As a small business owner and a nurse, this father and mother were comfortable but not rich, but they'd given their son everything they could. Yet, just a few days after the assassination, he proclaimed that Bhutto "deserved to die" for speaking on behalf of religious minorities. Days later, they still wondered how their son, well-educated and well-raised, could think such a thing. Given some of the alternative media narratives spun out from the killing, one could imagine how young men and women could see the extremists as liberators or heroes. Media coverage is a critical piece of the war on terror.

POSITIVE INFLUENCERS, EDUCATION AND GENDER EQUALITY

To effectively counter hate, we need to develop proven ways to undercut the extremists' recruitment narratives. One such strategy is the criminalization of insurgency groups. Revealing the hypocrisy and general ineffectiveness of extremist groups will help potential recruits see the organizations for what they really are. As the general popularity of extremist groups wanes, so too do their recruitment numbers. Revealing their weaknesses makes them weaker and is key to protecting the thin middle class in many of these key countries.

We also can unleash a battalion of positive influencers to counteract messages of hate. Interfaith leaders and women, especially mothers, comprise one of the most important constituencies in the fight against terrorism. Mothers' testimonials play a significant role in shaping their children's views on extremism and often can dissuade young men and women from going down this dark path. And faith-based engagement has proved effective for precisely the same reason recruitment ideology works — because religious leaders wield so much influence. The power of interfaith engagement can produce life-altering views that trickle down to large-scale communities. Some mosques will celebrate the Christmas and Passover holidays in a true appreciation for pluralism.

Education remains a key element in strategies to counter hate. Because extremists vehemently oppose nonsectarian education, they've made schools prime targets for years, especially in rural territories, including northern Pakistan. There, Islamic-powered fundamentalism forbids young women from attending classes altogether, but schools throughout the country have suffered religion-fueled violence. Despite the tragic deaths or injuries inflicted on teachers and children, the government's promises

THE POWER OF EMPOWERING WOMEN

BY CAPTAIN MOLLY MAE POTTER

Ms. Veteran America 2016, Veteran Affairs Commissioner for the City of Austin, and Dell Client Global Operations and Strategy Leader

Potter was deployed to Afghanistan in 2010 and sustained injuries that resulted in a traumatic brain injury and PTSD. The Air Force captain now advocates for treatment and resources to help veterans heal from the "invisible wounds of war."

If we listen to the needs of a community, we can find the answers. Unfortunately, one of the major barriers to empowering girls and women is the way in which society builds and develops its policies, opportunities and leadership programs. The inclusion of girls and women in programs and initiatives is too often an afterthought. And when any group of people feels isolated, they will shy away from supportive programs or group initiatives.

Consider, for example, how the U.S. military transitions female veterans after they return from their military service. Today, former military servicewomen have become the fastest-growing demographic of homelessness in the country. Many of the services for homeless veterans focus on single men, not women, and even fewer support women with children. What matters, of course, is how we meet and surpass the needs of all our returning veterans, but the most successful programs for women veterans were developed and designed around specific feedback from former servicewomen and their children. From their inception, these programs directly address issues that impact women and children. Openness to new solutions that address specific female vulnerabilities—such as the need for child care—can drastically change the way women view their role, empower them to be more involved, and take ownership of their situation.

Inclusion also means a chance to take a role in decision making. By enabling women from the beginning of the program-development process, we minimize feelings of isolation and unlock their capacity to transform themselves, their families and their communities through the strength of their voice, social power and ability to impact decisions. A great example of this can be found in the work of Nuru International, a U.S.-based nonprofit that seeks to eliminate extremism in Third World countries, implementing social programs that seek to end poverty. Founder and CEO Jake Harriman started the program with former U.S. Special Forces operators in the field, but they initially didn't include women with in-field operations. They soon learned that an all-male team could not effectively reach women leaders of the community and influence their home-life decisions. Jake and his team quickly realized that to decrease poverty and extremism in very rural African communities, they needed to include women and children of the villages in their outreach-support programs and their in-the-field leadership team. This helped bridge cultural barriers, made decision-making more inclusive, eliminated biases and resulted in greater overall support. The families and communities supported by Nuru now work as one team.

That solidarity with other women and networks of women is critical. Tradition, laws, customs and religion all can lead to isolation and profoundly weaken the role of women in society. Networks of women from similar traditions and cultures can empower them and reduce their isolation. Bonding over common stories and struggles can help boost the courage needed to seek support and services they might have avoided, and it can spur empowered women to reach out and provide support to others in need. Great allies and networks can accelerate a community's transformation, and those connections will play a major role in the empowerment of women — in the U.S. and around the world.

to track down the attackers go largely unfulfilled — as have pledges to rebuild destroyed buildings and fund replacement classroom materials. So, many children go without schooling or have to settle for improvised classrooms, shared textbooks and fewer educational resources.

This particularly heinous targeting of schools weakens an already shaky network of 150,000 public schools that educate more than 20 million Pakistani students. (More than 10 million children attend private institutions in the country.) Though Pakistan has made progress in boosting primary school enrollment, attendance rates remain the lowest in South Asia. And despite the national literacy rate moving upward in successive years, there are wide disparities in educational assets and resources from one school to the next. Urban schools receive more resources than rural schools; certain regions fare better than others. Graft, corruption, ineffective policy and mismanagement all play a part in depriving Pakistan's children of the valuable, life-enhancing benefits of education. In turn, this threatens the future prosperity and stability of the nation.

Gender-based disparities also appear throughout systems in Pakistan and other countries. In 10 of the most populous Muslim-majority countries, only half of the boys who enroll in primary school complete it. The situation for girls is even worse, with slightly more than 20 percent completing a primary education. High school dropout rates look even worse, with less than a third of teenagers receiving a secondary degree. And since Internet penetration rates are lower in most of these countries, few schools can use this primary communication channel as an educational resource.

Child labor too often impedes educational attainment, as well. In poor countries such as Pakistan or Indonesia, parents or circumstances often force children to give up school and work to help the family subsist. Education matters, but not as much as food and shelter. Accurate figures are hard to come by, but the United Nations Children's Fund (UNICEF) estimates that millions of poor and underprivileged children labor on farms or in workshops, factories and mines. A substantial number of children toil in the agricultural sector, as well as in urban centers where they weave carpets and produce sports equipment. Child labor accounts for as much as a quarter of the workforce in some developing countries.

And using cheap child labor pays off, as manufacturers gain a competitive advantage with cheaper goods for the export market.

U.S. laws prohibit imports made with child or slave labor, but enforcement is difficult and erratic. Children as young as four years old continue work in grimy factories, putting in long hours under Dickensian mistreatment by employers. Virtually everyone condemns this state of affairs, but the combination of razor-thin profit margins for manufacturers and intense global competition provides little hope for change anytime soon. Given the rapidly growing population across the Middle East, South Asia and Southeast Asia, the child labor market is more likely to expand.

As we've learned from existing research, the next generation of extremists probably won't emerge out of these factories. But terrorist groups will eagerly exploit the obvious injustice of child labor, further drive a cultural wedge between genders and attack schools and educators as the very real threat they are to these hateful organizations and philosophies. So yes, efforts to expose the hypocrisy of extremists will help guide impressionable youth toward a peaceful path. But for those of us who hope to counter hate — both in the West and in the many hotspots around the globe — we must address our own hypocrisies, as well.

CHAPTER 11

WHY PEOPLE BECOME EXTREMISTS

"These so-called extremists in Pakistan should be brought into the mainstream; if you marginalize them, you radicalize them."
— IMRAN KHAN
(Pakistani politician, former cricketer and philanthropist who leads the Pakistan Movement of Justice and serves as a member of the National Assembly)

A new shipment of hashish arrived from the north, and all the men in camp were cut liberal portions. After marshaling the shipment across a long day of travel, Tariq had that happy fatigue that comes with a job well done. The Haqqani network hired him for his leadership skills; he felt relieved and pleased to have justified their faith.

A sense of purpose and greater opportunity for upward mobility had drawn Tariq to Haqqani, a guerilla insurgent group that operated much like a private sector-entity, with subsidiaries all over the Pakistan-Afghanistan border region and specialized in logistics, pharmaceuticals and, most lucrative of all, illegal drugs. He'd attended a top law school in Kabul but switched career paths after spotting one of the slick social media advertisements Haqqani put out through its affiliates. The network would use imagery from the Afghan resistance of the late 1970s and 1980s — the Charlie Wilson era — a time when the Afghan *mujahideen* were lauded around the world for fighting the Soviets. Regional campaigns rife with religious symbolism bolstered the group's calls to the patriotic struggle, a mix that convinced many a young Afghan to sign up with this seemingly sophisticated organization. Marketing themselves as the special operations of indigenous asymmetric warfare and as a group dedicated to fighting on behalf of Afghans, the Haqqani network certainly meant business.

It conducted plenty of business, too. Running the drug trade in Afghanistan and Pakistan involved hundreds of people, from truck drivers to grunts in training camps to sophisticated investors who helped oversee the millions of dollars flowing through its financial network. Despite the illegality of its principal revenue generator, the corporation that Haqqani had become meant it could launder its profits and present itself as a force in the regional private sector.

Tariq had begun working for the corporation as a trader and middle-man, associating with a loose federation of Taliban and al-Qaeda that made up the terror ecosystem. He helped plan and execute attacks on U.S. and coalition forces operating in and around Kabul. But he really excelled at transporting "goods" from Point A to Point B. In recognition of his new-found specialty, Haqqani leaders promoted him, formally inducting him into the higher ranks of the Pakistani Taliban. When NATO put a bounty on his head — wanted: dead or alive — his prestige within the organization swelled. He took command of a cell, and over the next few years came to control a range of insurgent forces in several camps, reporting directly to the Grand Emir.

Tariq didn't come from abject poverty or repressive circumstances. He didn't lack for education or experience. Yet the lure of extremism still snared him, and he rose quickly up the ranks. He willingly became part of the growing global threat of extremism, hate and terror.

THE RIPPLE EFFECT OF SOCIAL MEDIA PROPAGANDA

Violent extremism isn't new, but the threat is growing for three reasons. First, there's the activity of extremist groups in the vacuum created by political transitions. Groups like ISIS are providing training grounds for foreign fighters developed to fill that vacuum, creating both a mid- to long-term risk of turbulence in several regions. Second, the Taliban, Boko Haram and other extremist groups are linking with like-minded groups at an alarming rate and expanding their skills and reach. As with the global-ization of Da'esh, these networks have become increasingly adaptable and able to share "lessons learned." Third, extremist recruiters are combining new information technologies and platforms with their traditional out-reach in a way that connects across borders. This allows them to reach a younger and more vulnerable segment of society wherever they reside.

The sheer number of foreign fighters streaming into Syria to join the struggle against the al-Assad regime put an intriguing twist on the conflict there. In early 2017, counterintelligence officials estimated more than 12,000 foreign fighters remained in Syria. While that had declined from a peak of 30,000 earlier in the conflict, that force still represented more than 90 different countries — many from the Middle East, but almost 3,400 reportedly from Europe or other Western states, including more than 150 from the U.S. The number eased after coalition forces put heavy military pressure on ISIS, which shifted gears and called for recruits to stay in their "native lands" to carry out operations. Many nations now worry about what citizens who traveled to the fight in Syria will do when they return home. And with good reason — attacks in Barcelona, Finland and elsewhere in Europe during 2017 reminded experts of the 2015 Paris attack, which came in retaliation for France's involvement in the Iraqi and Syrian wars. Led by Abdelhamid Abaaoud, a Belgian-Moroccan terrorist who joined ISIS in 2013 and subsequently operated as a link between the group's Middle East operations and its French terror cells, the attacks were, in the words of former President François Hollande, "planned in Syria, organized in Belgium (and) perpetrated on our soil with French complicity."

Local influence will always exert a strong force on hate. Abaaoud, for example, grew up in Molenbeek, a district of Brussels now notorious and scrutinized for its radical Salafist presence. But even as the influence of radical mosques eases — radicalization through mosques accounts for less than two per cent of documented cases in the U.K. — other local, personal factors exert a growing influence. Imprisonment has become an increasingly important factor in radicalization. Abaaoud spent time in prison, as did Michael Adebolajo, one of Lee Rigby's killers who converted to Islam in London and attended the meetings of the banned British terrorist organization al-Muhajiroun. In France, Muslims account for more than 50 percent of prisoners but only 10 percent of its population. Mental health and substance-abuse problems also exacerbate radicalization. The Chechen Tsarnaev brothers who perpetrated the Boston Marathon bombing claimed extremist Islamic beliefs as motivation, although they had no known affiliation with any particular organization. Analysts suggested their Caucasus sympathies and difficulty integrating into society might have played a greater role in their decisions.

These powerful local factors predispose individuals to the radical content they come across online. So, while social media itself might not drive the increase in young men and women joining extremist groups, it certainly accelerates and broadens the scope of the operation. Hate groups use refined movie-making and gamification techniques to appeal to potential Western recruits and to ensure their content is circulated on various social media platforms. Having such visual content readily sharable also makes their activities more newsworthy — or, in this case, more likely to get picked up by international media and "showcased" in the news. A *Vice* magazine article on young Britons waging extremist wars in Syria quoted fighter Abu Qa'qaa's Tumblr account, where he said: "Britain posting our pictures in newspapers. They don't realize it inspires more to come *religious extremism* and don't worry, we never wish to come back." He added a smiley face emoticon for effect. Such documentation on an international stage is what these once tiny, insignificant forces want, and it's a challenge recognized by some Western observers and media.

Foreign recruits have an especially complex, international relationship with social media. They are, of course, some of the most active participants in perpetuating the outreach tactics that captured their own interest. After all, they know full well how effective they are. They also use social media in a more direct manner to communicate with their families and with the families and friends of fallen comrades. In the latter case, they often supplement news of a death with an invitation for recipients to join them and avenge their loved ones. Imagining themselves on a path to *religious* paradise, they tend to send the most memorial tweets for those who've died in battles. Although Vice noted that, "One by one, these social media accounts have been going silent, presumably because their owners have been killed," the online connection provides these users with a psychological sense of purpose and a belief that their legacy, in more ways than one, will live on after their deaths.

Extremist groups also get help spreading their message from those who don't support or actively work against them. In the 24 hours after the Syrian chemical weapon attacks in the summer of 2013, most of the posted photos and videos documenting the horrible effects came from moderate or unaffiliated accounts. ISIS already made use of affiliated media outlets, which produced more than 625 Islamist propaganda videos from 2014 through 2017. The videos, produced in Arabic, English and multiple other languages, were easily sharable and spread quickly to a global audience. The most abhorrent clips, particularly the executions of U.S. journalists James Foley and Steven Sotloff, were some of the most widely viewed — in part because they were shared by thousands of completely unaffiliated users and groups.

Then there are the actors whom the London-based International Centre for the Study of Radicalisation and Political Violence (ICSR) call "disseminators." Most of these unaffiliated individuals live in Western Europe or the U.S., and they rarely show allegiance to any specific group. However, their social media accounts reveal a clear sympathy toward extremist causes. In many cases, particularly in Syria, they serve as Western media's key sources of information about the conflict, the events on the ground and the Islamist fighters participating in the battles. These disseminators are generally more personally responsive and more likely to build bonds with the fighters than an organization's official social media accounts, which usually don't engage online with supporters or detractors. The personal relationships the disseminators build gives them access to raw content from unauthorized and anecdotal sources — everything from fighters' private social media accounts to official reports coming from the Assad regime and NGOs. They then translate, edit and package the content into propaganda that travels worldwide, mainly through Facebook pages but also through Twitter and other channels.

A COUNTEROFFENSIVE FROM ALL ANGLES

The tsunami of extremist propaganda on social media feeds precisely the same elements that make the explosion of digital entertainment so crucial to those who seek to counter hate. It taps into a young and digitally engaged demographic. Discontented populations seek out these channels as an avenue for otherwise suppressed political expression. And they splinter conventional hierarchies into decentralized networks. In fact, the phenomenal and formidable digital success realized by extremist groups could become social media's undoing in many parts of the world, giving repressive governments and censors a prime excuse to monitor online

DEFUSE IT BEFORE IT BLOWS

BY MEHMOOD KAZMI
CEO, Pakistan Youth Change Agents (PYCA)

Kazmi is a partner with Share Investment Company in Maryland and serves on the Virginia Tech University Board of Visitors. He graduated top of his class from Harvard Business School and previously worked at Tipton Equity Partners, AIC Associates and America Online.

In times of perceived danger, humans are hardwired to seek the safety of the familiar. An extremist might not have to openly preach hatred, because simply heightening people's general sense of fear spurs a natural reaction to circle the proverbial wagons with their "own" in defense against "the other." Pressuring people to that point is like compressing flammable gas. The more afraid they become of even vaguely defined risks, the more the explosive potential of the group. Once it reaches a critical point, the tiniest spark of innuendo or subtle prejudice can ignite an inferno.

Lay observers often are confused. As they try to identify catalysts for an extremist's hateful attack, they tend to look for more obvious drivers, such as openly fascist or militant movements. In fact, the asymmetrical nature of the current battle is lost even on many a policy expert. However, in understanding this framework I believe we have ample opportunity to release the pressure and reduce the volatility—well before small incidents set citizens on paths that can burn down entire countries.

The efforts I found most interesting during my work in the U.S. and around the world were those that sought to dissipate the fear of change and the "enemization of the other"—reducing pressure before fears transform into oppression, hate crimes or violent action. In the U.S., I have seen the positive influence encouragement and empowerment can have on minority citizens. In Virginia, these efforts help young men and women resist alienation from political and civic life. This translates into active engagement with elected officials and prospective candidates, as well as an ability to approach others from shared business, healthcare, anti-poverty or public-safety platforms. By establishing our "sameness" on issues that affect all citizens, we take wind out of the sails of those who seek to define us as abjectly different. Part of this involves participating in healthy partisan political debate and electioneering, but it also involves exceptional service on the public boards and commissions that serve all citizens. Some of these efforts might be starting decades later than they should have, but wherever communities are taking these approaches we already see impressive results in appointments, hiring and even election of Muslim-Americans to key public service roles.

In a very different setting, I also helped lead a set of positive engagement projects for young adults in Pakistan. Much like the U.S. initiatives, we focused this effort on changing people's inter-communal fears, which are driven by ignorance or misinformation, and reducing the likelihood they will be poisoned against others. In these programs, university students from around the country trained to develop and execute public advocacy programs, and then sought to launch their own programs to promote inter-community understanding. The entrepreneurial nature of their tasks helped them realize they could be more than bystanders. And the winning student-run programs they launched addressed major social issues at grassroots levels even NGOs would have difficulty penetrating. By bringing together students from diverse backgrounds in the initial training, and by encouraging diverse teams to work together, the long-term social impact of the final projects spawned a new generation of civic leaders for the near future.

The recent electoral successes of xenophobic agendas and candidates might be less about the candidates and campaigns themselves, and more about the vacuum in which fear has perpetuated. I have seen approaches that work from Virginia to Pakistan, and I believe active engagement, especially in circles where one might be least comfortable, can defuse the capacity of vulnerable groups to transform frustrations into hate or violence.

communication and stifle their citizens' freedom of expression. So what can stem this tide?

The religious establishment has issued one counterblast. Particularly dismayed by the ISIS rampage, more-conservative and traditional Islamists around the Middle East have sought ways to generate effective counter-messaging. As the struggle in Syria has continued, locals also have complained about the "cowboys" who hijacked their struggle — the balaclava-wearing soldiers with automatic weapons and pickup trucks, urging others to join their sacred struggle against the tyrannical infidel.

Islamic authorities also have fired countermeasures. The Grand Mufti, head of a longstanding government-affiliated Islamist institute called Dar al-Ifta, spoke out against ISIS as far back as 2014, claiming that the extremists are "far from the correct understanding of Islam." The Dar al-Ifta, which also issues fatwas, launched an online campaign that urged media outlets to refrain from referring to the extremists as being associated with an "Islamic State," hoping that proper terminology would avoid the calcification of negative stereotypes. They instead suggested the term "al-Qaeda Separatists" and invited Facebook users to follow Dar al-Ifta's page to promote that initiative. "In keeping pace with the huge developments in the field of communications," its website said, "Dar al-Ifta undertakes huge tasks imposed by the qualitative transition brought about by the new era of means of communications." It now seeks to "achieve the 'highest degree of effective communication'" with the Islamic world. Its English-language Facebook page has more than 345,000 likes, and other historic Islamist watchdogs eventually followed its lead. Egyptian clerics at Al-Azhar, a Sunni institution founded in 970 A.D., leapfrogged into the 21st century with a YouTube channel designed to counter Islamist propaganda. Politicians have joined religious leaders, too. In a January 2015 speech at the Al-Zahar Islamic learning center in Cairo, Egyptian President Abdul Fatah Sisi called upon Islamist leaders to help combat extremism and radicalization through a more modern interpretation of Islam.

Of course, Western governments also call for more forceful and urgent action against ISIS and other extremist groups, although they typically encourage a secular approach. A growing army of private organizations and individuals have joined the public-sector counteroffensive, too. Together, they challenge terrorist tactics and hateful ideologies through the very same social media channels where hate spreads. However, they pursue an open online strategy and tend to vehemently oppose the idea of censorship or shutdowns of social media channels — the default option of many authoritarian governments. *This is a crucial point in the discussion about the benefits and pitfalls of social media: While ISIS certainly stands to gain from digital freedom, denying access to individuals across the region effectively silences their own criticism of radicalism.*

And that criticism takes some extremely effective forms. In one favorite ISIS strategy, its operatives abuse popular trending hashtags to hype their message to a fresh and broad international audience. So netizens have turned their own hashtags against them. For example, the hashtag #amessagefromISIStoUS, initially appeared in 2014 with different threats and menacing photos of its supporters. Westerners quickly hijacked the idea, adding jokes or insults and returning the favor by mocking ISIS with their own hashtag: #amessagefromUStoISIS. ISIS had not accounted for the satirical return volleys that a huge and varied audience might fire back at it. And on it went: Poking fun at ISIS's open and obliging outreach strategy on sites like Ask.fm, British comedian Lee Hurst started the satirical hashtag #AskIslamicState in August 2014, kicking off an onslaught of hilariously ridiculous questions for ISIS. Filled with satirical questions about First-World problems and other trivialities, #AskIslamicState became the second most popular hashtag on Twitter that month, speaking to the power of laughter in the midst of a deadly serious situation. Not even barbaric murderers are immune to trolling.

Some groups took a more earnest approach in their fight back. The #NotInMyName campaign, organized by the Active Change Foundation, uses the popular hashtag to give individuals a chance to declare that ISIS does not speak for all Muslims. (We believe much of the campaign's power derives from the fact that Dar al-Ifta propounds the exact same message.) In the wake of the November 2015 Paris attacks, the Anonymous hacker collective declared war on ISIS via their French arm's YouTube page: "We will hunt you down. … We as a collective will bring an end to your reign of terror. We will no longer turn a blind eye to your cruel and inhumane acts of terrorism. ... The War Is On." Their #OpISIS campaign has scored direct hits already — roughly 100 ISIS and ISIS-related Twitter accounts seized; social media accounts hacked; more than 100,000 Twitter accounts flagged for removal; 5,000 propaganda videos reported; and "denial of service" strikes that brought down the main ISIS website. One major Anonymous Twitter account, @GroupAnon, announced, "We won't stop opposing #IslamicState. We're also better hackers."

All these efforts to counter hate found remarkable successes on their own. What sort of impact would they have if they could join in a strong, unified coalition of government, private sector and civil society actors? This is what we must build if we are to truly challenge the sophisticated extremist narrative and properly confront the presence of these groups on social media. This need not be a capitulation by any faction — Anonymous might continue to antagonize Western governments, if they so choose — but a multilateral approach must include a coordinated effort to mitigate a potential "us versus them" mentality within global hot zones. For example, if we educate all partners about the theological basis used by extremists to justify terrorism and hatred, we can collectively devise strategies that will reduce demand for radical content, rather than simply countering the radicalization already in progress. A sound agenda should include the creation of a multilateral forum to deal with online extremism. This strategy should set out to improve digital literacy in schools, promote critical thinking, activate social media accounts that debunk propaganda and clarify official policies, and establish a central body to fund and train grassroots counter-extremism specialists.

Social media is but one piece of the challenge posed by hate and instability, but the scale of support, power and funding that flows to these extremist groups through their social media outreach cannot be allowed to continue unchallenged. In a world where one hacked Twitter account can cause billions of dollars of damage — the Syrian Electronic Army's hacked tweet about a White House attack sparked a $136 billion dollar selloff on the New York Stock Exchange — the cost of further inaction or ineffectiveness will only escalate.

CHAPTER 12

WHAT LEADERS CAN LEARN
FROM EXTREMISTS

*"The trouble with the world is not that people know too little;
it's that they know so many things that just aren't so."*
— MARK TWAIN

A rmored jeeps draped in black flags rolled along the eerily silent, rubble-strewn suburban streets of southern Raqqa, passing unaware past three students hidden in an abandoned house, one of many there that had been pounded with shoulder-launched rockets and heavy-caliber gunfire. As the then-dominant ISIS forces canvassed the ruins of their de facto capital, looking for dissidents, their loudspeakers crackled with invitations for cowards to come forward so the local enforcement squad could have mercy on them. The students, hunched over their laptops, ignored the offer.

The three young men were members of Raqqa Is Being Slaughtered Silently (RBSS), a citizen-journalist group that initially formed to oppose the bloodthirsty Assad regime, but which pivoted to chronicle the ISIS atrocities after the terrorist group's 2014 takeover of the city. RBSS set out to become an uncensored news source for concerned parties outside of Syria. While it would've seemed galaxies away from the three men in that damaged house, the group hoped to establish a transnational community to put international pressure on Assad and ISIS. It already had inspired other resistance groups in Syria and Iraq. In fact, since the start of the occupation, RBSS had been instilling an increasing level of fear among the

ISIS elite. With orders to spare no one, the extremists made a public show of hunting down and slaughtering all the group's members they could find.

This RBSS cell was generating a live video feed from concealed cameras, documenting the latest ISIS purge with visuals that others could use as a meme and send to fellow anti-ISIS activists around the world. Earlier, one of the members, Hussam, had slipped outside, pretending to be a farmhand heading to market. Inside his basket was a GoPro camera filming ISIS vehicles and their loudspeaker harangues. The video automatically uploaded to the group's cloud-based storage account, and in less than 20 minutes would be edited and packaged for distribution via Facebook, Twitter and sister blogs like Mosul Eye. Hussam considered live-streaming the latest ISIS roundup over Facebook, but he realized doing so might reveal his location to enemies monitoring the web.

The latest technology could spell a death warrant for him and his colleagues, so Hussam opted to expose the abject lack of support ISIS had on the ground in Raqqa. RBSS used an active Telegram channel and, back at the house, Hussam's colleagues put their latest short visuals on Snapchat. One of Hussam's postings on Facebook generated hundreds of thousands of hits in less than 24 hours. The dozen or so RBSS operatives had inflicted more damage than any guerrilla force ISIS had faced on the battlefield. With their seat-of-the-pants journalism on a virtually nonexistent budget, these young resistance fighters made themselves a force. This ragtag coterie of undercover citizen-journalists humiliated ISIS on a global stage. International media outlets sought out and ran their videos, often producing stories based primarily on the group's reports — including the time RBSS members used Google Earth to pinpoint the exact location where downed Jordanian pilot Moaz al-Kasaesbeh was burned to death in a cage in 2015. In that case, a German digital outlet picked up the latest "wire" from Hussam and his RBSS team, wrote it up and quickly had it translated into French and Dutch. Later the same day, the story made its way into a three-minute segment on the BBC. TRT World dedicated two of its journalists to liaise with RBSS members and use their incoming stories as features in primetime. Turkish audiences, especially, craved the news reports from RBSS.

Within minutes, Hussam and his brethren could reach 11 million people in eight countries. It marked a new day for the power of the press. Now, when ISIS indiscriminately killed innocent people or bared their bald-faced corruption, a global audience knew about it—often with the support of disturbingly visceral video evidence. RBSS initiated multiple viral reports, building up a 21st-century media powerhouse that almost no one had heard of.

FIVE MYTHS OF EXTREMISM

Groups like RBSS have learned key insights from ISIS and other extremist groups, and they've put those lessons to good use. But these local resistance groups also have another advantage that few Western governments, NGOs or individuals fully understand. By virtue of their on-the-ground presence and their lifetimes of experience in regions where extremism often propagates, they already know enough to reject the five key myths of extremism that are prevalent in the West:

Myth One: *Extremists are creating a market*—The prevailing narrative suggests that extremist groups' sophisticated use of social media lures young men and women who otherwise would stay home with their families, playing video games or reading. That's just not true. It's not the stylized violence in ISIS videos that motivates potential recruits. It's frustration, ideological alienation, chronic unemployment, lack of education and a life with very few outlets for free expression. Corruption and a lack of opportunity already breeds cynicism and despair. ISIS didn't create a new "market," it's cynically exploiting an existing one.

Myth Two: *Technology is the answer to extremism*—Technology, on its own, cannot counter violent extremism. In fact, as we've seen in prior chapters, technology often exacerbates the problem. The fact that technology and access to information are so inexpensive and widely available means young people now have a virtual community within which they can find others who share and amplify their grievances. Twitter is great for venting, but there isn't a Muslim Peace Corps or equivalent movement to channel this energy. Extremist groups provide a concrete, real-world alternative.

Myth Three: *Poverty causes militancy and extremism* — A closer look at the backgrounds of the young men and women who join extremist groups proves they're rarely destitute and desperate. Poor people don't join ISIS in droves. More often, recruits come from a middle-class background — young, educated people who come from households that earn $1,000 to $1,500 a month. They don't sign on to extremist mentalities to escape poverty, but to advance upward, satisfy grievances, adhere to a certain ideology and break free from what seems like a confined position in life.

Myth Four: *Extremists are selling a medieval, dark narrative* — One can see the falsity in this statement by simply looking at the way ISIS publicly markets itself. Their recruitment videos portray a consumerist lifestyle and a Western-modeled, efficient governance structure free of corruption. This isn't a medieval return to the Dark Ages with archaic traditions. This is the new caliphate on steroids, bigger and better than the Ottoman dynasty.

Myth Five: *It's all about religion* — Many observers in the Middle East, North Africa and around the world rue the fact that the Arab Spring didn't produce the change revolutionaries had sought. For those within the upheavals or watching from afar, the movement's dissipation heightened the belief that playing by the rules of the game will never work. Especially in that environment, religion offers a change narrative that provides a practical outlet to "walk the walk" and take part in something bigger. The challenge from a messaging standpoint is to promote credible, local religious voices who offer a more compelling alternative to hate.

WHAT LEADERS CAN LEARN FROM
EXTREMISTS' STRATEGIES

To say most American business leaders and citizens have little understanding of extremist groups — let alone detailed insights about their propaganda tactics, recruiting initiatives and the allure they hold for young men and women — is a vast understatement. Almost without fail, general conversations about terrorism fall back into one or more versions of these five myths. To effectively counter these groups and individuals, we need to move beyond these stereotypes, because they blind us to the things we

THE THREE LEVELS OF ISSUES MANAGEMENT

BY RAYMOND F. "RAY" KERINS JR.
Senior Vice President and Head of Communications,
Government Relations & Policy for Bayer Corporation

In nearly 25 years of leading crisis- and issues-management programs for major *Fortune* 100 companies and governments, I was regularly surprised by senior management's limited engagement in pre-crisis planning. Even today, as planning becomes increasingly important, many leaders' fail to appreciate the potential impact that a crisis could have on their organization's reputation. Understanding how to handle these challenges starts with accepting the three levels of issues management:

- *Problem:* All organizations can identify dozens, if not hundreds, of day-to-day operational problems that exist and don't necessarily have a material impact on the organization, but they can become serious issues if not managed properly.

- *Issues:* These are the topics that can impact an organization's reputation. Issues are often larger, more significant problems that often aren't taken seriously.

- *Crisis:* These serious challenges to an organization could cripple a company or government, often resulting in problems such as bankruptcy, jail time and/or billions of dollars paid in restitution.

It is often said that people don't remember the actual crisis, but they never forget the response. Look no further than the last few major international crises. The public will tell you about the executive and what they said or didn't say, the government that was too slow to react, or the NGO that didn't take the years of rumors or accusations seriously. Think about any major crisis that has circulated on the front pages of newspapers or burned up the social media channels, and you'll find situations that could have been managed very differently—in many cases, simply by engaging in appropriate scenario planning. So here are Five Steps to Reputation Management as an initial guide:

- *Listen:* Social media has given a true gift to the organization willing to listen to the problems and issues roiling in and around it.

- *Plot:* Categorize your topics into the three levels of issues management.

- *Monitor:* Keep a close watch on these issues, as they can change levels very quickly.

- *Plan:* At minimum, invest the time to develop a strategy for your crisis and issues, and then "war game" various scenarios. Better to pressure-test the organization's readiness prior to a real challenge.

- *Engage:* The public is forgiving if treated with respect. Be honest, remorseful and, most importantly, have a plan to ensure that these issues do not repeat themselves.

Reputations are built over years and can be lost in seconds. If truly handled with the public's best interest in mind, most potentially negative issues can have a positive impact on an organization's reputation.

really can learn about and from these organizations. And there's much we can learn:

Go Local — What resonates well in Pakistan might fall flat in Jordan. With limited resources, those fighting extremists in different countries or cities need to ensure messaging and programs are tailored for those targeted audiences. For example, just like ISIS thinks about segmented audiences, we need to produce different media in different national and regional vernacular. This organic approach adds authenticity and carries more force among viewers.

Monitor, Monitor, Monitor — Effective media content requires time-intensive work with local partners to ensure proper storyboarding, tone and language. ISIS doesn't simply outsource things to contractors. They have a rapid fan base (ISIL fan boys) that are passionate about media, and much of the content they produce goes through rigorous pre-testing, including focus groups.

Portray the Narrative Visually — Music, drama and animation are game-changers. ISIS, for example, has its own "Game of Thrones," web games and choose your own adventure fantasy games. We can do it better. The ability to visually tell dramatic stories and tragedies of terrorism resonates with key audiences.

Find Key Influencers for Partners — We need to amplify credible voices and partner with locally rooted groups. Media partners who are well-respected and notable leaders in their field, whether documentaries, music, interfaith or animation, move the needle. These influences can deliver a positive message in a way that resonates with our target audiences.

Know Your Audience — We need to counter structural advantages in the feedback loops that violent extremist groups enjoy. Since these groups are integrated into local communities, they can deploy communications and social welfare programs, immediately sense which efforts work best, and then adapt their plans based on that learning. Whether big governments or big corporations, organizations with less access and a bigger bureaucracy will not learn and adapt as quickly. Many items in this book reflect an effort to build constant feedback mechanisms and fast learning cycles within counter-hate initiatives.

Link Multimedia Platforms — Linking multimedia platforms resonates with audiences. With many TV dramas, such as Selfie, the top-rated program in the Middle East in 2016, producers link the TV and radio versions, and viewers follow both. Feedback mechanisms, including SMS and social media platforms, allowed for additional interactive engagement with viewers.

Employ a Range of Interventions — One of the main takeaways from looking at extremist groups is the need to deploy a range of inhibitor messaging to prevent individuals from moving down the path toward extremist violence. A range of media products present multiple tipping points for changing behavior and channeling grievances toward more productive actions. This range of interventions allow us to present more balanced content to viewers when and where they're ready to receive it.

Focus on the Positive and the Negative — To attract audiences, anti-hate programming needs to inspire positive outcomes as well as discourage extremism. Presenting alternative narratives of young people who have succeeded in life against great odds attracts audiences to the programming and portrays alternatives to extremism.

Research, Research, Research — Rock music resonates in Egypt, but not as well in Malaysia. Research provides these sorts of insights, guiding us on what kinds of programming to organize in which locations and enabling groups on the ground to constantly retool content based on regular feedback.

Seek out Public-Private Partnerships — Fiscal realities dictate that local and international stakeholders will have to do more with less in the coming years. Increasingly, efforts to combat hate will need to overlap with NGOs and private-sector interests, combining various efforts and working to unleash more volunteerism.

Fund Projects using a Startup Model — To be sustainable, efforts to counter extremism should adopt a startup model, in which organizations gather international resources and use seed funding to help a project take shape and get it off the ground.

UNLOCKING INNOVATION IN UNEXPECTED PLACES

BY WAJAHAT ALI

New York Times contributor, playwright, writer, media personality

It's easy to be cynical and nihilistic, snarky and perpetually outraged when countering hate. To sit on the sidelines and do nothing but throw social media grenades and emojis. Cynicism requires zero work and investment. It's cheap and lazy. Hope requires work. It also requires vulnerability, because you risk exposing yourself to failure and pain. But hope is needed. Hope can fuel a new narrative and vision in which our kids, regardless of their multisyllabic name, their religion, their sexuality, their national origin, can stand up and throw down with humble swagger and contribute a verse to the evolving rough draft that is America. I'll be damned if they end up as antagonists, sidekicks, tokens, footnotes, or worse of all, excised completely and existing only as a number in a camp.

There are several factors that drive hate in general and anti-Muslim bigotry in modern America. For brevity, it really boils down to the following: ignorance and misperceptions. Specifically, Muslims have been in America since the 16th century (some would say even earlier). However, that marked the first major arrival of black slaves who were forcibly brought to this country against their will. Estimates suggest nearly 5 to 30 percent of these slaves were Muslim. So, even though our blood, sweat, labor, dreams, lives, stories fertilize this country's soil, nearly 65 percent of Americans say they don't "know" a Muslim in 2017.

Let that sink in for a moment.

Muslims are also the most diverse religious communities in America, in terms of ethnic background, religious sects, national origin and so forth. Muslim women are the most educated women of any religious group just behind Jewish American women. But the mainstream image of a Muslim women is silent, oppressed, walking tragedy shrouded in a black veil.

The current anti-Muslim trend seems like a remake. Tag, Muslims are it. But, back in the day, the bogeymen were Jews, Catholics and Japanese Americans. If you remove what some haters say about Muslims right now and simply replace it with Jew or Catholic, you will have a near perfect mirror of the conversations that were taking place in America during the '30s, '40s and '50s. White supremacy and bigotry is a helluva drug.

We need more education. More awareness. More allies and people of good faith coming together to inoculate their community and children from fear and hate. We need schools to strengthen their anti-bullying measures. We need equal standards—not double standards—across the board when it comes to employ- ment, housing, media representation and the label of "terrorism," which has been rendered almost meaningless with its lopsided application to only Muslim suspects.

The goal in countering hate is to unlock innovation in unexpected places. And, yes, that sounds like a sexy tweet and branding gimmick, but we mean it. The way to go about doing that is by identifying and working with passionate individuals on the ground, from the community, who are actually dealing with these challenges on a daily basis. Whether it's religious intolerance, online bullying, anti-LGBT harassment, misogyny, lack of economic resources, or violent extremism.

Specifically, we did social impact hackathons with Facebook and Google around the world to come up with some impactful and sustainable solutions to combat hate. Hackathons are intense, organized experiences in which teams compete with each other in a fast-paced race against the clock (usually 2.5 days or less) to "hack" (creatively solve) a challenge and develop prototype tools, products, narratives, and initiatives.

Let's build solutions and counter hate together. What's next?

Focus on Refugees and Displaced Persons — In several conflict-ridden areas, refugees and internally-displaced persons, especially youth, are particularly vulnerable to recruitment into ISIS and affiliated extremist groups. This includes refugees who leave the region entirely, including those displaced to Europe. Insurgent groups capitalize on this dynamic, recruiting heavily in these areas and camps. We need to develop rapid-response teams that enable a swift scale-up of counter-hate programming to support refugees and internally displaced persons as such situations arise.

Elevate Education as a Priority — In some settings, educational institutions can incubate violent extremist ideology, but they also can serve as antidotes to such views. Evidence shows that critical-thinking skills, civic education and sports engagement can help to prevent or mitigate violence among school-aged youth. Because the ability to speak English can reduce extremism in certain communities, increased investment to meet the demand for English-language education could help combat hate, as well.

Build a Cadre of Countering Hate Fanboys and Fangirls — These young activists will explore new opportunities with local partners, develop innovative programming and build relationships with key influencers. These programs can reach vulnerable youth populations in places of concern.

Develop a Countering Hate Toolkit — There aren't many practical guides on the market, and this book is just one attempt to educate readers about the tools available to counter hate. Few initiatives use analytic tools to understand local manifestations of violent extremism or to develop programmatic options to counter them. This is why the data.world initiative is so vital. This site includes options for understanding local drivers of extremism, characteristics of displaced persons, target-audience focus groups and templates of successful interventions — as well as guidance on metrics and evaluation.

Build our Own Countering Hate Networks — This can be done by launching Digital Train/Sustain, a state-of-the-art technological platform for linking like-minded, youth-relevant networks who seek to counter extremism and encourage dialogue on peace and conflict resolution. There are many examples like the Peer to Peer network (sponsored by Facebook) and the AVE (Against Violent Extremism) network initially seeded by

Google. These networks would include a digital platform for young people to talk about peace, conflict resolution and other measures.

Make Exchanges Work — Explore ways to continually engage a worldwide "alumni" community of offline and online exchanges. These networks are some of the best resources we have for countering violent extremism, building and amplifying positive campaigns through social media connections and constant outreach initiatives.

CHAPTER 13

THE SILICON VEIL

"Advertising people who ignore research are as dangerous as generals who ignore decodes of enemy signals."
— DAVID OGILVY

S ilicon Valley companies are racing to develop the best products and services technology will allow. The extremists hiding behind the Silicon Veil are racing, too. They don't care about valuations or the buzz of a Recode or Tech Crunch story. They don't file for patents, publish papers or dream of launching an IPO. But the people and groups on both sides are doing what they need to do to win: outsmart their opponents and expose their weaknesses, uncover new ways to reach customers/recruits, and unleash products that disrupt the status quo. Both sides employ brilliant engineers and programmers, layering their own ideas on existing platforms or just creating their own platforms. In many ways, it's the same race. They have vastly different motivations and goals in mind, of course, but they differ in another key way, as well. Silicon Valley is transparent. You have to be if you want to raise money, recruit top talent, increase your share price or report to Wall Street. The Silicon Veil is silent. You have to be if you want to exchange money illegally, recruit soldiers, stoke your members' hatred and plan ways to inflict harm on innocent people.

The veil maintains its silence and its strength by maintaining focus on three key factors—disinformation, encryption and anonymization. Disinformation acts as a smoke screen to mislead Western governments and citizens; sometimes it even stokes dissension among the enemy.

Encryption allows for secrets of any type to flow discreetly and avoid detection. Anonymization protects bad actors from the consequences of identification by authorities. It's a three-legged stool of hate-driven innovation, one that allows those who engage in hate and extremist behavior to hide in plain sight.

DISINFORMATION

The breathless coverage of the recent U.S. elections and the sheer wonder at the fact that Russia might interfere with the U.S. election shows either ignorance of what's happening everyday around the world, a disregard for history or a combination of both. Perhaps ratings get in the way, perhaps reporters just fall short in their efforts to study and educate themselves and readers. Either way, a report by Citizen Lab at the University of Toronto concluded that Russia focused recent disinformation campaigns on at least 39 countries, including our own. They targeted government, military, industry, journalists, academics and multiple other groups. One common tactic involved the theft of emails and the subsequent leak of them to the media. The Russian efforts targeted officials in Afghanistan, Armenia, Austria, Cambodia, Egypt, Georgia, Kazakhstan, Kyrgyzstan, Latvia, Peru, Russia, Slovakia, Slovenia, Sudan, Thailand, Turkey, Ukraine, Uzbekistan and Vietnam, the report said. If you just read the U.S. media for the last year or two, you'd think that this was a new phenomenon and the U.S. was a sole target. Turns out we weren't so special.

The sheer volume of disinformation campaigns and their long, long history might surprise most of us, though. Russia formed its "special disinformation office" back in 1923, nearly a century ago. In fact, the actual word, disinformation, is a translation of the Russian word *dezinformatsiya*. Our ignorance encompasses virtually every mode of disinformation, too. For example, most U.S. residents think of hackers working from China, Russia or Eastern Europe. Yet, a 2017 Internet security report by Akimai, the leading content-delivery network in the world with 15 to 30 percent of all Web traffic, found that no country originated more attacks than the U.S. itself. The top ten source countries for attacks were the U.S., China, Brazil, the Netherlands, India, Ukraine, Russia, France, Germany and Canada. The U.S., China and Brazil accounted for more than one-third of all attacks. (That said, experts tell us that anywhere from 50,000 to 100,000 people in China work professionally as hackers. We believe Russia has a similar approach, although the number is unclear.)

As we define it, disinformation comes in many forms. It might include straight-up propaganda and fake news reports, but we also include hackers, malware and denial-of-service attacks in this category, as all gum up the flow of legitimate information. The broader definition considers how antagonists deploy technological or marketing innovations to either distract us, hurt us financially or disrupt our daily lives. It results in wasted time, money and resources. To be sure, it's on the mild side of the terroristic spectrum, and it should remind us that what we read might not be true, that our files might not be safe, and that our work environment could become dangerous or shut down.

Terrorism forces you to consider how much worse it could get. Disinformation has a similar, but much subtler, effect.

ENCRYPTION

It might feel like a cliché to call something "the Facebook of...," but VK does have a similar platform and it is Russia's largest social media platform, with more than 410 million accounts as of early 2017. So, the label fits.

Pavel Durov founded the site, but unlike Mark Zuckerberg, he was forced out and eventually created another company called Telegram Messenger, a cloud-based messaging platform. He scored another hit with the new firm. Telegram's advanced encryption allows users to share content for free from any device, store it in the cloud and feel certain that your information will stay secure. He and his colleagues made it easy to build new tools for the platform, making the powerful encryption available to a range of users and developers. It sounds much like a successful startup in Silicon Valley, but it has become a prime example of how the combination of capital, different societal values and technological innovation can create the perfect environment for nefarious behavior. The big X factor is Durov himself — and his views of right and wrong.

Durov butted heads with Russian authorities on several occasions. In 2011, he stonewalled police who demanded that the site take down pages

STOPPING THE PROFITABILITY OF HATE

BY JOSH LIPSKY
Senior advisor to Christine Lagarde, International Monetary Fund

The idea of "startup" culture has spread from Silicon Valley to nearly every corner of the globe. During my time at the State Department, I met with entrepreneurs representing dozens of countries, each of them eager to develop the next great app or leave a positive impact on their communities. But what we have to understand when it comes to extremism is that many of these hate groups have adopted startup culture as well. They understand the persuasive power of the Internet. They rely on young people to fuel their movement. They organize in small, mobile cells with little central leadership.

If we think of extremists in this way then the follow-up question has to be how can we disrupt their business model? How can we stop the profitability of hate? One answer is to bring their message out of the shadows, shine a spotlight and reveal the hypocritical and self-serving motivations of those who peddle in divisiveness.

Look at social media, for example. Many accounts—from white nationalist groups to ISIS—can be and have been shut down. But the ideas these groups promote will always find a way into the Twitter, Facebook and Google ecosystems. Every person can take on these messages in their own way and use their own voice to make a difference. Each tweet, post and dangerous video should have a rebuttal. Not from a U.S. government official, but from any concerned person in the world who sees something wrong and can take a moment to simply say: "This person does not speak for me."

The collective power of this kind of response is more potent than any single program, campaign or strategy. And when done in coordination and cooperation, these counter-narratives can cut-off the life source for the business of extremism—new recruits.

for opposition politicians. Some three years later, he refused a security agency's demand for information about Ukrainian protestors. Five days later, he was dismissed as VK's CEO. He left the country, vowed to never return, established citizenship in Saint Kitts and Nevis and launched Telegram. As an avowed libertarian, and given his past run-ins with the Russian government, his decision to create a platform that authorities can't track makes perfect sense.

While older chat and messaging apps encrypted messages as far as the servers, using a protocol called SSL, that technology was designed to defeat hackers who would eavesdrop on traffic over Wi-Fi networks and the like. Once the messages reached servers, however, they were stored in an unencrypted format because companies considered them safe from hackers at that point. Of course, law enforcement could still obtain the messages with a court order, something that would not have sat well with Durov. Today, newer chat apps encrypt messages all the way down to the recipient's device, and Telegram was one of the earliest platforms to support this end-to-end encryption. Only end users, with a private key, can decrypt the information on Telegram and similar services. Authorities might still demand and get metadata — who sent messages to whom — but they no longer have access to the content of the messages themselves.

These days, most messaging apps have added the feature, from Apple's iMessage and the Facebook-owned WhatsApp to several smaller services. The code converts a message, even entire files, to encrypted text that can be sent, copied or pasted anywhere. For all intents and purposes, there's no difference in security between this technology, called PGP, and "military grade encryption." So individuals can post these encrypted messages, and even the NSA can't access them. There is a misconception that intelligence agencies like the NSA are able to crack any encryption.

As one might imagine, ISIS and other extremist groups immediately took advantage of the near-perfect security for messaging. [See Box 13.1] U.S. media called Telegram the ISIS "app of choice." And the groups flaunt their use of it and other encryption apps, too. For example, because the encryption uses "public-key cryptography" — through which a message encrypted by one key can only be decrypted by the other, mathematically related key — the publishers of the Al-Qa`ida's *Inspire* magazine can publish one of the keys publicly. Anyone who wants to send them a private message can use the key to encrypt it, and only they have the sister key to decrypt it.

BOX 13.1   **A SAMPLING OF ENCRYPTION TECHNOLOGIES**
DEVELOPED BY EXTREMIST GROUPS

Extremist groups and the engineers and coders they employ have created an array of platforms and apps to help encrypt and hide their online interactions:

- **Tashfeer al-Jawwal**—A mobile encryption platform developed by the Global Islamic Media Front (GIMF); released September 2013.

- **Asrar al-Ghurabaa**—Another alternative encryption program developed by the Islamic State of Iraq and Al-Sham; released November 2013, around the same time the group broke away from the main Al-Qaeda organization following a power struggle.

- **Amn al-Mujahid**—An encryption software program developed by the Al-Fajr Technical Committee, a mainstream Al-Qaeda organization; released December 2013.

- **I-Qaeda (AQ)**—A series of encryption product releases since at least 2014; these releases have strengthened a hypothesis that the Edward Snowden leaks influenced Al-Qaeda's crypto-product innovation.

- **The main Al-Qaeda media house**—GIMF and Al-Fajr are not using home-brewed crypto-algorithms, as validated through a combination of open source and reverse engineering techniques. There are rumors of Al-Qaeda software being infested with backdoors.

Opsec Methods

Encryption isn't the only way to hide. The terrorists who perpetrated the Paris attacks congregated in Belgian safe houses to plan. Some had downloaded encrypted messaging apps, such as Telegram, but many simply used burner phones, prepaid mobile phones that are easily wiped and discarded. Technologists often refer to this approach as "opsec," or operational security.

Most chat apps, such as Telegram and Wickr, now have a feature where old messages automatically self-destruct after a certain period. So, for items not manually deleted, this feature will get rid of any incriminating evidence automatically, without any interaction by the user. So even if law enforcement agents can obtain a terrorist's phone, the evidence they need might already be gone. Desktop and laptop PC users can get Windows Washer, software that wipes disks and rids them of remaining information. Another option is Tails, a live USB flash drive that effectively works like a removable operating system. The user boots up on the Tails drive and, once it's removed, leaves no trace of activity on the computer itself. Perhaps most important, Tails reduces the chance that the user will make a mistake because no evidence can be left behind accidentally once the USB drive is removed and the computer is shut down.

ANONYMIZATION

In 2013, Edward Snowden released top-secret NSA documents that revealed widespread mass surveillance, even of U.S. citizens. This agency did not eavesdrop on the phone calls of people in the United States, instead collecting metadata about the calls. Some reports suggest U.S. forces have used intelligence from these sources to target drone strikes at overseas terrorists. A survey of terrorist publications and details that emerged from interrogations suggest that terrorists have become at least as concerned about hiding metadata as they are about encrypting communications. But the various chat apps and services now available on the market do little to hide metadata. In almost all current protocols, servers must know the address or phone number to know where to send a message.

There are, however, tools to help obscure pathways. Tor, which stands for "the Onion Router," might be the most popular of them. Tor passes encrypted web traffic through multiple proxy servers across the Internet, each of the proxies controlled by different organizations or individuals. Bouncing the message around can make it extremely difficult, sometimes virtually impossible, to identify the source. The process isn't foolproof; it requires that the user pay attention. A member of the Anonymous hacker faction once logged into a chat room before enabling the tool—a single slip out of hundreds of uses, but enough to reveal his Internet address to investigators. Nor is it perfect even when in use. When the FBI went after Jeremy Hammond, the perpetrator of the Anonymous Stratfor attack, they collected traffic on both ends and then matched the Tor traffic coming from his home with activity by the targeted hacker in a chat room. The correlation was robust enough to secure the necessary court orders.

For intelligence services, Tor is a double-edged sword. Reports suggest U.S. government agencies had a hand in its development and provided funding for it. The documents leaked by Snowden and others show the agencies often use Tor to hide their own activities. Yet, when terrorists use it, the very same authorities spend significant resources trying to counter it.

CHAPTER 14

THE WEAPONS OF HATE

"There is nothing either good or bad, but thinking makes it so."
— WILLIAM SHAKESPEARE

Rashid Rehman had his routine down, and the morning of May 7, 2014, went like so many before it. He woke up early, read the newspaper over a cup of hot tea and a light breakfast, and got to his office in Multan around 7 a.m. A prominent human rights lawyer in Pakistan, Rehman was preparing his next major case, in which he would defend a local professor charged with violations of the country's blasphemy laws. Students had accused the professor of insulting religion on social media, and clips taken out of context by extremist groups went viral. Rehman immediately realized this was another case of extremists trying to intimidate. He knew he could win and clear the innocent professor's name.

Throughout the rest of the day, Rehman met with several different clients. He often worked into the night, so the people knocking at 8:30 p.m. didn't seem unusual. He assumed it was the light dinner he ordered. But before he could get up to open his office door, two extremists walked in and opened fire, shooting indiscriminately. They gunned down Rehman on the spot, and they injured several of his employees.

The terrorists who killed Rehman used real guns that fired bullets that evening, but the virtual information war against him had begun weeks earlier. Extremist groups unleashed a virtual arsenal on him, deploying all their weapons of hate. They won their battle long before the two gunmen burst into his office. If we don't find an effective way to neutralize these virtual weapons, we have little hope of rerouting a recruit's Pre-Hate Journey and combatting the kind of hate that killed Rehman. And we can't counter the attacks on the information battlefield until we understand how extremists deploy these information weapons.

TWITTER

Twitter came online in 2006 and made its first mark on the Islamic world three years later, during the Green Revolution in Iran. Liberal Islamist and opposition groups used Twitter's geolocation to help organize events or coordinate denial-of-service (DoS) Web attacks against the Iranian establishment. Recognizing how important it was to opposition efforts, the Iranian government temporarily blocked the site. It could not maintain the jam for long.

Twitter's power lies in its efficient sharing of information and links in tweets of 140 characters or less. (Twitter hiked the limit to 280 characters for some users as we wrote this book.) But the platform also provides users the ability to rapidly organize on-the-ground mobilizations, flash mobs and coordinated demonstrations. As one participant in the 2011 Tahrir Square protests described in an essay published at Medium.com: "When I arrived [home], the Twitter hash #jan25 lit up. Someone said that earlier tweets had been deliberately planted as decoys to mislead authorities. Now, in dozens of real locations throughout the city, protesters had begun to mobilize. I ran out the door and took the subway back to Tahrir Square."

Twitter's speed, versatility and encouragement of intense but pithy interactions have made it one of the world's most widely used digital platforms. Governments and opposition groups both use it. It's a regular channel for peace-promoting NGOs and extremists alike. Malaysian Prime Minister Najib Razak had more than 3.6 million followers as of August 2017. The Sunni Islamist militia Jabhat al-Nusra had more than 300,000 followers on its affiliated sites. The Muslim Brotherhood's English-language account, @ikhwanweb, had more than 145,000 followers. According to a report in *The Economist*, four of the 10 most-followed Twitter accounts in Saudi Arabia were clerics. The person with the most followers in the Middle East wasn't an actor, a popular singer or a politician; it was Muhammed Al-Arefe, a religious cleric, with more than 18 million followers on Twitter and other social media services. Based in Saudi Arabia, Arefe has become a major pro-ISIS sympathizer and influencer, and many ISIS defectors cited him as the reason they decided to pack up their belongings and join the Islamic State.

The fact that many Twitter users accept tweets as truth grants the platform huge popularity and power, especially when it coalesces attention on a particular issue. The widespread use of hashtags enables instant searchability and content coherence. Simple "hashtag campaigns," in which followers tweet certain hashtags at certain times of the day in an effort to make the topic a top trend across Twitter, significantly boost profile and participation. A hashtag might garner a thousand appearances within a few hours. Hot-button issues can generate 100,000 tweets an hour, with tweets and retweets driving the excitement or outrage. Hashtags also give both Islamists and extremists a direct line to their audience's concerns. Even ISIS has been known to conduct focus-group research via Twitter, for instance when proposing a rebrand that would focus its name on the rebirth of an Islamic caliphate. The angry, acrimonious response convinced ISIS to abandon the idea.

Twitter became a choice platform for Islamists and extremists because it rarely issued takedowns or restricted user access. Free Internet usage groups lauded Twitter's noninterventionist approach, but several governments and security-based NGOs derided the policy. The tragic case of James Foley, a journalist whose execution video at the hands of ISIS went viral in 2014, convinced the company to take a more hardline stance on images and objectionable content. And in March 2015, Twitter took the dramatic step of taking down 10,000 extremist accounts. In fact, many extremist groups use Twitter with the precise understanding that they will get shut down, knowing they can simply change a letter or symbol in their account name and be back online within twenty minutes. One of the most notorious is the al-Shabaab press office's English-language Twitter account, originally set up in 2011. It continually posts extremist content, is continually blocked, and continually regenerates under slightly different usernames. During al-Shabaab's attack on a Kenyan shopping mall in 2013, for instance, the group live-tweeted the attack's progress despite

Twitter's best efforts at clamping down on their real-time glorifying posts. The group sprang up as @HSM_PressOffice, @HSMPress, and other names during the incident, successfully spreading terror and justifying its actions to a global audience.

Dealing with Twitter extremists requires something of a "whack-a-mole" approach by the platforms. Extremist groups do not simply sit back and wait for their followers to tweet and retweet content. They create, inflate and control the message themselves. In fact, ISIS effectively "gamed" Twitter with its official Arabic-language Twitter app, "The Dawn of Glad Tidings" (or simply "Dawn"), which was unveiled on Google Play in April 2014. Before it was removed that June, the app had been downloaded more than 10,000 times. It helps users stay informed with ISIS-related news, keeps track of their daily prayers and provides access to short sayings or scriptural references encouraging religious war. But it also automatically tweets content scripted by the ISIS social media squad on users' own Twitter accounts, spaced well enough apart to evade Twitter's anti-spam algorithms. This has allowed for tweet blitzes that can reach into the tens of thousands per day, swarming the Twittersphere with intimidating updates from the front line and evidence of atrocities committed. One such blitz used the meme "Baghdad we are coming!" and included a 2014 Photoshopped picture of a jihadi looking at the ISIS flag fluttering from the top of Baghdad's Palestine Hotel (the hotel long favored by Western media personnel). It popped to the top results of multiple searches.

Despite the many shutdowns and account removals, ISIS is winning the extremist Twitter war. In February 2017, its hashtags generated more than 12,000 mentions a day, far more than the 2,500 to 5,000 that referred to the al-Nusra group.

YOUTUBE

With more than 1.5 billion active users a month, a great number of them young men and women, YouTube ranks only behind Twitter in terms of social media importance for Islamic groups in the Middle East and South Asia. It was one of their early big-hitters, bursting onto the Islamic scene the year after its 2005 founding when the Jamaat-e-Islami in Pakistan began uploading nasheed, the traditional songs that, at the time, weren't being played anymore on Pakistani TV. Believers considered the content a source of inspiration, and the videos featured photos of the breathtaking views from around Pakistan. One often would see the videos playing in barber shops and cafés.

Not only does YouTube serve as a distributor of film and video content — minus the inconvenient and often repressive production executives — it also enables easy uploading of clips and full-length videos. These can stretch into hours-long affairs, especially if they're sermons or religious teachings. The site has become so influential that most Muslim majority-world regimes go to YouTube for intelligence and counterpropaganda campaigns, always neatly packing them with disinformation. YouTube gives both Islamists and extremists the ability to visually impart their narrative, toy with their audience's emotions and spread their propaganda. The platform's strict DoS regulations usually means extremist content, such as videos depicting or advocating extreme violence and bloodshed, are removed swiftly. So, Islamists take a more straightforward approach to their use of the site. They avoid posting overtly violent content, and thus avoid the platform's flagging system. Instead, they post videos that depict their enemies' horrible acts to elicit sympathy and outrage. The YouTube pages of the al-Nusra Front and the Free Syrian Army ("FSAHelp") have also featured instructional videos on the proper use and maintenance of firearms, stealth tactics and hand-to-hand combat — a questionable, but still permissible, dissemination of educational material.

Furthermore, as YouTube stores content on its own servers, it greatly facilitates the uploading of videos taken on mobile phones, which have very limited storage space. In recent years, this feature has made it hugely popular with Islamist groups, which rely on mobile technologies. In fact, phone users account for almost 55 percent of total YouTube consumption, another reason why the video-sharing platform is so popular.

FACEBOOK

Facebook is the behemoth of social networking sites, with more than 2 billion active monthly users who generate more than 3.5 billion "likes" every day. More than 1.3 billion people log on every 24 hours. Because it's a full-fledged multimedia platform — users can post material of any length and any kind, whether text, pictures, videos, PDFs, links or comments — it has played a major role in various seismic events across the Muslim world. It played a central role in the anti-government movement in Tunisia during the country's 2011 Jasmine Revolution, as visceral images and words swayed hearts and minds across the country and around the globe. Various Islamist groups, such as Ennahda, used Facebook to rally potential volunteers, recruit district-level workers and spread awareness on government repression of the movement. More than 20,000 related posts went up on Facebook in a two-month period focused on the organization of Jasmine movement teams. Islamists also posted details and mobile phone footage of demonstrations and injuries to protestors, sending an undeniable message that ordinary people were willing to participate in rallies against the establishment.

Facebook appeals to many Islamists because its size and fame helps generate TV, newspaper and web coverage, and the platform's hybrid media axis gives political parties and actors a significant recognition and popularity boost. However, even as Facebook proved to be an extremely effective forum for organizing activities and actively engaging more people during the Arab Spring, many more radical groups are wary of its built-in propensity to connect people, places and events. Its facial recognition technology and monitoring techniques have made some groups cautious about operating an official Facebook account. So, despite all of Facebook's power to drive extremist messages and motivate hateful action, many terrorist groups' pages are operated by supporters or individuals who want to identify with the organization, such as the al-Battar Media Battalion and Nukhbat al-I'lam al-Jihadi. Facebook's strict authentication process and its vigilant 24/7 anti-extremist team limits extremist use to connections with like-minded sympathizers, rather than allowing it to become a source for active recruitment and propaganda.

BLOGS

Paid readership of print newspapers has been dwindling for almost 20 years in Western countries. In Muslim-majority nations, newspaper penetration peaked at roughly 20 percent, although papers often were

TRUST IS THE NEW BLACK

BY JEFF JARVIS

Director of the News Integrity Initiative and professor for the
CUNY Graduate School of Journalism

To join the News Integrity Initiative as a funder or participant, please contact us at: generalinfo@journalism.cuny.edu

"Trust is the new black," Craig Newmark likes to say when asked about the state of news at the many journalism conferences he and I attend. At one, soon after the 2016 election, Craig invited a proposal from me and the CUNY Graduate School of Journalism to tackle the crisis in trust in news. He has put journalism at the heart of his philanthropic efforts.

We started the News Integrity Initiative and Facebook called soon after, looking for guidance in its efforts to aid journalism. It gave more funding, as did the Ford Foundation. Now our director, Molly de Aguiar, is administering a $14 million fund to support research, projects and partnerships.

We see manipulation of news and of the public conversation—by trolls, political extremists and foreign agents—as the short-term issue and trust as the long-term challenge. In this connected age, the real mission of journalism—a goal that should be shared by the platforms—is to convene communities into civil, informed and constructive conversation, helping the public find common ground in fact over fear to reduce the polarization tearing at the nation's soul.

Journalism can accomplish this by learning to listen to, empathize with, reflect, connect and serve communities that for too long have been unheard in mass media. (That is the founding principle of a new degree in Social Journalism I started at CUNY.) The social platforms can help by creating safe spaces where people can connect, making strangers less strange and robbing the polarizers of their most potent weapon: the other. Together, we are just beginning our work.

passed around communities and families, perhaps belying point-of-sale calculations. Meanwhile, blogs and online newspapers have come into their own, especially among young people who use smart phones to access daily news and editorials in a more immediate and less censored manner. These online publications have become the channel for journalism that no longer can find a robust audience in print.

Egyptian journalist and writer Ahmed Naji updated his blog almost daily as he documented life during the overthrow of President Hosni Mubarak. While many sites were banned or found it difficult to get up-to-date information, Naji provided incisive commentary. His site garnered thousands of hits a day and often became a key source for TV, radio and international reporting on Egypt. Mada Masr, an independent online newspaper, set up shop in 2013, after the demise of the *Egypt Independent*. In the years since, it has become one of Egypt's most-influential news sources, despite — or maybe, in part, because — it was shut down by the authorities for criticizing the country's Supreme Council. Mada Masr thrives on "a different kind of journalism," especially important in times of crisis and in Egypt where, since the military coup, there is renewed pressure on journalists to toe the party line.

With the right skills, blogs and websites can host any content, and with enough cash they can establish themselves quickly and persist for a long time. They can attract a great deal of attention — garnering links from different platforms and picking up attention from traditional media worldwide — but they also can fly under the radar of regime watchdogs at the same time. That makes them an attractive, albeit somewhat more complicated, option for Islamists and extremists. For Islamic policymakers, the ability to track traffic and page views provides incredibly valuable data. For extremists, interaction between bloggers and visitors could facilitate the kinds of connections that win over a niche audience.

TUMBLR

This interactive microblogging site has become increasingly popular with different Islamist and extremist groups for their high-powered recruitment campaigns. Tumblr's power lies in its customization. Its users can easily create a unique viewing experience, posting images, links and notes on their page. They can choose other blogs to follow, a linkage that peppers the dashboard with things they've posted, constantly feeding it new stories. It makes a true feast for the eyes, with wall-to-wall color and its famous near-continuous scrolling. The platform also makes it very easy to search for specific subjects and have the results screen populated by enticing images, perfect for religious-oriented outreach to specific audiences. ISIS frequently used Tumblr text and video postings to show the "exciting" and "adventurous" life of jihadists participating in the Iraq and Syria conflicts. It was an extremist's dream: easy to use, visually rich, password-protected and encryption friendly. As such, it's not surprising that Tumblr postings are known to be responsible for inspiring many young people to carry out "lone wolf" acts of terror from Islamabad to London, Copenhagen to Sydney, and New York to Texas.

ASK.FM

"You've got questions, we've got answers." So went the old Radio Shack slogan — now updated for the 21st century by Ask.fm, a website on which anyone can create a cloaked profile and post questions for other anonymous users to answer. It's an electronic hotbed of extremist recruitment, providing a way for groups to reach a captive audience of one, even as countless others can view the thread. It has become an especially valuable tool for targeting young Westerners who naturally have many questions about how different life is in the Muslim world. Sometimes questions can be more contentious, such as those once posed to the Jordanian Muslim Brotherhood group: "Do you want to overthrow the government?" and "How is it Islamic to criticize other Muslims in the political process?"

The questions and answers frequently become more detailed, and exclusive. Often, the interrogatives have to do with living standards for *mujahideen* fighters or ISIS members ("Are the bugs a problem?" or "Can I buy a smartphone there?"). Others ask about how people can join the various conflicts in the Muslim world. As with almost all Islamic recruitment and PR campaigns, the Ask.fm responses focus less on religious doctrine and more on how *jihad* is the cool cutting-edge of modern Islam. Extremists make outlandish promises, with all the high-pressure sincerity of a used-car salesperson, and, unfortunately, many impressionable youth take those promises on faith. Recruiters become guides and mentors, following up with private individual communications in which they can be (or at least seem to be) direct and candid. Step by step, the target comes around to enlisting in the religious cause.

Ask.fm became particularly notorious in the West for its apparently laissez-faire attitude to cyber-bullying, which tragically led some young people to take their own lives. Initially, the site went almost entirely unmoderated and had no tracking or reporting systems in place — a gold mine for propaganda-touting extremists and bullies alike. It since has put a raft of reporting and blocking features in place, including a limit on extremist content. When an extended conversation goes over the line, the offending account is banned, but usually not before the Islamists have interacted with a range of new contacts, many of whom already have converted.

MESSAGING APPS AND SMS

Mobile phones have become ubiquitous across the Middle East and South Asia, and now the region is seeing a huge increase in the use of smartphones, particularly in the 15- to 34-year-old age bracket, which accounts for about three-quarters of the total users. Mobile phone penetration in the region hovers around 57 percent today, making sure SMS and web-based messaging remains a critical component of Islamist and extremist social media strategies. Text messaging is the most basic and straightforward means of electronic communication, with the added advantage of not requiring an internet connection or Web-enabled phone. Several studies have also shown that Islamists and extremists use text messaging because it is the most personal and appropriate way to interact with someone, especially of the opposite sex. In some countries and situations, extremists have bombarded women with twenty to twenty-five messages per day, often encouraging them to come to Syria as foreign fighters or to become wives of the believers.

Extremists also text information on the many occasions someone in the West insults Islam, intending to incite and enrage their followers. Islamists, by contrast, use texting more sensitively and regularly. For example, they will send daily *hadith* sayings that extol the virtue of dedicating time and service in the path of God — and they'll include subtler hints about duty to the organization. Instant alerts and texts about breaking news also serve the purpose of creating broader awareness. However, whereas the Islamists' use of text messaging seems to garner a good response and take-up rate, the tactical use of text messages by extremists had met with limited success, according to recent tracking of high-volume text message traffic by anti-extremist NGOs and human rights groups.

Even in cases of limited success, instant messaging enables direct and personal contact with either one person or a whole address book full of contacts. Islamists have been known to acquire bulk lots of phone numbers within targeted areas from spammers and hackers, yet another way that the sharing of information on the Internet can benefit these groups. Both Islamists and extremists are highly attuned to both established and new instant messaging apps, including WhatsApp, WeChat, Telegram, Threma, LINE, Viber and Hookt. Always seeking personal contact to make the sale, Islamic recruiters are quick with their requests to "Kik me" (a phrase originating with the Canadian messaging app Kik, and meaning "send me a private message") across various forums, chat rooms, blogs and other social media platforms.

Extremist groups need end-to-end encryption, which ensures a much higher degree of security and privacy, so they often use programs such as WhatsApp, which has become very popular in Turkey, Pakistan and North and East Africa. WhatsApp serves its purpose all too well, helping pull in and radicalize multiple young men who have gone on to the battlegrounds of Syria and Iraq, Afghanistan and Pakistan. As a result, security officials in major nations, including China, Saudi Arabia, Russia and the United States, have expressed deep concerns about these instant messaging apps. Authorities in these and other countries regard such apps as central to terrorist "grooming" of impressionable and susceptible youth. Anti-terrorism efforts have infiltrated these sites, though with uneven results to date.

In the wake of the game-changing NSA leaks by Edward Snowden in 2013, and the resulting increase in internet surveillance, a considerable amount of instant messaging traffic has switched over to encrypted or self-destructing messaging apps. For example, photos sent via Snapchat can reach any number of designated recipients, but disappear within seconds — frequently before the server even knows it was there. Some data shows that Snapchat engenders a higher engagement per piece of social media than other platforms. And Snapchat's unique linear storytelling has appealed to young millennials — even key influencer religious clerics like Mohammed Al-Arefe have done "Snapfatwas," giving eight-second religious decrees. Wicker, Telegram and certain extremist-owned messaging apps utilize highly sophisticated military-grade encryption protocols that allow for truly undecipherable communications.

There are now several dozen similar apps in different languages that give recruits tools to communicate with others, have their questions answered and connect them with counselors and mentors. For Islamists and extremists, apps are a great way to design and build a sense of community.

JUSTPASTE.IT

JustPaste.it is a favorite of Islamists and extremists. Operating out of Poland, the app is a labor of love for developer Mariusz Żurawek, a young entrepreneur who holds degrees in informatics and econometrics. Żurawek works "out of his bedroom" — shades of the Silicon Valley entrepreneurs in their garages — but the site, which launched in 2013, has amassed more than five million users a month. The simple format allows users to attach text, images and videos to an anonymous page, creating a "note" that anyone can see. The site does not require registration, there is password and encryption protection, there is no internal search feature and Żurawek, as the lone administrator, does no real content management on the site. As a result, its anonymous users can flout laws and upload anything they like — illegal pornography, stolen financial data, details of drugs for purchase and other underground links and services. The site is a secure haven for extremist material, and, within the last couple of years, JustPaste.it has become a particular favorite of ISIS and the Taliban.

Part of the site's popularity in the Middle East stems from the fact that it works well with right-to-left scripts, such as Arabic. And since it doesn't use ads or pop-ups, the site runs smoothly even over slow Internet connections. Even more important, the site's multimedia capability gives the extremists a platform for posting write-ups, images, videos and links to breaking news. One can find minute-by-minute battle reports, which regularly include images of gruesome death and wanton destruction, as well as graphic images of beheadings by ISIS fighters. Some of the pictures are so horrific, authorities regularly issue JustPaste.it takedown notices. If the request comes from law enforcement agencies (e.g. Interpol, the U.K. Metropolitan Police's anti-terrorism unit or Pakistan's ISI), the offending material *might* be removed, albeit slowly. Of course, the original poster or someone else can simply re-paste the deleted material in a new note, and it starts all over again. It really is like electronic graffiti: a scandalous way to rub your message in the face of the establishment, leave it for all to see and get away with it.

Żurawek's success with JustPaste.it has inspired legions of other text-paste sites, most of them low-budget, highly obscure and hard to find. Most are used for messaging followers, whether a call to street demonstrations or to arrange a meeting, and once the information has been sent and received it is automatically deleted. It's a fast, run-and-gun system, completely anonymous, easier to use than most blogs and nowhere near as heavily patrolled by content monitors as the big names. These are the websites that often continue to carry links to videos that were removed from the closely managed social media giants.

INSTAGRAM

With more than 700 million active users as of late 2017, the picture- and video-sharing site Instagram has become a major player in the social media landscape. Islamists and terrorist groups, among the platform's earliest adopters, flocked to it for its ability to humanize otherwise faceless or forbidding groups, to facilitate image-building campaigns and to glorify selfie-loving extremists. One iconic Instagram photo depicts old weapons — a gun and a knife — alongside a mobile phone with Instagram pulled up on its screen. The message is clear: This is the new weapon of choice.

It has proved to be an effective way of targeting young people, too. Extremists post memorial montages of martyrs that look like family photo albums. They show the upbeat young men in casual, even intimate scenes, with no indication of the bloodthirsty acts for which they gave their lives. Extremists tout their guns, beaming, in countless photos. Not all the extremists' videos are warm and fuzzy. Footage depicts young boys in *mujahideen* uniforms, firing shoulder-launched missiles, gunning down prisoners, carrying out vicious attacks, beheadings and other grotesque executions. The images are meant to goad susceptible Muslims into action, and frighten everyone else.

The globally ubiquitous Instagram also raises the real possibility of Westerners stumbling upon content that celebrates more extreme religious thinking—something that extremist groups are fully aware of and aim to exploit. The hashtag function on Instagram allows users to sift the material easily and bring up a smorgasbord of related images, as on Twitter. (In fact, many photos are posted on both sites concurrently, with Twitter links updating Instagram.) Although Twitter content managers have become increasingly aggressive at removing extremist material and banning those who post it, Instagram managers have been criticized for the slowness of their reactions. And, because pictures are often tougher to monitor than words, artsy photos by Islamists and extremists often stay up on Instagram for longer than authorities would like. They are subtle and often layered with meaning, and many of them speak effectively to a precisely targeted young audience.

SOUNDCLOUD

Designed as a way for musicians to share and promote their tracks, the audio-distribution service SoundCloud had around 177 million unique monthly listeners as of late 2017. It hosted far more than musical talent, though. For extremists, SoundCloud offered an ideal place to post audio of sermons and religious speeches. The speaker might be a famed cleric from the past, although most of SoundCloud's talks and lectures come from newer and more violently strident leaders, such as the American-Yemeni militant imam Anwar al-Awlaki, who was killed by an American drone in 2011. Islamists will post political rally videos and broadcast public service messages about their campaigns; for example, Anwar Ibrahim's People's Justice Party (PKR) in Malaysia used SoundCloud to publicize one of his lectures at a campaign rally, and it went viral.

Extremists also have used SoundCloud to upload scandalous audio to embarrass political leaders and expose corruption in high places. In early 2014, a series of intercepted phone calls were posted to the site, making public a very private set of conversations between Turkish Prime Minister Recep Tayyip Erdoğan, local politicians and business elites, all of whom were discussing a bribery scheme. The Turkish government promptly blocked access to SoundCloud, and refused to lift the ban until all the material had been deleted. By then, though, untold thousands of users already had copied the clandestine recordings.

Because users can easily link content between it and other social media sites, such as Twitter, SoundCloud has become the primary platform to disseminate high-quality audio across the widest possible online audience. Within the last year, an ISIS radio service began broadcasting out of Mosul, spreading the call to *jihad* via pop tunes, anthems and battle songs. It refers listeners to SoundCloud for more of the same material, and their visits there enable direct recruitment contact. To date, SoundCloud moderators have moved slowly when extremists post objectionable content, even though such material violates its terms of use.

REDDIT

The massive interactive discussion forum and entertainment and news website Reddit acts as a rambunctious town hall for all comers. The site consists of bulletin-board posts submitted by registered users, divided into hundreds of categories and subcategories, called "subreddits." Users cast up or down votes on posts, pushing the best or most popular material to the top. Almost all the posts are read by someone — hence, the brand's pun on the phrase "read it" — and that guarantees at least a modicum of exposure.

Yet Reddit is one platform that, in many ways, has countered the spread of toxic rhetoric. While it has eliminated certain subreddits in the past, its chief weapon against extremist materials has been the presence of informed counter-messaging by the vast Reddit community. This is one site where the Islamists regularly run into robust criticism, and they've had trouble gaining a firm foothold. Many Reddit account holders, especially the active posters, hail from Western countries. They tend to be well-informed and engaged in current affairs, policy matters and global events. So, whenever a post or comment takes on an extremist tone, users jump in with counterarguments attacking and deconstructing the radical argument, often with witty putdowns. Reddit is in the vanguard, along with a few other websites, in pushing back against extremist propaganda.

That said, extremist groups have scored some modest successes. One foreign fighter with the extremist group Jabhat al-Nusra signed up on Reddit to answer questions about living in Syria. The soldier had an excellent command of English — he probably was from the U.K. — and did an effective job of answering both simple and complex questions about marriage, what to pack, daily life, the availability of Nutella and how the group members kept clean. Thousands of people read the answers, which provided an easygoing, humorous and very romanticized view of going abroad.

POSTSCRIPT: HATE IS SPREADING AS FAST AS SOCIAL MEDIA CAN CARRY IT

In the late 1990s, extremist groups used only twelve known websites for recruitment and radicalization efforts. Today, they have more than 10,000 websites and forums — and that doesn't even include social media platforms. This extraordinary growth tells its own story about the critical importance of online activity to the rise of hate, and to efforts to combat its spread. It's on these sites and social media networks, which draw greater levels of interactive engagement, that we most clearly see the mobilization prowess of these extremist organizations.

CHAPTER 15

THE BUSINESS OF DISINFORMATION

"The point of modern propaganda isn't only to misinform or push an agenda. It is to exhaust your critical thinking, to annihilate truth."
— GARRY KASPAROV (former world chess champion, writer and activist)

Disinformation comes in many forms and often carries huge consequences, especially on the information battlefield.

So it was when news of two attacks on U.S. outposts abroad filtered back on Sept. 11, 2012, shocking Americans already raw on the 11th anniversary of the 9/11 terrorist attacks in New York City. In one, a protest at the U.S. embassy in Cairo ended with protestors scaling the walls and removing the American flag. And in what would become a hot-button issue on Capitol Hill for years to come, the second, an attack on the consulate in Benghazi, Libya, ended with the death of American ambassador Christopher Stevens. Initial reports claimed the attacks were prompted by two similar 14-minute YouTube videos called "Innocence of Muslims." The videos were billed as trailers for a forthcoming film, with the first, an English-language version, uploaded in July and a subsequent Arabic version appearing in early September. The videos' laughably poor production values could not disguise the deeply offensive nature of its content. Claiming to be a biopic of the Prophet Muhammad, it depicted him as an oafish lecher with a taste for underage girls. The original scenes were overdubbed with Islamophobic content, against the original intent of the actors.

"Innocence of Muslims" struck a chord across the globe. Research shows that much of the viral buzz and discussion about the video did little more than spread disinformation designed to rile emotional and identity issues. Protests erupted in more than 40 cities in September 2012, with most occurring in majority-Muslim countries or cities with large Muslim populations. Yet, other Muslim countries that were very much aware of the video did not erupt in violent protest. Why?

Although the U.S. eventually determined the Benghazi attack had nothing to do with the video, the Cairo incident and some fatal protests less than two weeks later in Pakistan can teach us much about the dynamics of the Muslim world and the outsized role disinformation can play there. But to understand that, we first must consider the competition for power and influence that rages between religious figures and political parties in Muslim-majority countries — and the varying role that social media content played in their jousting over "Innocence of Muslims."

TWITTER AND THE BIRTH OF A PROTEST

Unsurprisingly given its subject matter and its producers' lack of a platform, the original "Innocence of Muslims" video languished in obscurity until it was discovered by two ideologues on opposite ends of the spectrum. Florida pastor Terry Jones, infamous in both the U.S. and the Muslim world for his repeated attacks on Islam, endorsed the video. (Around the same time, it appeared on the Arabic-language blog of Morris Sadek, an émigré Egyptian Copt and noted Islamophobe.) Shortly after, on Sept. 8, Sheikh Khalid Abdallah — one of a new breed of vociferous hardline Salafi religious TV personalities competing for viewers' attention — featured it during his daily program on Al Nas, the Salafi satellite channel. Although a man who was quick to interpret any event as an attack on Islam itself and who was motivated by his profit-seeking TV channel, Abdallah didn't appear to fully grasp the incendiary material he had in his hands. He buried the video in the final third of his program, and he played just two and a half minutes of it. His inflammatory rhetoric, not the clip itself, appeared to launch "Innocence of Muslims" into the popular Egyptian awareness. And launch it did; the video became a rallying cry.

The story's rapid course through Egyptian society can be traced most easily on Twitter, which offers far more robust archival tools than other social media platforms such as Facebook. Al Nas didn't even tweet about the video until Abdallah featured it again a couple days later. Other actors led the charge in the interim. *Al Youm*, one of Egypt's major dailies, published a story on the morning of September 9, describing the video and pinning blame for it directly on expatriate Copts. The story slowly gathered steam on Twitter throughout the day, with tweets linking to the paper rather than Al Nas' social media. Some of the other early interjections came from very significant figures, including the Grand Mufti of Egypt, Dr. Ali Gomaa. A major figure in Egyptian politics with more than 1.8 million Twitter followers, Gomaa weighed in on his own account at 5 p.m. local time, which would have brought the film to a broad new level of awareness among Egyptian Twitter users.

But one of the most seismic interventions came from another TV channel, a direct competitor of Al Nas. Al Hekma is a religious TV channel with links to Egypt's main Salafist party, al-Nour. Its founder, chairman and most prominent onscreen presenter, Dr. Wessam El-Haddad (also known as Wessam Abdel Wareth), posted a tweet about the film at 5:38 p.m. local time on September 8, referencing it in a plug for an upcoming TV appearance. El-Haddad has long used his position as the head of Al Hekma to promote himself and his support for the increased Islamization of Egypt and increased power for Salafi political parties. His views are conservative rather than extremist. Before "Innocence of Muslims" came along, for example, he was campaigning on TV and social media on behalf of Egyptian army and police officers who were prevented from growing beards, which many Salafis view as a religious requirement.

The following evening, El Haddad took to Twitter to announce that a new group, the Dar al-Hekma ("House of Wisdom"), had been founded to defend Islam against those who would "ride roughshod" over it. The name of the new coalition was clearly intended to elevate El Haddad's television station, and the link between the man, his channel and the video would continue throughout the controversy's life. No other religious station's Twitter feeds mentioned the issue directly, at the most responding to the growing ferment with mostly anodyne salutations of the Prophet. After all, why use your own feed to direct viewers toward a competitor?

El Haddad exploited his monopoly on the controversy of the day, tweeting about the coalition constantly over the course of the afternoon of September 10, updating his followers on prominent figures who had announced their support and linking to newspaper articles, which prominently featured his picture, of course. He even crowdsourced slogan production, asking his followers for ideas about what to chant at a protest the coalition was organizing at the American embassy the following day. And, at 2:11 p.m., he announced a major coup: The Salafist Call, Egypt's main Salafi group, and its political arm, al-Nour, had joined the coalition.

This significantly altered the stakes for the social media campaign and the protest. Nader Bakkar, a leader of al-Nour, had almost 1.1 million Twitter followers — about half as many as the Grand Mufti, but nearly twelve times more than El Haddad. His announcements about the coalition and the protest that afternoon were retweeted hundreds of times. If El Haddad was something of a political gadfly, Bakkar was a true power broker leading a party with huge organization capacity and on the political ascendancy after its surprise success in the 2012 parliamentary elections. His involvement turned the House of Wisdom Coalition from a fringe group into a national movement.

On September 11, during the embassy protest itself, the movement's leaders were remarkably silent, with Bakkar's only words a quick tweet around 7:30 p.m. local time, in which he informed his followers that the Salafist Call had ended its participation in the event shortly before. Dozens of ordinary Egyptians who attended the protests provided real-time reporting on the action, tweeting the address of the embassy, updating followers on the movement of the protests and, most spectacularly, apprising Twitter of the removal of the Stars and Stripes from the embassy's roof. However, social media was never the main tool of those organizing the Cairo embassy protests. Given the relatively shallow penetration of Twitter in Egypt, and the involvement of the established party, one can safely assume that the real organizational effort took place offline.

And this was a key lesson for observers: El Haddad and Bakkar represented two distinctly different types of influence. El Haddad's power lived and died by his ability to create controversy and draw notice. Bakkar was a politician who presided over a more robust base with a more entrenched power structure. Yet, both were necessary to bring the Egyptian protests to life — El Haddad to create a controversy that could pay off for both himself Bakker, and Bakker to provide the people in the streets necessary to turn an Internet scandal into a geopolitical crisis.

TWITTER CARRIES THE CONTROVERSY TO PAKISTAN

Jamaat-ud-Dawa (JuD), a Pakistani extremist organization rebuilt from the scraps of the banned terrorist group Lashkar-e-Taiba, was one of the many Pakistani Twitter feeds to hop on the story and urge action. On the afternoon of September 13, JuD's official account announced the organization would hold an emergency meeting to discuss the issue, with a press conference to follow. It provocatively linked to a website recounting how two Muslims assassinated Ka'b bin al-Ashraf, a Seventh-Century Jewish Arab in Medina who wrote poetry defaming the Prophet Muhammad. Using the hashtags #BanInnocenceofMuslims and #HurmateRasool (or "the sanctity of the Prophet"), JuD used its account to issue ringing condemnations of the video, to call for its removal, to demand its makers be brought to justice, to link to videos of worldwide protests, and to instigate similar protests in Pakistan. The JuD Twitter feed closely followed the course of protests around the country the following day (September 14, a Friday), giving would-be protesters information about where they could take part and issuing a stream of passionate tweets calling upon Muslims to defend the honor of the Prophet. It wouldn't take a giant leap of the imagination to interpret some of the tweets as a call to violence.

While the protests that Friday ended peacefully, they served as a preview to larger events across Khyber–Pakhtunkhwa on September 18, and throughout Islamabad and Karachi three days later. As it had the previous week, JuD used its Twitter account to raise awareness of the protests. Besides organizing the action, the JuD account offered followers material to deepen their understanding of the issues at stake, such as a religious scholar's video blog about the importance of protecting the sanctity of the Prophet. Naveed Qamar, the *amir* of JuD's Karachi branch, tweeted calls to the Pakistani government to cut off trade and diplomatic relations with the countries responsible for the video, and he encouraged his listeners to boycott those products from those countries. As it had the previous week, the official JuD account tracked the protests' progress throughout Pakistan's cities. And when they turned violent, JuD quickly turned to Twitter to disavow any association with them, emphasizing that its own protests were both peaceful and nonsectarian, having been held in conjunction with a protest led by a Shiite student organization. At the same time, the JuD tweeted excerpts (in Urdu) from the speeches that party leaders gave at JuD rallies which, while not mentioning violence, used more inflammatory language than that found in the English-language tweets, indicating that the JuD modified the messages it intended for different audiences.

Of course, the JuD account was just one of many Pakistani Twitter accounts tweeting about "Innocence of Muslims" at the time. A search for Pakistani tweets that included hashtags related to the video and protests returned more than 11,000 hits for the period between Sept. 12-23. Almost 8,000 of them appeared on September 21 — which is Ishq-e-Rasool (a day that celebrates "Love of Prophet Muhammad"). That same day, dozens of Pakistanis were killed or injured in clashes with police.

TWITTER'S VARIED ROLE IN PROTESTS
AROUND THE MUSLIM WORLD

The protests continued in Indonesia, a country with a huge moderate Muslim population and a large cohort of Web-connected urbanites despite an Internet penetration rate of just 50 percent. Jakarta, however, is widely considered to be the most active city on Twitter. There is evidence that the "Innocence of Muslims" video was widely viewed within Indonesia, particularly as the Indonesian government demanded that YouTube remove or ban the video for Indonesian users. While searches for the video trended on Google throughout the country's Muslim-majority provinces, the protests that erupted on September 17 were concentrated primarily in urban areas.

The main organizers of the protests in Jakarta were the Forum Umat Islam (FUI) and the Islam Defenders Front (FPI), both members of the Indonesian Ulema Council, the national clerical body. While the FUI and

FPI both have little presence on social media (less than 500 Twitter follow-ers each), information about the protests quickly spread through tweets about the time and location of the protests. That helped give rise to a decentralized, student-led and truly viral protest at the U.S. embassy, with similar demonstrations held in front of widely known American firms.

In Tunis, protests that broke out on September 14 appear to have been instigated and organized by Saif-Allah Benhassine, a cleric at the al-Fatah mosque and the leader of the Tunisian chapter of the Salafist organization Ansar al-Sharia — a group thought to be tied to the Benghazi attacks. Benhassine is thought to have delivered an inflammatory sermon at the al-Fatah mosque, calling for the resignations of Ennahda officials who, he claimed, had abandoned devout Muslims. Compared with the 2010–11 social media-led protests against then-president Zine El Abidine Ben Ali, which found French-speaking moderates and more extreme Islamists working together, the 2012 protestors were almost exclusively Salafi. There was scarce media and social media coverage of the protests, likely a function of the conservative nature of the Salafi movement and the lack of support from Francophone moderates. Since social media did not play as large a role, the protests were consequently smaller.

In India, the protests varied widely because of the subcontinent's complicated ethno-religious makeup. The most intense protests occurred in Chennai, capital of the southern, Muslim-minority state Tamil Nadu. There, "Innocence of Muslims" was the most popular search term for September 2012, even though Muslims account for less than 6 percent of the statewide population. A coalition of Islamic political organizations, including the Tamil Nadu Muslim Munnetra Kazhagam and the Popular Front of India, organized the protests held on September 15. Comparing online data with protest reports across India, it again appeared that the relationship between viral searches, Islamist participation and the pro-tests had no direct correlation. As Internet penetration in India stands at around 34 percent, Indian political organizations, especially in rural areas, still rely on conventional political networks — though this has changed somewhat since the successful social media campaign of Prime Minister Narendra Modi.

In Sudan, the public outcry over the video was substantial, despite the country's low social media and Internet penetration rates. The independence movement in South Sudan and the resultant economic crisis in 2012 provided the country plenty of experience with the protests organized via social media. Those campaigns targeted relatively wealthy young people with photos of police brutality and economic strife. However, in the days following the release of "Innocence of Muslims," the 5,000 or so protestors who gathered around several embassies in Khartoum were older and highly sectarian, and reports stated that the protests were both larger and more fervent than anti-government rallies earlier in the year. There was little use of social media. Rather, during midday prayers, several clerics had called for the crowds to gather, even as they forbade their congregations from committing the blasphemous act of actually watching the video. Thus, in Sudan, it appeared that the video's viral status aggravated the protests, rather than the protests making the video go viral. In fact, many observers now believe the Sudanese protests came in response to the controversy over a Danish newspaper's cartoon that offended Muslims worldwide with its depictions of the Prophet Muhammad.

Yemen, like Sudan, saw intense and violent protests on September 13, but little record of them exists on social media, likely due to the low internet penetration in the country. However, the Sana'a rallies were far more violent than those in Khartoum and Pakistan, breaching the grounds of the American embassy—one thing even al-Qaeda had failed to do in 2008. Massive dismissals of political actors and military personnel from the national government followed, suggesting that the Yemeni protests were aggravated to alleviate pressure on the troubled Saleh administration. As in Egypt, the protests in Yemen and Sudan are something of a testament to the power of religious authorities in translating online controversy into on-the-ground action, acting as a sort of internet connection for the masses and protecting their status with Luddite rhetoric. Or, perhaps more accurately, they used a viral sensation as a *casus belli* for a premeditated attack.

THE IMPORTANCE OF MODERATES IN HEALING OUR FAITH-BASED COMMUNITIES

BY ABDULLAH ANTEPLI
Chief Representative of Muslim Affairs,
Duke University/Adjunct Faculty of Islamic Studies

One of the first things faith communities do is to acknowledge how faith could be a source of division, how that toxic and destructive role plays out in each of their respected faith communities and fight against it with a strong moral courage and prophetic voice. This has been the hallmark of my work in renewing Muslim Jewish relations and building institutions for young leaders from both communities. There is a great deal of denial and apathy going on regretfully in this regard. Every serious recovery and healing process first starts with acknowledging the problem and creating a willpower to solve it. Faith and faith communities contribute to division in two major ways:

First, crazies and nut jobs of our faith communities hijack the faith as they zealously promote the narrow, exclusive and even violent interpretations of our faith traditions. Each and every faith has more than enough "rich" body of scriptures and teachings that could be the source of a hateful, divisive, and violent theology and religious understanding. No religion is "richer" or "poorer" than others in this regard. As loud and sensational as these nut jobs are, they are often fringes and never represent the majority in any faith tradition.

The second and more important role that the faith communities contribute to the division and many other evil social cancers is apathy and laziness. Regretfully, the overwhelming majority of Muslims, Christians, Jews, Hindus, Buddhists, and all other faith traditions are so-called moderates. Moderates often are never as hard-working and determined as radicals. Most people arrive to be moderate in their faith tradition and stop there, as if being moderate doesn't require any real ethical, moral commitment, as if all the problems of the faith and faith communities are only extremist minorities and not the lazy, inactive and apathetic majority. Until and unless we shake the imagination of the lazy moderate majority, turn them into radical peace makers, bridge builders and healers, we won't see the real role of faith in healing our global communities from division and from all other social, spiritual and any other diseases. Only when moderates of all faiths start paying as much attention as their crazies, working as hard as them, becoming as determined as them, will you see the faith revealing the best of its ideals in action. All faith communities can turn their religions and traditions into such power of positive transformation but it will not happen on its own. Members and leaders of their communities have to learn how to activate that potential within.

Both Judaism, Islam, and all other faiths teach you that hate primarily corrupts and destroys the bearer before it becomes a threat to the subject of that hate. Hate is a cancer; it eats up your morals and ethics. It rots your soul if it goes unhealed and unchallenged for a very long time. It makes you vulnerable to so many other diseases such as violence and extremism. Hate prevents one from upholding the ideals of one's faith and enables them to reveal the worst of that tradition, not the best of that tradition. So as someone who LOVES Islam and my Muslim faith I would never want such a calamity to happen to my beautiful tradition. That's why fighting against anti-Semitism has been increasingly central to my ministry and work.

PLOTTING THE GOOGLE DISINFORMATION COURSE

The phrase "Innocence of Muslims" never came close to "Gangnam Style" and its position atop the global Google Zeitgeist rankings for 2012. However, when disaggregated by country, "Innocence of Muslims" was a far bigger deal in the Muslim world than the overall figures might suggest. Of the ten countries in which the video's title was searched most often, six are majority Muslim, and another is almost half Muslim. Yet, except for Pakistan and, to a certain extent, Bangladesh, the countries that experienced the most unrest over the video weren't the ones where the search was most popular. There are a few possible explanations for this apparent disconnect:

- It's possible many of the people who searched for the video weren't upset by it, were interested in understanding what the controversy was about, or simply were able to shrug it off.

- It's likely that people living in countries where the video was a huge deal didn't have to search. Given its viral nature, many probably received links to the video in email or messaging apps. Others might have viewed it in groups with family or religious leaders.

- A third reason might lie in the problem of comparing countries with huge variances in Internet connectivity and population sizes.

- The difference between reactions in Pakistan and Indonesia might be attributed to the presence of interest groups in the former. Some of those groups saw an advantage to be gained from fanning the flames. (That's not to suggest that every religious or political leader who called for protests did so with ulterior motives. But when interests and passions align, the result can be explosive.)

Twitter users picked up on the "Innocence of Muslims" phenomenon slowly. But once the controversy erupted, the channel raised the awareness and prominence of the videos throughout the world. What started as a low hum of activity burst into the forefront on September 21, when the phrase "Innocence of Muslims" appeared in Twitter feeds more than 130 million times. As with Google searches, those who tweeted about the issue were disproportionately located in the Muslim world. Remarkably, the far smaller total number of Twitter users in Pakistan and Saudi Arabia used the phrase "Innocence of Muslims" roughly as often as those in the United States or Indonesia.

While tweets clearly associated with "Innocence of Muslims" accounted for just 0.005 percent of worldwide Twitter traffic during the height of the controversy, in Pakistan they accounted for more than four percent. However, to put things in perspective, Pakistani searches for both "Innocence of Muslims" and "Gangnam Style" fell far short of the sheer number of searches for "Unblock YouTube" — an increasingly popular search after the Pakistani government cut off access to the site on September 17, 2012.

In the end, both "Gangnam Style" and "Innocence of Muslims" were niche interests. Compared to searches for "Facebook," neither of them figures at all. Furthermore, "Innocence of Muslims" wasn't the first example — and won't be the last — of how disinformation can inflame Muslims and spur extremists into action. Gleaning the role of social media in spreading awareness and perpetuating this anger, however, is essential if we are to understand the differences in how hate is cultivated and utilized.

CHAPTER 16

THE TOP LESSONS FROM MARKETING

*"Education is the most powerful weapon which you can
use to change the world".*
— NELSON MANDELA

W e can't solve problems if we don't understand them, whether in business or in our efforts to counter hate. Segmenting both audiences and messengers is critical to defeating extremists and the pro-hate agenda. Messaging only to mass audiences will sway no one, so we need to make sure positive counter-messaging reaches four key audiences — fence sitters, immediate influencers, cultural influencers and the general public.

When reaching out to fence-sitters, the tiny fraction of the world's 1.6 billion Muslims who seriously consider joining ISIS or other organizations, messengers who hold extreme ideological views but don't support extremist groups can have the greatest influence. Such messengers include ISIS defectors and members of groups that have condemned other extremist organizations. Because ideological justifications push many fence-sitters to act, our messaging should demonstrate the damage ISIS and other groups are inflicting on Islam and Muslims. We might also open attractive avenues for fence-sitters with messaging about positive, alternative paths, such as humanitarian efforts to address suffering of Muslims. Government-sponsored messages will have the least influence, because most fence-sitters have little trust for governmental authorities.

Authentic statements from friends and family members impacted by terrorist violence will resonate with fence-sitters and immediate influencers alike. By aligning our efforts with immediate influencers, we can leverage their bonds to amplify a positive message to susceptible young men and women. As we widen the lens to integrate cultural influencers and general audiences, positive messaging will have greater influence when targeted at the very start of the Pre-Hate Journey — guiding young minds toward mutually beneficial pursuits from the start. Ideally, this messaging should come from non-governmental sources, but government messaging also can exert a positive influence with these target audiences, who are less likely to dismiss it as propaganda.

In addition to segmentation by level of radicalization, audiences should be segmented by geography. ISIS messages, for example, vary depending on the region they're targeting. In the Arab World, their narrative is largely sectarian, arguing that Sunni Muslims have an obligation to end Shia abuses against Muslims in Iraq and Syria. In addressing European audiences, ISIS emphasizes alienation and discrimination faced by some Muslim communities there. In addressing American and Canadian audiences, ISIS challenges Muslims to leave their comfortable living conditions and to "fill the spiritual voids" in their lives by defending fellow Muslims suffering elsewhere.

THE CHIEF STRATEGY OFFICER'S GUIDE TO DEFEATING EXTREMIST GROUPS

Because of its online sophistication and current influence on the Middle East, ISIS provides a good example of how we might segment audiences on the information battlefield. Here we blend what we know of ISIS and similar extremist groups with our expertise in sophisticated corporate marketing strategies. What results is a breakdown of what top marketers would build into their strategy pitch in defeating ISIS, using top-of-the-line positive counter-messaging. Think of it as a chief strategy officer's guide to countering hate:

Highlighting former radicals and victims of terrorism

Messaging should erode the terrorists' credibility by using local images and voices to graphically illustrate how ISIS and other groups are killing mostly Muslims, including women and children, rather than defending the Muslim *Ummah* (world-wide community). Family members of victims and terrorists, former foreign fighters and former radicals can provide testimonials about how participation in extremist causes destroyed their lives. Footage of ordinary people describing life under formerly-ISIS areas could be particularly compelling. Counter-hate teams can title and compile these in ways that ensure they appear as top hits on Web and social media searches. And, in addition to conversations about terms of service, government authorities should convene with internet service providers to establish the best way to elevate counter-extremist content in online search results.

"De-glamorizing" ISIS and amplifying its battlefield losses

In addition to making clear that ISIS is not a Caliphate, content should highlight the organizations battlefield losses, including through video footage and maps. These messages should deglamorize the foreign fighter lifestyle, revealing the miserable living conditions that fighters and those living under ISIS must endure. They should highlight internal divisions and counter the notion that the group has succeeded in unifying Muslims under a new Caliphate.

Amplifying the Islamic response to extremists to stem recruiting

Messaging generated by partners could address the grievances cited in extremist materials, potentially concluding with powerful messages about the "proper" faith-based response. These could include calls to assist humanitarian efforts and other productive initiatives. Such content could include references to the theologically proscribed punishments for those who kill innocent people. Direct-to-camera videos of qualified Islamic scholars making religious arguments are important but insufficient. These materials must also provide a credible hook and a sense of purpose and obligation. Because many Muslims hold romantic notions of past caliphates and an eventual return to this system, new media content must include materials in which Muslim leaders stress that ISIS is not "Islamic," not a state and not a true Caliphate. Messages should note that its efforts will fail, that it has flagrantly violated principles established by the early Caliphs of Islam, and that joining ISIS is *haraam* (prohibited in Islam).

Highlighting positive narratives

Counter-hate campaigns can combat the narrative that devout youth cannot succeed in the modern world. By highlighting similarly situated young men and women who overcome odds and succeed, these messages could help others find constructive ways to express their grievances and channel their energies. Such materials should highlight Muslims engaged in humanitarian work that directly benefits people suffering from poverty, disease and war. Those who gain experience in creating and publishing such content will form an invaluable cadre of experts who help in other settings, including de-radicalization programming.

Across each of these strategies, counter-hate messaging should not only counter ISIS or al Qaeda, it should affirmatively address the many common ideological tropes that extremist groups will continue to advance. In many instances, counter-content will be most credible when it's not seen as counter-content, but as an affirmative and positive narrative of what Muslim youth can do to address the grievances that extremists articulate. Like hateful messaging, counter-content can draw in youth with emotional images, themes and religious content that acknowledges Muslim suffering, particularly in places such as Syria. But it also can help foster a deeper, positive sense of purpose, belonging and religious obligation. To do that, producers of counter-content should keep three main objectives in mind: 1) provide positive Islamic alternatives into which young men and women can channel their energies and passions; 2) alienate extremists with imagery and religious content that demonstrates how they hurt Muslims and betray Islam; and 3) integrate the power of testimonials from former fighters, former radicals, victims of terrorism and credible scholars and thought influencers.

A SKETCHBOOK OF SAMPLE PROGRAMS THAT COULD HELP COUNTER HATE

To ensure the creation and dissemination of credible content and to support positive alternatives to ISIS and other organizations, we need to work with partner countries, private-sector firms and NGOs to develop flexible, innovative strategies that can evolve as extremist groups do. Keeping in mind our broader guidelines above, we sketched out a few sample

CHOOSING A BETTER PATH

BY JIM WEISS
Founder and CEO, W2O Group

Like a lot of people growing up, I experienced hate in many forms. Being raised in a small community, there was often a lack of connectivity and sensitivity regarding things such as race, religion or even economic means. This often led to a lack of trust and fear of the unknown, resulting in disrespect, acts of animosity and even confrontation toward me.

While the details of those circumstances are irrelevant today, what is import-ant in any hate-related situation is how *you* choose to deal with it. At its core, hate is psychological, a deep and extreme emotional dislike. But what I've seen is that hate also is based on fear—fear of what you don't know, fear of what you don't believe and even fear of yourself. In effect, a lack of mutual understanding triggers negative feelings from jealously to violence. And people who act or talk in a hateful manner often are attempting to suppress feelings of inadequacy, injustice, ignorance, helplessness and even self-worth.

In each instance, dating back to childhood, my response to hate has been to deal with it directly and pragmatically. The reason is very clear: I truly believe the line between hate and love is very thin. If you look closely, hate and love are mirror images of one another. One allows you to live productively and con-fidently. The other destructively and anxiously. Dealing with hate head-on has resulted in turning negative situations into achieving common ground, lowering the temperature of an escalating argument or agreeing to disagree and moving on. The common trait in all those examples is that time was taken to listen, to be empathetic, to learn and to grow as a human being. It's really all about curiosity, truly getting to know what drives someone's behaviors and thinking.

Believe me it's not easy. Hate breeds hate. But often, engaging with someone who was aggressive toward me or my beliefs not only forced a different response, it also spawned new relationships—many that have survived the test of time. This approach also served me well in my business. Establishing and growing a marketing communications firm with a global reach is a true challenge. You will always hit snags or need to address a difficult client or staff problem. Tackling these issues head-on, listening intently, and always being empathetic, provides an opportunity to struggle towards a mutually beneficial solution.

John Steinbeck said it best: "Try to understand men. If you understand each other you will be kind to each other. Knowing a man well never leads to hate and almost always leads to love."

Certainly, words that I've tried to live by.

initiatives based on our experience in global diplomacy and business. These are examples, but many of them include grains that have already shown promise in other initiatives.

Support for Messaging Centers

Governments and NGOs fund and support counter-messaging centers that operate on both covert and overt channels. Ideally, foreign entities run foreign centers independently. The U.S. and its partners provide training, exchanges and technical expertise, and they facilitate collaboration with Western technology, Internet and social media companies to help establish the centers.

Content Creation Grants

Every country offers grants to fund the creation of countering violent extremism (CVE) content on social media and other channels. Governments and NGOs offer funding to both individuals and groups that build organizations to disseminate CVE messages. This initiative helps spur regional entrepreneurship and creates jobs for many of the thousands of talented young graduates in global hotspots.

Regional Conferences

Countries in the Arab League or the Organization of Islamic Cooperation (OIC) convene events similar to the December 2014 Hedayah Expo, which brought together leaders from media, social media, foundations, private-sector companies and religious organizations. Multiple conferences in the Middle East, Southeast Asia and North Africa establish mechanisms for creating positive content that's both broad, covering all audiences, and targeted for particular regions, countries and cities.

Online Competitions

Countries and NGO partners hold national, pan-Arab and OIC-wide contests online to incentivize the creation of both anti-extremist and affirmatively positive content. The competition spurs ideas tailored to specific localities and generates ideas applicable to both specific and broad audiences.

A "Muslim Peace Corps" and Positive Alternatives to Address Conflict and Humanitarian Need

Arab countries and NGO partners highlight the efforts of volunteers and those making peaceful and constructive contributions to the humanitarian situation in Syria, Jordan and beyond. With an open and thoughtful approach, regional partners create and possibly fund a Muslim Peace Corps, through which young men and women of any nationality contribute to humanitarian efforts in the Muslim world.

Influential anti-ISIS Figures

Jordan currently hosts many tribal and religious leaders with deep ties to the Sunni communities in Iraq and Syria. In partnership with other counter-hate allies, these leaders use their influence to disseminate anti-ISIS messaging and to dissuade Syrians and Iraqis from joining the organization. As part of a counter-narrative campaign, these refugees in Jordan use their unique positions to proclaim ISIS actions as so repugnant that even other extremist groups and leaders reject them. (ISIS has declared on social media that it will "soon bring the Islamic state" to "brothers in Jordan". According to reports, Jordan is using two influential extremist clerics as part of a counter-narrative campaign. Both Abu Qatada and Abu Muhammad al-Maqdisi have significant followings in extremist circles and already have condemned the ISIS beheadings and other actions as un-Islamic.)

Protection of Religious Minorities

A group of prominent Muslim scholars is working on a project to create a declaration on standards and protocols for the protection of religious minorities in the Muslim world. They already gathered for a series of meetings convened by the Ministers of Religious Affairs in North Africa. As part of a separate initiative, Jordan's King Abdullah is supporting an interreligious effort to create a "global covenant" that denounces violence in the name of religion. Its steering group includes Prince Ghazi of Jordan and officials from the Vatican. As the next step, the U.S. and other Western countries help these regional and global partners promote these indigenous, affirmative messages and, wherever possible, formalize them in policy.

Information Ministries

The U.S. asks national public affairs entities, including information ministries, to highlight positive narratives and profile strong role models around the Muslim world. New special-purpose ministries promote beneficial channels and underscore the destructive impact of terrorism on Muslim communities. Content includes stories of former radicals and foreign fighters who condemn ISIS, its actions and its philosophies. Governments that exert significant influence over television broadcasting, including pan-Arab satellite channels, use their pull to disseminate these messages to the broadest possible audience. Western government, entertainment, business and NGO officials provide training and exchanges for public affairs officials seeking to build capacity and frame messaging efforts.

Religious Affairs and Education Ministries

Religious-affairs ministries already help formulate and coordinate Friday sermon content and mosque programming. Now, they encourage imams to focus on anti-extremist messaging, including religious-based explanations for why joining ISIS or other organizations is *haram*. Ministries also sponsor rapid response teams of high-level scholars, who travel together to regions where extremism is gaining a foothold. Individual statements remain important, but delegations of the most influential international imams coming together with a common message are more visible and powerful.

Traditionally, some countries have discouraged leading religious figures from participating in international events because they see their countries as more appropriate hosts. The Saudis, as custodians of the two Holy Mosques, have been particularly protective of their country's authority over Islamic issues. In this new strategy, global government leaders ask these countries to encourage leading figures, such as the Grand Mufti and the imam of the Grand Mosque, to travel widely and join others in spreading an anti-hate and anti-terrorism message around the Muslim world. In addition, the role of education ministries takes a longer-term view and goes beyond messaging — to broader improvements in education and enhanced access to schools, textbooks and curricula that avoids negative portrayals of religious minorities and reinforces the notion that violence is an unacceptable response to political and other grievances.

Supporting De-Radicalization Programs

Some de-radicalization programs, when conducted well, have been effective at addressing the terrorists' rationale for terrorism. So, the U.S. encourages partners in the Muslim world to explore the development of more effective de-radicalization programs. These initiatives create a talent pool of voices with a unique expertise for combating terrorist narratives, including those online. The experts and former radicals are then used in a range of effective intervention programs.

CHAPTER 17

HOW TO DECREASE SALES

"The moment there is suspicion about a person's motives,
everything he does becomes tainted."
— MAHATMA GANDHI

This might be the first book in history with a chapter called "How to decrease sales." Yet, as we merge our marketing knowledge with our diplomatic expertise in the fight against hate, we hope to do exactly that—reduce the supply of people willing to join extremist groups and disrupt their ability to fulfill demand for new converts. However, much like increasing sales for a global brand, we can't decrease the sale of hate if we isolate ourselves in silos. It doesn't work if each country does its own thing. It doesn't work if we can't use the broadest and deepest insights to create the right programs and outreach. It only works when we cooperate globally and share our models, insights, successes and failures.

We can decrease sales, but we need a collaborative effort—one that allows us to avoid stereotypes, borrows time-tested models from the business world, and combines the deep pool of talent at NGOs, government agencies and businesses around the world.

THE PROBLEM WITH STEREOTYPING

There is no way to tell which person will join a terrorist or extremist group in advance. We deploy the best artificial intelligence, the greatest access to data and any resource available on earth, and we still can't

accurately predict why some people merely get angry and others devolve
into hate and terror.

Profile information certainly doesn't tip the scales one'way or the
other. Just imagine meeting a well-heeled professional gentleman over
coffee one day. He speaks four languages, has lived in multiple countries
around the world and got his bachelor of science in mechanical engineering at a U.S. university. He tells you about his family and his happy
childhood in Pakistan, where his father was a lay preacher. Drawn back
to his home, he attended University of the Punjab in Lahore to get a master's degree in Islamic Culture and History, and then moved his family
to Qatar after landing a project engineering job at the Qatari Ministry of
Electricity and Water.

Only later do you find out he also joined the Muslim Brotherhood.
Even though many Muslims join that organization, perhaps your impression starts to change. After he received his undergraduate degree, you
learn, he traveled to Peshawar to fight with the *mujahedeen* forces in the
Afghanistan-Russia war. Not as many people did that, but you figure that
was cool given the nature of that Soviet invasion. Then, it comes to your
attention that he also found time to attend the Sada training camp run by
Sheikh Abdallah Azzam before working at a magazine called *al-Bunyan
al-Marsous*, which was created for the Islamic Union for the Liberation
of Afghanistan. Oh, and his nephew was Ramzi Yousef, one of the main
actors in the 1993 World Trade Center bombing. At this point, you're
probably not so sure about this guy — good thing, too, because this profile
belongs to Khalid Sheikh Mohammed, the principal architect of the 9/11
terrorist attacks.

He didn't have to go this way, and neither did any of the men and
women recruited into extremist organizations. Ayman Al-Zawahiri, the
current leader of Al-Qaeda, comes from a family of scholars and doctors.
Several other key members would make fine electrical engineers if they'd
opted to work in Silicon Valley. They are poor, rich, smart, not so smart,
upper class, middle class, lower class — there is no single type of person
who decides to hate at such extreme levels. We can't predict who will
become an extremist bent on hurting innocent people, who will simply

be angry, or who will prosper and become productive members of society. And yet, that doesn't stop us from stereotyping.

Stereotypes make it easier to process our crazy, diverse and complicated world. We simplify, in part, so we can understand. And although we can think and do better, we take the easy road. To successfully counter hate, we need to change paths, and to do that we need to first accept that our own brains will get in the way of our progress. Humans, after all, are capable of tremendously destructive subconscious behavior. A study of college students revealed as much in 2015.

A Stanford University research team led by management Professor Margaret Neale and psychology Professor Geoffrey L. Cohen set out to discover whether a classification with certain groups would influence behavior. In essence, they asked, would someone in a stereotyped cohort naturally conform with those stereotypes? The simple answer was yes, the researchers said: "People are more likely to lie, cheat, steal or endorse doing so when they feel that they are being devalued simply because they belong to particular groups. The more the college students worried or expected stereotyping, the more likely they were to report engaging in delinquent behavior, like skipping classes, verbally abusing someone or vandalizing school property." Speaking to a writer for the Stanford Graduate School of Business newsletter, Neale said she hoped the research would help people understand that "the responsibility for criminal and deviant behavior lies not only with individuals, but with society. We tend to make criminal behavior a dispositional attribute—a quality of the individual. But maybe we are part of the problem that is expressed by those people behaving badly."

To combat extremism, we need to at least acknowledge the role we and the rest of global society play in the growth of hate. Better yet, we ought to take a few cues from Neale and her colleagues and ask ourselves a few key questions:

- *Do we think logically or emotionally?*—How do we become more aware of what is happening inside the mind of those who may become extremists? What can we learn from those who've traveled the length of the Pre-Hate Journey and joined terrorist organizations?

- *Who joins a group?* — Why do people give up on normal society to join a gang or hate group? How has Maslow's hierarchy of needs played out in their lives?

- *Who joins a full-blown terrorist organization?* — What myths can we shatter to better understand who joins these groups and why? What is their motivation? What do the data and evidence tell us?

A LOGICAL VERSUS EMOTIONAL MINDSET

Most rational people are astonished when they see Neo-Nazis demonstrate and hear the racist comments they spew. We find it repugnant. We recoil. And inside our minds, we erect a shield to protect ourselves against it. We know this has nothing to do with who we are. We know these people are bad. Our narratives save us, in a way, from the difficulty of thinking more deeply about the problem and potential solutions to it. Unfortunately, this natural defense mechanism also prevents us from understanding why a person could hurt so much that they turn to hate. We need to push ourselves out of our emotional comfort zone and into the logical side of the equation.

In business, we call this walking in the customer's shoes. We force ourselves to think like a customer, imagine what they would do, how they would act and why they might adopt certain viewpoints that we want to change. We map the customer journey, going through the process of their daily lives — what they watch, listen to and interact with. We get to know them so well that we can map out how they will engage with certain content, form their opinions about a brand and eventually act over the course of several years. Mapping out the same for someone's Pre-Hate Journey could provide us with powerful insight to counter hate, but it's an extremely difficult task.

In fact, it's not easy to do in any context. Companies have committed millions of dollars and degrees upon degrees of marketing expertise to mapping out their customers' journeys, even if they're just trying to figure out why customers might buy a new energy drink with extra Vitamin C. It's even harder when we try to get inside the head of people we don't know, don't like or whose environment we can't understand. We push until we encounter the blockades in our brains, and then we stop learning.

THE NEUROSCIENCE OF HATE

BY SCOTT MCDONALD, PhD
President and CEO, Advertising Research Foundation

I lead an organization that was founded to advance the scientific study of marketing, media and advertising. As such, we tend to study why people like things more than why they dislike them. And when we study persuasion, we usually study how to get people to act affirmatively rather than negatively. So, when the authors of this book asked me to pen a note about the neuroscience of hate, I was not entirely sure I would have much to say. The ARF has encouraged greater use of the tools of neuroscience to study unexpressed, sub-verbal emotions, and these emotions frequently run a gamut from like to dislike. But hate?

Checking the literature and consulting with some practitioners both in private practice and in academia, it's clear the neuroscience of hate has not been sufficiently studied. Interestingly, whenever hate is studied in this context, it usually is paired with studies of the biological basis of love. Both emotions tend to unmoor people from their usual restraints and from their rational footing. Both activate measurable changes in the autonomic nervous system—usually measured by skin conductance, heart rate and significant changes in the prefrontal cortex.

For example, in 2008, researchers at the Wellcome Laboratory of Neurobiology at University College London showed seventeen experimental subjects photos of someone they loved and someone they hated while closely monitoring their brain activity. Showing a photo of the hated person activated distinct parts of the prefrontal cortex and sub-cortex—the areas dubbed the "hate circuit" by the researchers. These activations were different from those related to emotions such as aggression or disgust. Interestingly, they shared some of the characteristics associated with the passions around romantic love—specifically the activation of brain substructures known as the putamen and the insula, both connected to our ways of managing distress. But the patterns of activation were different.

As explained by Professor Semir Zeki who led the research: "A marked difference in the cortical pattern produced by these two sentiments of love and hate is that, whereas with love large parts of the cerebral cortex associated with judgment and reasoning become deactivated, with hate only a small zone, located in the frontal cortex, becomes deactivated. This may seem surprising since hate can also be an all-consuming passion, just like love. But whereas in romantic love, the lover is often less critical and judgmental regarding the loved person, it is more likely that in the context of hate the hater may want to exercise judgment in calculating moves to harm, injure or otherwise extract revenge."

The tools that permit researchers to map how our brains respond to emotions have not been around very long, and their application to the study of hate has thus far been sparse. With a bit more time and effort, however, they could provide an important key to our understanding of hatred and our ability to reduce this most primitive and destructive of emotions.

HOW TO "TREAT" BIAS AND HATE IN THE PHYSICIAN'S OFFICE

NABA SHARIF, MD, FAAAAI, FACAAI
Adult and Pediatric Allergy, Asthma and Immunology Specialist

In the medical profession, clinicians pride ourselves on treating all patients without discrimination. Regardless of race, gender, sexual orientation or religion, we ascribe to an ideal of professionally and compassionately caring for those who are ill. We see this as an ethical obligation and sometimes, as in the care of emergency departments, a legal obligation to not turn away sick patients. But what of patients who discriminate, carry bias against or even refuse care from physicians who might look different, pray differently or have a different gender?

A 2017 survey of nearly 1,200 physicians showed that about 60% had experienced a patient encounter with discrimination against their age, gender, race, ethnicity, religion, etc. In the survey, titled "Patient Prejudice: When Credentials Aren't Enough" and published by WebMD and Medscape, nearly half of all physicians surveyed have even had a patient request a different provider due to the above biases. A recent video that went internationally viral showed a woman repeatedly screaming that she only wanted a "white doctor" at a walk-in clinic in Canada. Unfortunately, these incidents are not isolated ones.

Guidelines for dealing with these types of patients are minimal. We are often taught techniques for dealing with the "difficult patient" during our medical training, but not specifically for the racist patient or patient with hateful speech. The fear of turning ill, albeit, prejudiced patients away due to our perceived and known ethical obligations, and the lack of reporting guidelines, put providers in these scenarios in a precarious dilemma. However, physician burnout is likely much more common if repeatedly having to encounter painful and insulting abuses from the very patients they service—a burden that is intrinsically unfair, and one that may hurt the entire physician workforce.

With this in mind, a 2016 article in the New England Journal of Medicine attempted to provide a framework for "Dealing with Racist Patients," prioritizing the patient's medical condition and the medical setting, and then looking at negotiating care to put the patient's best interests first. It acknowledges that "no ethical obligation is absolute", and that reasonable limits may be placed on unacceptable patient conduct towards providers in order to protect the providers. Ultimately, employees of health care institutions also have the right to a workplace free from discrimination according to Title VII of the 1964 Civil Rights Act.

Practically speaking, what does this mean for minority physicians? As a young, female, brown, Muslim-American subspecialist caring for both children and adults, when I am faced with these degrading patient encounters, my first thought will be to put the patient first. But if there is the risk of significant emotional distress to myself or my staff, I must recognize that I can only provide the best care to my patients when there is mutual respect. When that respect is repeatedly undermined, I will have no choice but to safely transfer or decline further patient care. I will undoubtedly rely on my non-minority colleagues and staff to also intervene and advocate against hate. Pressure must be applied to health care systems to support minority physicians and ensure that hospitals and clinic policies are in place to keep physicians safe against hateful speech or behavior. Ultimately, only when we as a medical community speak out against these injustices and refuse to tolerate discriminatory behavior, can patients one day recognize that they cannot bite the hand that treats them.

Addiction provides a useful allegory for how hard it is to think beyond our initial reactions and find ways around our mental roadblocks. Approximately one in every ten people suffers from some form of addiction, so we all know someone fighting to stay clean and sober. For those of us in the fortunate 90 percent, we often find it difficult to sympathize with addicts, especially those who live on the cusp of society and panhandle or steal to fund their next fix. Since they often live in this state of angst, we just as often write them off, once again dealing with the issue at a surface level and allowing ourselves to avoid questions about what actually happens inside this fellow human. A short post that made the rounds on Facebook and other social media and Internet channels in July 2017 put the addict's struggle in far more sympathetic terms than most of us ever do:

> *"You see heroin, I see low self-esteem. You see cocaine, I see fear. You see alcohol, I see social anxiety. You see track marks, I see depression. You see a junkie, I see someone's son. You see a prostitute, I see someone's daughter caught in addiction. You see self-centeredness, I see the disease. You see a pill head, I see over-prescribing of opiates. You see someone unwilling to change, I see someone hasn't connected with them yet. You see denial, I see someone hurting. You see someone nodding out, I see God showing us they need help. You see the end, I see the beginning. You see a dope fiend, I see a future success story. You see them, I see me."*

It shouldn't take a tremendous leap in imagination and cognition to understand problems from this viewpoint, but it remains a rarity. Viewed conscientiously through the eyes of the other person, we begin to realize one bad incident or situation alone rarely breaks someone's will. The process is more complicated and longer term, and gaining any nuanced understanding of it requires that we think of each person as a multidimensional human being caught in their own struggles. That's a rare enough courtesy for sober people to grant to addicts they know; it's all but nonexistent for terrorists whose actions we can't or don't want to fathom. Yet, virtually no one goes to kindergarten hoping they can become a Neo-Nazi or a member of Al-Qaeda:

"You see a person to avoid, I see a person who doesn't like me because of my religion or color. You see a poor person to be careful around, I see a future employer who will never hire me. You see someone to yell at, I want to respond but can't lest the abuse escalate. You read stories about how bad my neighborhood is, I see a family trying to work their way out of that same neighborhood. You see an unemployed person, I see someone who wants to work but doesn't know where to go. You see a beggar, I see a mother desperate to make some money for her family. You see my religion as a problem, I see the local religious leader as one of the few people who treats me with respect. You see college, a job and starting a family, I see chronic unemployment for my life and wonder what else I need to do to gain respect. You see a crazy person, I just want to belong to a group that matters. You see the end, I see the beginning. You see them, I see me."

BOX 17.1   **DISCRIMINATION, EMPATHY AND THE NEED TO BELONG**

Remember a time when someone harrassed, intimidated or made fun of you. Take a moment to put yourself back there and recall how you felt at that moment. How many other times can you remember having those same feelings? A handful? Dozens? If it happened on a daily basis, would you be the same person you are today?

Now, flip the scenario around. Recall a time you made fun of someone, dogged them or put them down. Again, take a bit of time to recall how you felt in that moment. And if you did this on a daily basis to relieve the stress in your life, would you be the same person you are today?

Finally, remember the good role models in your life—your favorite teacher, your mom or dad, a mentor or teacher. Did the people who boosted your confidence and raised your ceiling possess something special, or did they merely support, encourage and empathize with you?

For better or worse, most of us have plenty of memories about all three of these scenarios—the times we were hurt, hurt someone else, or were healed by someone else. We can still wince at the first two, and fondly remember the third. It all kind of burns into our soul, and we wish we could take back the bad and become more of the good. And that's for the generally privileged few who are reading these words. For a young boy or girl growing up in a community rife with harrassment and intimidation—and the survival instinct to inflict the same on others—the presence of the empathetic role model becomes all the more alluring. In that environment, one rarely forgets the day someone approaches and says: "Hey, why don't you hang out with us for a meeting? We think you're a good kid. We could use a person like you. You would be great at what we do."

For impressionable and vulnerable youth, it might not even matter what the meeting is about. That young man or women just got a chance to break out of a demeaning narrative, to believe that maybe this is the group that will respect you for who you are or want to become. So you join and, next thing you know, the rhetoric escalates. You start to think about things you never considered before, and you put faith in the respected leader who took you under his or her wing. You want the truth. You want to be part of the team. You want respect. Now, you're getting it.

It doesn't take a giant leap of imagination to get from here back to your teenage parties, when you and your friends chugged beer after beer because you wanted to look cool. You threw up that night, felt horrible the next morning, but you weren't a chump. Maybe some of your friends drove home that night; maybe you did—decisions that easily could've killed yourself and an innocent mother, father or child.

The young man who decides to strap on a suicide belt or pick up a gun might have different motivations and a willingness to go to far more hateful extremes. He might act out of sheer spite, rather than peer pressure to stick with the "in" crowd. But these aren't always differences in kind so much as scale: One can remember the handful of cringe-worthy incidents he suffered throughout his life; the other can remember only a handful of days he got by without one.

WHY WE JOIN GROUPS

The Los Angeles Police Department has to keep track of more than 1,350 gangs with 120,000-plus members. They have a pretty good idea of why people join gangs. Some of the reasons they identify as key motivations tell us a lot about why we make that decision:

- *Identity or recognition* — You achieve a level of status that's not present in daily life.

- *Protection* — You have a team to protect you, whether from violence in your neighborhood or insults from the other side.

- *Fellowship and brotherhood* — The group serves as an extension of one's family, and often includes family members within it.

- *Intimidation* — You don't feel you have a choice, so you join the group to avoid intense pressure, discomfort or even pain.

North American gangs almost exclusively recruit youth, who tend to see only benefits and can't properly assess the full risks inherent in their choices. They would look at the LAPD's list from a clearly affirmative perspective — joining the gang makes me cool; my fellow members care about me; we make some money, have some fun and protect each other when things get rough.

The motivations of 2,032 people who joined Al-Qaeda as foreign fighters look similar to the LAPD list in some respects, but quite different in others, according to research compiled in an excellent U.S. Institute of Peace report written by Col. John M. "Matt" Venhaus. Col. Venhaus, a Jennings Randolph Army Fellow, is a career psychological operations officer experienced with foreign media-influence operations throughout Europe, the Middle East and South Asia. His study married his academic research as a Senior Service College Fellow with the operational experience he gained while commanding the Joint Psychological Operations Task Force, the missions of which included reducing the flow of foreign fighters in the U.S. Central Command's area of responsibility.

His report gave us a deeper appreciation for the powerful sense of belonging within extremist groups. But from a business perspective, it also confronted us with the fact that Al-Qaeda wields a remarkably sophisticated marketing machine. To underscore just how adept the terrorist organization has become, we put Venhaus' findings into a more corporate marketing context here. Put simply, this is what Al-Qaeda is doing well:

- *The Narrative is Patriotic* — We are fighting anti-Muslim oppression. If you join us, you can help us establish the Islamic Caliphate that will counter this oppression.

- *Customer Experience and Support* — When the underwear bomber, Umar Farouk Abdulmutallab, wrote in an online forum, "I do not have a friend, I have no one to speak to, no one to consult, no one to support me, and I feel depressed and lonely. I do not know what to do," Al-Qaeda knew how to reach him — just like marketers do for major brands.

- *Customer Segmentation* — Brands figure out which micro-segments to target based on extensive research. Al-Qaeda knows that recruits have an unfulfilled need, whether based on a need to seek revenge, to improve one's status, to join a group that cares about you or to experience new adventures. The organization picks from the menu and matches its messages to your needs.

- *Selling the "why"* — Since most fighters have led normal lives and are leaving the safety and security of their homes, they must believe in a cause that will allow them to de-personalize the plight of others and focus their actions on harming innocent people. In this respect, Al-Qaeda's operation is similar to the way many countries prepare their soldiers for war. No one gets to know the enemy before they hit the battlefield.

As the Venhaus report shows, the collective outreach efforts of Al-Qaeda are well thought out. It's also clear they work hard to establish a global narrative that can be regionalized or localized to meet the needs of those they hope to activate. Most of Al-Qaeda's recruits join because it gives them purpose, a sense of direction and an identity at a critical time in their personal development — not unlike the reasons young men and women join gangs in the West. In fact, we all join various groups for fundamentally similar reasons.

We can use this similarity as a launching point for getting over the hurdles that keep us from truly walking in the shoes of those who hate. If we know where this journey starts and can see the basic direction of the path, we'd be remiss if we didn't push ourselves further and develop the more detailed map of the Pre-Hate Journey. If we collectively do the hard work, we begin to see why youth evolve and, over the years, reach a point where they might make the decision to join an extremist group. And we can identify the points at which we can intervene and provide the information, activities or outlets that can sway these young men and women towards more beneficial pursuits.

This is one of those times where you realize we really can counter hate and substantially decrease it. All it takes is our unrelenting focus on developing intense customer journeys and our commitment of resources on reaching people at the right times in the right places with the right content and ideas.

Getting to the answer isn't always easy. The execution is extremely hard for even the largest companies in the world. It requires a shared knowledge of what to do, and an intense coordination of resources and teams.

It is why we must counter hate together.

BOX 17.2   **FOUR MYTHS AND A MOMENT OF TRUTH**

Col. Venhaus' key report on Al-Qaeda obliterated many of the myths surrounding the organization. These four truths reveal just how far off much of our thinking had been.

- **Healthy minds are important**: Crazy people are not of interest. Like any organization, Al-Qaeda wants to attract the best and the brightest who are willing to further its goals.

- **Economics are the least cited reason for joining**: Motivation to help the cause far outweighs economics. The study does not show a correlation between poverty and joining the *jihad*.

- **Religious zeal is not the driver to join**: Many recruits aren't very religious. They don't know the Koran so are more susceptible to an interpretation they hear for the first time. If you start with a narrow interpretation of Islamic teachings and this is all you know, you just assume this is the right body of knowledge.

- **Peers drive our decisions**: Just like everyone else in the world, we listen closely to our peers and often make decisions similar to theirs. Recruits are much more likely to follow their friends than react solely to Al-Qaeda recruitment tactics.

The Venhaus report also included a telling anecdote about the sensibilities that prompt young men and women to look for a sympathetic ear. It's worth recounting here:

"The young North African who travels to Europe in search of better wages or a better life. When he arrives, he finds only menial work, though the pay is much greater than in his home country. He dutifully sends money home, all the while seething over the fact that he is restricted to certain sections of town or certain jobs by a society that is interested in him only as cheap labor. One young Moroccan proclaimed, 'I was like a slave in France. I could work in the kitchen but was not welcome in the dining room. When I left my neighborhood, people avoided me on the street as if I were unclean.' Young men in these situations believe that they have value and abilities and a worth to the world that their position in society doesn't reflect."

A NEW COALITION OF EXPERTISE

We propose a new coalition of expertise that can develop a more nuanced map of the Pre-Hate Journey *and* craft effective interventions to steer global youth toward healthier outcomes. This coalition should represent a mashup of government and NGO intelligence and mapping expertise of private-sector marketers — all focused on making sure extremist groups can't complete the sale.

The marketing expertise of corporations

Marketers might create charts that look super intense and complicated, but the fundamental elements of the customer journey are straightforward. After all, we're just trying to understand how fellow human beings make decisions over time. We can boil that decision-making journey down to five key phases, each of which we can adapt and apply to a counter-hate strategy:

- *Awareness* — We want to know when you become aware of our brand/topic and how you learn about us. Which channel? What content do you see? What is the story you learn about us? By understanding this first set of interactions, we can see how we should improve how we initially "meet." We also know it's vital that you keep hearing about us, because you might not make a decision for years.

- *Consideration* — Did you start your research via Google or Bing? Are you joining certain forums or dark net groups to learn more? Your actions tell us that you consider us an important part of your world, so we need to know how we educate you at the point of interest. What is our mobile experience like? Is our story inspiring you to learn more? The groups you join can tell us how serious you are, so we might introduce you to some new groups and see if you convert — just like companies give you reasons to click and find out more about their brands.

- *Purchase* — You decided we're worth the effort and you join a key online forum or confidential group. As an extremist recruit, you don't make a purchase in the traditional sense, but we both know you're part of the team for now. We want to make sure we provide what you need, so we can help you achieve higher status, seek revenge or enact whatever you believe is important.

- *Retention* — We need to keep building our relationship, so we're going to look for more ways to interact with you and engage your passions, both online and offline. So, we want to keep providing you content to gauge what interests you. If we can build the right momentum, you're more likely to become an active member. And we identify your friends, too, because they also might consider joining — another element that would solidify your interest.

- *Advocacy* — You're now fully on board and want to help us recruit others. You start with your friends and people you know and trust in your hometown. We'll work hard to make you look good, so your friends can see the value of joining you. You now have a role, so we'll help you tell our story successfully. You're all in — and in our view of the world, there's no turning back now.

The anti-extremist expertise of NGOs

When we began to consider the breadth of this new anti-extremist coalition, we first wanted to integrate the groups and individuals who know extremist groups better than anyone. We quickly realized that the NGOs dedicated to fighting hate and extremism around the world have unparalleled insight. We seek to learn from this vast collection of NGOs, which includes the European Network Against Racism (Belgium), the Center for Prevention of Exclusion (Denmark), the Jewish Community of Rome (Italy), the Federation of SOS Racism (Spain) and the Anti-Defamation League (United States) among many others.

Through our work at The Marketing College, the U.S. State Department and normal life, we've worked with hundreds of NGOs dedicated to the battle against extremism. We know these hidden heroes understand how extremist groups work, who drives their stories, what their messages are, who has influence, which media channels they use and more. They typically have the best view into this world, because they think about it every day while we go off to our day jobs. This is their day job, and they do it very well (as we note in our next chapter).

The mashup

We have a window between birth and 25 years old — and a prime opportunity during the teenage years — during which we can make a difference in the lives of young men and women. But we can counter hate far more effectively if we know *precisely* how and when to intervene with the best messaging and the most-innovative marketing techniques in the world. This is why we launched our website, www.counteringhate.com, and it's why we have our dataset community at data.world. We can't achieve this goal if we simply agree something needs to be done and then go back to working in silos.

Former Viacom CEO, Tom Freston framed the challenge well: "Innovation is taking two things that already exist and putting them together in a new way." Whether we work for the government, an NGO or a private-sector company, we need to make a conscious and concerted effort to combine forces and create the most innovative approaches to countering hate.

CHAPTER 18

MENTAL TOUGHNESS, NGOS AND YOUR ROLE

"Knowing is not enough; we must apply.
Willing is not enough; we must do."
—Johann Wolfgang von Goethe (German writer and statesman)

I spotted the pickup truck a block or two away and watched it slowly cruise down Tate Street in Greensboro, North Carolina. I didn't pay it much attention at first. After all, it was one of those sunny, languid autumn days, when it feels like everybody and everything takes it just a little bit easier — no need to flee summer's heat; no care to rush into winter's chill.

And then, the whole atmosphere around me (Bob) instantly froze. I'd seen the white hoods first, then saw the group of men in the bed of that approaching pickup, their arms all raised in protest. The crowd yelled, and the Klansmen reveled in the attention. No more than 15 seconds elapsed, noisy and chaotic before they disappeared down the way, but it felt like hours. The whole scene still runs in slow motion when I remember it today.

The hair on the back of my neck rose up, and a chill colder than winter's wind ran down my spine. I don't know what sort of expression I wore on my face at that moment, but I know that I, like the rest of the people on the street, were left speechless by the sight. Seeing raw hate that close left me shaken, and with little idea what I should do next. I'd grown up in New Jersey and read plenty about the Ku Klux Klan, but in my mind it always remained abstract and anachronistic — forever stuck in another place and time.

Rationally, it shouldn't have shocked me as deeply as it did. Not even a full year earlier, an anti-KKK demonstration march by the Communist Workers' Party devolved into a gun fight with Klansmen and the American Nazi Party. The infamous Greensboro massacre on November 3, 1979, left five people dead, four of them members of the Communist party, and another 11 injured. While the shooters were acquitted in criminal trials, a civil jury found the Klan and Nazi shooters liable for one death — and found that the Greensboro Police Department failed to prevent the shootings.

The fallout and weight of the massacre still hung over the city the following autumn, but nothing drilled into my psyche and soul like this firsthand brush with hate at the extreme. It made me wonder about who defends us. How does someone decide they won't go into banking, launch a small business or become a doctor, and instead choose to dedicate their lives to the terrorization of innocent others? Why would a gang of angry white men put on white robes and try to intimidate a crowd on an otherwise beautiful day? How could this feel more relevant and rewarding than playing ball with their kids or going to work?

And why, I wondered, were my fellow classmates and I walking back to classes at our safe campus? Why didn't we have the awareness and the fortitude to do something about it?

THE MENTAL TOUGHNESS OF GLOBAL NGOS

To really connect with the audience you hope to reach, you need to study them, understand them, think like them and obsess over ways to build bonds with them. It requires a focus that goes beyond discipline. It requires a type of mental toughness that defines a truly effective Non Governmental Organization (NGO), but doesn't always pervade the ranks of successful corporations or government agencies. NGOs walk in the shoes of those they expect to impact. They figure out how people become hateful so they can try to intervene. They know they will fail far more than they succeed, yet the continue to get their hands dirty.

Many people describe members of NGOs as zealots and true believers. They are, just like you are for the passions of your personal and professional lives. That sort of passion is powerful when channeled correctly, and NGOs focus like few other types of organizations. And in that sense, they're akin to the world's great brands. Nike produces a range of sports equipment and apparel; they don't try to sell us cars, computers or cordless drills. A top NGO focused on anti-semitism won't ever veer from its initiatives to prevent anti-semitism.

We can silently applaud their efforts, but tacit support won't effect true change. It's like watching the Klan drive by and then simply walking back to class. Instead, we can share our knowledge directly with NGOs to ensure that these heroes have the tools they need to win the soft war against bias, hate and extremism. We can develop ways to integrate NGOs and our business and diplomatic expertise, so collectively we can leverage the best of each to make a real difference.

A NEW GLOBAL WORKSPACE FOR ANTI-EXTREMIST NGOS

We talked to hundreds of people about our ideas for countering hate, and we got the same reply from virtually all of them: "How can I help?" The overhelming support persuaded us not only to write this book, but to accelerate our timeline for finishing it.

The remarkable response also convinced us to develop a platform where all of us could learn the best and next practices for everything from communications to marketing, and technology to behavioral research. But we also realized we needed to help integrate all of this with the world's anti-extremist NGOs, which bring both deep front-line experiences with extreme hate, as well as the mental toughness to keep fighting it.

Our site, www.counteringhate.com, provides a platform where anyone can provide the types of expertise, insights, models or resources that can help NGOs counter hate:

- *Facebook Page* — At the global page in Facebook called "Countering Hate," you can share insights and determine the best way you can share your knowledge with the wider group. The workspace also provides a forum for NGOs to seek help, so we know where to focus. It will be a two-way street.

- *data.world* — We also established the "Countering Hate" community on data.world, the leading online space for sharing public datasets. Imagine what happens if we gather all the public data sets related to bias, hate and extremism and give data scientists around the world a chance to develop anti-hate insights for cities, states, countries and regions?

INNOVATION AT THE COMMUNITY LEVEL

BY SEBASTIAN JOHNA
Project leader for Migration und Integration, Goethe-Institut (Munich, Germany)

The Goethe-Institut is the cultural institute of the Federal Republic of Germany. Through its global reach, the institute helps promote knowledge of the German language abroad and fosters cultural cooperation.

I always find myself amazed by the inventiveness and effectiveness of Islamist groups when it comes to placing messages, advertising for themselves and recruiting new blood. Much of what I read and encounter follows shockingly simple templates and concepts. A large amount of it, in fact, is innovative, very well-tailored and directed straight to young Muslims, and groups can bring it up quickly and cost-effectively. That forces us to reassess our own work time and time again.

The Goethe-Institut's work on the role of Islam in Germany is expensive and complicated. We must stick to the rules and procedures, continuing to work hard so we can appear credible and provide long-term points of access to Islamic communities. Obstacles such as these do not affect extremist groups, which operate fluidly and in loose networks, a situation that gives them a competitive edge.

I have therefore set myself the goal of removing these obstacles to give my projects their own freedom to operate—in terms of both content and finances. This will require some work to convince others within our own organization and among our partners, on which I depend. Three approaches have shown themselves to be particularly convincing and successful here:

- *Asking for content instead of pre-determining it:* Our work takes a participatory approach. We start new projects not by setting content but by setting questions. I want to know what motivates the people with whom I work, and then start building with that. I look for direct conversations whenever possible, so I visit participants and their organizations on the ground and make efforts to build relationships that allow for open discussions.

- *Working based on religion but not fixed on religion:* Our projects reach out to Muslims, but religion is not a specific topic of our work. We have kept it up surprisingly well, so I can say—even five years on—that I have not staged a single event on a specific theological or religious theme of Islam. That is a decision on principle that others might make differently. For me, however, it has turned out to be very positive. Our work has been freed from questions that we could not settle in the first place, making room for issues such as social and civic engagement, education and youth work. The participants also are unburdened, allowing them to focus on problems within their area of activity and really contribute to their solution. In my experience, themes of action potentially motivated by religion have the most impact when religion is in the background.

- *Delivering messages rather than achievements:* Naturally, our projects are geared to specific goals in the field, which makes it possible for both the Goethe-Institut and others, such as funding bodies, to measure the success of our work. Practically speaking, I consistently end up stumbling over this, as the work goes differently than planned, the general conditions suddenly change or I make mistakes. I have come up with an approach that enables me to deal with it very openly. I regret every failure and try to learn from it, but that is only one level of my work.

On another level for me, it is not a matter of hitting specific targets, but sending messages, drawing attention to needs and problems as well as opportunities. Only these messages will make sure our work takes effect and ensures sustainability. Our day-to-day efforts, with their successes and failures, support our credibility along the way. But ultimately, it takes second priority after these messages.

- *New Groups & Insights* — Spread the word. On any of these forums, you can recommend groups we ought to invite, or just invite them yourself. Share insights directly or point us in the direction of key material.

The Facebook Community will include curated links to the most progressive approaches we find on social media, media, NGO and other channels. This can get us started, but we also will ask experts from around the world to proactively share their top thinking on a variety of strategies — how to counter disinformation; how to improve a search position; how to know who has influence in the media; or how to reach people most effectively via video.

At one time or another, we've all been that person on the street corner, stunned by the scene unfolding in front of us and not knowing what to do about it. Now, we will know — now, when we're at that crossroads, a collective knowledge, power and mental toughness will be there with us. We will know where, when and how to intervene, so we positively influence young men and women before they put hoods over their faces, climb onto the back of a pickup truck and set out to harrass, intimidate or kill.

CHAPTER 19

THE MEDIA CAMPFIRE:
10 IMPORTANT TRENDS

"We thought that we had the answers,
it was the questions we had wrong."
— BONO

The looks give it away, the all-too-familiar mix of anxiety and resignation. You finally start the meeting, even though half of your team hasn't arrived. Your friend walks in just as you started to gather your things to leave. And then you see it on their faces — the city is on alert again, the stress of threats and the delays blending into the numbing recognition that this won't be the last time heavily armed police and military officers patrol the subways, squares, buses and airports. We appreciate the need for security, despite all its daily hassles, but each officer carrying an Uzi reminds us again of how far we have to go to combat extremism.

What happens next happens far too often. Business and government leaders with amazing careers, awesome intellectual capability and a wealth of resources devolve into the usual chatter. We should start the next War Advertising Council, like the original in 1941. We should invest in public service announcements to convince young *extremists* they made a poor decision. Maybe we should just round up those who might join *religious extremism* and send them back to their home country. (Never mind that they already are in their home country.) On the one hand, it's mindless chitchat before the meeting can really begin. On the other, it shows the remarkable lack of interest in truly contemplating the problem

223

that confronts us. Too many of us live in a world where we still believe a great advertising campaign would make the difference. If we could just flood the airwaves with our view of the story, we would win!

We already know none of it works. We see the failure anew every time we see that too-familiar blend of anxiety and resignation on our colleagues' and friends' faces. But now, with our emerging capability to combine data science with behavioral analytics, we're starting to find effective ways to counter hate. Yes, we still have a long way to go to reduce extremism around the world, and no one would suggest we can eliminate it entirely anyway. But these new technologies and insights have started to reveal the critical, overlooked questions we need to address if we expect to wage a more effective battle against terror and hate.

THE TOP 10 QUESTIONS TO ANSWER

Bono was right, we were asking the wrong questions. No matter how smart an answer we developed, it never could've solved the problem we really faced. We need to recast all our questions, building them from the ground up based on rigorous big-data analysis and the merged expertise of private-sector, government and NGO leaders. Some of the higher-level expertise can be found in these pages. The data sets and analysis are on our workgroup at data.world. On the Facebook Community, we have a variety of private-sector learnings, including excerpts from *PreCommerce* and *Storytizing* (Bob's previous books).

Based on our research and analyses to date, we've developed the Top 10 Questions we need to answer to develop and enhance a successful countering hate strategy. (You can find more data and research on each of these at our "Countering Hate" workspace on Facebook.) Here are the questions and some tips for starting to answer them:

1. AUDIENCE—Who are we trying to reach, and when is our message most important to them?

Ed Tazzia and Kip Knight, leaders of The Marketing College, have outlined the tried-and-true approach they and countless private-sector marketing professionals have used throughout their careers. Beginning with this "ABCDE Model" provides a foundation for the rest of the questions to follow.

- *Audience:* Identify the strategic target. "Peel the onion" to define the prime prospect. Spend the time to understand your target audience's habits, beliefs, practices and attitudes. Get to know them as well as you know yourself and your organization.

- *Behavioral Objectives:* Clearly articulate the specific action step you want the audience to take. When you get this granular, you know whether you've clearly identified what you want to have happen. If you don't, go back. Specificity matters.

- *Content:* Make clear, concise and meaningful choices at every point. Identify the promise of what your product or service will do. Give the audience a reason to believe. And then make sure you strike the right tone, attitude and look of the message.

- *Design and delivery:* What are the best media vehicles given our audience, behavioral objectives and messages? What additional events or platforms can be utilized to deliver our messages?

- *Evaluation:* Set specific and tangible measures of success. We need to know what works and when, so we can revise our shortcomings and amplify our successes.

2. DEVICE—What is their main vehicle to consume content?

Most young men and women around the world prefer mobile devices, so we need to design our content as mobile-first. If it does not play well on phones and similar devices, don't do it. We need to be more involved in open communities where we might see conversations, topics and trends build on Snapchat, Instagram and other channels, even if content will quickly disappear after it's consumed.

- *Text:* The favorite way for youth to consume and share content, thanks to its speed, privacy and ease of use.

- *Outlets that erase history:* Snapchat, Instagram or any service that erases history is favored. No need for a digital trail.

- *The phone is the new TV:* New content, apps, entertainment and games need to be created for mobile devices.

- *Focus search on first three links:* The top-of-page effect on Google and other search engines narrows even further on mobile devices. Users focus on the first three links, with limited interest in what shows up after the first screen.

3. SEARCH—Where do I go to answer my questions?

Think of Google and Bing and other search engines as the brain of the web. If we need to know the answer for something, we type in our question or query. We do this in relative privacy. But we can see the topics for which other people search, so we should be experts in what's happening and how to leverage Internet and other social media trends. At a minimum, we need to know these three items:

- *Search trends:* We can identify the 10 most common ways people ask questions about extremist groups or related issues. What do they find from the top results for those searches? How do you make sure your anti-extremist message shows up and provides a counter-view on the first few links?

- *Search influencers:* Search engines simply organize people and outlets who share content. The search companies' algorithms organize this for us, but we need to conduct the deeper analysis. Who are the people and organizations that are on the first screens for the queries you care about? Keep expanding out from 10 queries to 100 and see what that universe looks like.

- *Impacting Search:* You already have a lot of content for your organization, or at least you can find it readily. If you know the right keywords that are linked to the searches people are making, you can see what keywords you should tag your content with, so your story starts showing up more often.

4. LOCATION—What public channels and places are most important?

We used to think in terms of newspapers and television channels, but that's not where our audience resides. If we're trying to reach youth who might shift towards hate and extremism, we need to use the same channels they do—social media and text-based services. They are not reading newspapers, listening to cable commentators or tuning in for the latest news show. They could care less.

We also can see exactly where people go, thanks to geo-specific listening tools. Yes, people can turn off sensors and make this tracking difficult, but we still can generally identify where actions are occurring online at the city, town and even neighborhood level. So, while we need to know what content our target audience consumes beyond our messaging and issues, we also need to know where to share our content both on earned and shared (social) media:

- *Social channels:* Accept that social channels are the main way to reach our target audiences. In fact, governments, such as Iran, are way ahead of the Western world on this count. Their news channels broadcast direct via Facebook. YouTube is the equivalent of TV for many viewers. People regularly share news by social channels on mobile phones.

- *Geo-location:* Enough people who utilize Twitter share their geo-locations. The same goes for a range of other social channels. In general, people are either proud of where they live or, through their online conversations, make it easy to figure out their location. We can see where conversations and actions occur over time.

5. INFLUENCERS—To whom does our audience listen and why?

The powerful 1,9,90 model reveals a lot about a target audience and the sites, organizations and individuals that influence them. We share more details on the Countering Hate website, but at a high level it shows that the top market influencers—those who continually produce content—account for just 1 percent of the audience. Another 9 percent include the people and groups that move the content around, sharing it via social media and the like. The rest of us, the 90 percent, lurk and learn. We use search to inform us or listen to inside communities, but we don't say much. Our search trail, however, shows what we care about. So, what we want to do is identify the 1 percent and the 9 percent.

- *The 1 percent:* Identify the people who routinely write about your topic.
- *The 9 percent:* Identify the people who follow the 1 percent and actively share their content.

You can do this for positive and negative topics, and it's not an overwhelming task to identify these two key groups. The 1 percent doesn't include more than 50 people who drive a particular topic in a particular country. And if you can identify the top 250 people in the 9 percent, you're in great shape.

6. THE COUNTER STORY — How are the antagonists telling their story?

Call this respect. It's important to diagnose exactly what antagonists say to recruit people to their cause. How do they position their argument? What symbolism do they use? Why is it compelling for certain people causing them to join? It feels good when someone recruits you for a cause. They show you respect when they do so. So, we encourage you to show the same respect in understanding why your nemesis is succeeding. We need to show that same respect for the recruits our enemy targets, but also for our enemies, themselves, so we can understand the underlying reasons for their success and counteract them.

One simple exercise to help in this regard: Go through the ABCDE process in No. 1 above, but do it from the perspective of an extremist group. If you can, compare your notes with other allies in the battle against hate, and then collectively analyze them against what the data show. A better picture of our enemies' successes can help us improve our interventions.

7. NEW CAMPFIRES — Where can you meet up privately?

The dark net provides a wide range of options of private forums and sites. Telegram and services like it provide ways to share content that's encrypted from end to end. We haven't set out here to try to infiltrate private, encrypted communities. It won't happen, at least not at any effective scale. Rather, our goal is to understand human behavior well enough to know that someone excited enough about hiding their actions eventually feels a need to share, brag or update their peers. Again, we're talking primarily about teenagers and young adults, for whom the need for self-identification and ego support is heightened. Here's a few ways we can keep tabs on extremists when they emerge from the shadows of the dark web:

- *Understanding Signals:* No one will surface on a social channel and say: "Hey, all of my neo-Nazi friends, let's meet up at the Blue Fin Tavern at 6 p.m. so we can plan our next protest." But they might say: "Hey, guys, Blue Fin, 6 p.m., let's catch up." If we accept that most of what we want to know happens privately now, then we become expert at listening for clues, signals or changes in behavior.

- *Recognizing Patterns:* Humans always follow patterns, even the smartest ones. What are the patterns of the people we want to watch? Do posts on Facebook increase just before protests? Do certain groups appear to align with one another across cities or countries. Who follows whom on social media? The clues are there.

- *Rethinking Policies:* We need to think about the specific, tangible goals of our campaign and how they improve the world. We can draw these goals out from various starting points, including public policy, but we need to make sure we're willing to open our minds about how we achieve them. For example, we might not shut down every new site we find, leaving some as bait to see whom they attract and the patterns we can draw from the activity surrounding them. From a policy perspective, we need to reconsider use of aggregated metadata, the analysis of which might help us identify trends of hate and extremism. This can allow us to narrow our focus enough that local law enforcement can investigate in a manner consistent with due process or other laws.

- *New Standards:* This relates to metadata, in that we need to talk about and actually write out the standards we would accept if they would allow us to learn more about extremism. Share those with your peers, see if you agree and see whether we might build enough consensus to take our ideas to elected officials. Be willing to think through how far you need to go to reach your goal, while still protecting the privacy of individuals who don't participate in terror or hate.

8. LANGUAGE — What is the importance of keywords and actual language?

When you search online for information, you ask a question that shows the words of interest to you. When we look at thousands or millions of like-minded people, the "language of search" becomes obvious for any given topic. And we can see this language, at least in part, with a Google Analytics account. As we analyze these search trends, here are markers we can watch out for:

- *Supply chain of language:* Once you know the words most often used in search, you can tag all your content on your website, social channels,

INSIGHTS FROM THE U.S. MARKETING COMMUNICATION COLLEGE

BY KIP KNIGHT
Senior Vice President, H&R Block

I've had the pleasure of teaching at the U.S. Marketing Communication College over the past 10 years with Ed Tazzia and other professionals from across the country. We've had more than 500 "students" from U.S. embassies and consulates around the globe. It's been very gratifying to work with such a talented group of State Department professionals who, to many Americans, are unknown and unappreciated for all the hard work they do.

There are three insights I've gained in doing this over the past decade:

- *We desperately need to be less country-centered and more open to other points of view:* I'm as proud as any U.S. citizen of my country, but having traveled and worked in more than 60 countries around the world, I'm continually impressed and sometimes amazed at what we could learn from others in the global community. We have plenty to be proud of in our nation, but let's give our fellow humans a bit more credit on being pretty awesome in a number of ways as well.

- *We can be a lot more impactful if we take the time to listen first, then respond:* I started my career in marketing research and continue to use the skills I learned in that role on a daily basis. Challenge your biases and assumptions when working with others, especially if they are from a different culture or country. Be open minded on their behaviors and attitudes; there are probably strong reasons they do what they do and believe what they believe. Our odds of success in communicating with anyone go up dramatically if we first ask some basic questions, such as "Why do you feel that way?" and "What makes you say that?"

- Despite the current sad state of global affairs, I remain an optimist at heart in terms of our collective future: I'm optimistic primarily because I've been around enough young people to know that most of them are more open-minded and willing to challenge historical biases and hatred. We could learn a lot from the way in which they engage with their counterparts, both in person and online. They are our best hope for getting to a better place, so let's give them all the support and help we can muster.

press releases or any public form of content you share. This will help people find your messaging. Perhaps even more important, if we share these keywords with allied groups, they could use the same keywords and leverage the effect. This would have the impact of multiple groups impacting search far faster and better than if you do it individually. Search engine optimization (SEO) can be a team sport.

- *Accelerator and detractor words:* if we look at a community closely, we can see which words accelerate search behavior and which ones decelerate it. We can continually improve our understanding of how to speak in ways that align with the audience we want to reach.

- *When keywords change:* If you are following the top 50 influencers for your topic, you'll notice when they start discussing a new topic and/or start using different language. Normally, influencers are one or two months ahead of the general marketplace. So, if you see them using new words, you might want to start retagging your content with those words, and perhaps start addressing their key topics earlier than ever before.

9. ALIGNMENT—Why is it important to work as a team, even if our causes are different?

When we think of alignment and the Media Campfire—the places where people come together to converse—we really do want to have a Kumbaya moment. The original meaning of Kumbaya is "come by here," and the lyrics derive from a spiritual song that was an appeal to God to come and help those in fellowship and in need. When it comes to marketing, we all are in need, so here are a few simple ways we can align around the Media Campfire:

- *Keyword sharing:* As noted above, share the keywords that matter so you can all use the right words and more effectively impact search for the greater good.

- *Follow each other:* If another group in your country or another country anywhere in the world is aligned with your cause, follow them on Twitter, Facebook, LinkedIn, Instagram and any other channel you utilize. Share key follower lists with each other, or simply look at the followers of like-minded groups and start routinely following their most ardent fans. This makes a more powerful media ecosystem, so if one group speaks, a much wider audience hears what you are saying.

- *Accelerate learning:* We set up a Facebook community so we can all share, learn and grow together. We all can learn from our successes and our failures, and it might be more important to share the latter for the greater good.

- *Tracking trends:* Your group might see certain antagonists rise up more often, or you might notice an uptick in recruitment in a given city. You might see things that merely interest you, but reveal a critical trend when combined with the insights of 30 other groups battling the same issue. Often, we can identify trends just by sharing notes among different locations worldwide.

10. FUTURE RISKS — What is the risk if we do not work together in the world of media?

Extremists appreciate our fragmented and uncoordinated counter-hate initiatives. Most terrorist groups already coordinate far better than we do, and they do it across the globe, too. It's really not all that complicated.

When Walmart founder Sam Walton was asked why his company had become so successful, he replied simply but powerfully: "We're all working together; that's the secret."

Let's make that our secret too.

CHAPTER 20

IMAGINE OUR WAY FORWARD

*"You may say I'm a dreamer
But I'm not the only one
I hope some day you'll join us
And the world will be as one"*

—John Lennon

Imagine you were born today. You probably arrived in a part of the world where you and your family will struggle, either financially or socially. As you grow into a teenager and young adult, local authorities will trample upon your rights, or at least leave you feeling oppressed by the local culture, religion or state. You will look around and recognize that your elders are unemployed and resigned to a life that doesn't look all that promising. And you'll start to wonder where your life will go next.

What you won't think about is whether to go to Oxford or Yale, which new car you might get, or what summer job you'd like to score. Your concerns for the future are far more fundamental: *Will this life get better? Whom should I trust? Why does the world seem pitted against me?*

Many people will compete for your attention as you mature, each trying to feed you answers to those questions. Some have great intentions; some know you're vulnerable and ripe for manipulation. Those people, whether well-intentioned or not, will help shape your outlook right as you're figuring out who you are and what you stand for.

You'll have plenty of help no matter where you live, and so will they. You'll have a phone, so you can meet new friends around the world via social media. Each day, their words, actions and approach to their lives will help you define what's important for yours. The unique set of messages from local media and the government will shape your outlooks on society and authority. When you leave your house, you'll have times where you are teased, ostracized, yelled at and ignored by the very people you thought you could trust. You might pretend it doesn't matter, but either way it hurts. You'll frustrate your parents — as all teenagers do — but they'll compete for your attention and try to guide you, anyway.

Slowly, haltingly, you'll start down the road you want to take. And as you commence the journey, you'll form memories and habits that will shape your view of yourself and the world around you for the rest of your life — as everyone does from birth to 25 years old. Will you love, or will you hate?

| ▌ ▌ |

If you're reading this book, you can make a difference. *We* can make a difference. We can become one of the online voices that makes a positive impact. We can support groups who reach out and become the new friends that make a difference. We can support parents in the hardest job of their lives: raising their children. Through sports, entertainment, education and all the other activities that every child anywhere in the world enjoys, we can help our young men and women form memories and habits that lead to lives of peace and fulfillment.

But none of this happens if we nod in agreement as you put this book back on the shelf, and then go back to the daily grind. The world doesn't improve if we all tacitly agree and refuse to act. So, join and support an NGO. Donate to an organization that works to counter hate. Share your knowledge in the Facebook community to help fight extremism around the world. Donate your time to help one child at a time. Ask one friend to join us in helping others.

This threat of extreme hate and all its manifestations can overwhelm us if we think we need to solve it all at once. Start with the idea of saving one young man or woman. Just take that one small action. After all, with 7.5 billion of us around the world, we have the law of large numbers working in our favor. If we focus on this goal together, we will guide generations of youth toward productive, peaceful ways to process and express the feelings and contradictions of adolescence. It really is up to us.

| | ▌ | |

The Dave Matthews Band has a song called "Funny the Way It Is," and its lyrics remind us of just how urgent our mission is:

"Funny the way it is, if you think about it
One kid walks 10 miles to school, another's dropping out
Funny the way it is, not right or wrong
On a soldier's last breath, his baby's being born
Funny the way it is, not right or wrong
Somebody's broken heart become your favorite song
Funny the way it is, if you think about it
One kid walks 10 miles to school, another's dropping out"

Imagine you were born today. Like every other child across the globe, you won't begin your life on an irreversible path toward hate and extremism. Yet, in today's world, a growing number of your peers will take that route—unless the rest of us join together and help the amazing organizations and individuals who've dedicated their lives to making the world a more peaceful place.

We look forward to countering hate with you.

BOB PEARSON | HAROON K. ULLAH

ACKNOWLEDGMENTS

We have been continually humbled and inspired by the leadership and commitment of our colleagues in government, NGOs and the private sector to make our world a safer place.

Great initiatives neither happen overnight, nor are they the work of a single person, which is why we would like to say thank you to all of the teachers who have found time to share their insights as part of the U.S. Marketing College. Starting in August 2008, this group has included Kip Knight, Ed Tazzia, Jim Nyce, Mike Ribero, Gary Briggs, Elana Gold, Rachel Makool, Griff Griffity, Nigel Hollis, Matt Ackley, Shawn Mielke, Mark Kleinman, Eureka Ranch, Norm Levy, Cassidy Dale, David Knight, Gordon Wyner, Klon Kitchen, Victoria Romero, Kelly Hlavinka, George Perlov, Mike Linto, Dave Wallinga, Stan Slap, Andrea Cherng, Rob Malcolm, Terry Villines, Nancy Zwiers, Tim Love, Pete Carter and Kimberly Doebereiner.

In particular, Ed Tazzia, Kip Knight, Jim Nyce, Gary Briggs and Mike Ribero deserve a second round of applause for being part of this illustrious group since its formation.

Of course, none of this happens without strong coordination on the State Department side, as well. We would like to thank the entire team who has been involved.

As authors, we enjoy writing and will continue to write as long as the ideas are flowing. What we appreciate as much as our writing is the editing that can make the difference in a book. And for this, we are very thankful to have partnered with Dan Zehr, who is an excellent editor, thinker and just a fun person with whom to conceptualize a book. For Bob, this is his third book written with Dan's support.

This book, as you know, is about so much more than we could hope to tackle in one sitting, which is why we are honored to have sidebars written by such a powerful and smart group of global leaders. We thank each and every one of them for taking the time to stop, contemplate and add insights that have made us all think about how we counter hate.

The making of the book has involved several key leaders who operate behind the scenes for the reader, but certainly not for us. Tamara Dever, who leads the book-making process for us at TLC Graphics, along with Monica Thomas have done their usual amazing job.

Vanessa Hess, who is Bob's colleague at W2O Group, has been our project manager, ensuring we stay on schedule, have regular update calls and, when the book started to take form, jump right in (as she always does) to help us with everything from formatting the final manuscript to outlining our incoming side bars.

We then get to the cover and when we talk about the cover, all we can say is "wow!" Paulo Simas, the chief creative officer for W2O Group, has this innate ability to listen to us and then come back and say, "Is this what you meant?" We can only look at his creation and say "Well, actually, you went way beyond what we were saying and just nailed it." Paulo's gift with art pushed us to match his cover with our words. We hope we did alright.

Each of us had to put aside many personal activities to complete this book, which is normal, of course, but still leads us to thank those who have supported us. Bob would like to thank his wife, Donna, for listening to concepts, reacting to ideas and offering encouragement during weekends or evenings when the caffeine has worn off, but a concept still needs completion.

And finally, and most importantly, we thank all of our friends, colleagues and people who we have never met, but who gave their lives in the fight against extremism. You might not be here physically, but you are here in spirit, and we are doing our best to represent you for the future. In your memories, we will donate the proceeds of this book to Vetted, a new organization led by Michael Sarraille, which is creating an innovative educational curriculum and transition program for military veterans who leave the field of battle and return home to begin a new chapter in their lives.

May we all join together to listen, learn and act to make our world a safer place.

BOB PEARSON | HAROON K. ULLAH

March 15, 2018

ABOUT THE AUTHORS

BOB PEARSON

Bob is Vice Chair and Chief of Innovation for W2O Group. He has written two books on digital innovation (*PreCommerce* and *Storytizing*). Prior to W2O Group, Bob developed the Fortune 500's first global social media function at Dell and served as Head of Global Corporate Communications and Head of Global Pharma Communications at Novartis in Basel, Switzerland. His board service includes The Advertising Research Foundation, the MedicAlert Foundation, and the Vetted Foundation. Bob resides in Austin, Texas with his wife Donna and two daughters, Nicole and Brittany.

HAROON K. ULLAH

Haroon is Chief Strategy Officer for The Broadcasting Board of Governors. He previously worked on Secretary of State Rex Tillerson's Policy Planning Staff covering digital innovation, public diplomacy and public/private partnerships. He previously advised three Secretaries of State, traveled with Ambassador Richard Holbrooke's Afghanistan/Pakistan team, and started the first-ever public diplomacy countering violent extremism office at an American Embassy as the Director of the Community Engagement Office at the U.S. Embassy in Pakistan.

A visiting professor at Georgetown University and a Term Member of the Council on Foreign Relations, Haroon has written award-winning books, including *Vying for Allah's Vote* (Georgetown University Press), *The Bargain from the Bazaar* (Public Affairs Books), and the *Digital World War* (Yale University Press), which focuses on new uses for technology, transmedia, and digital content. Haroon resides in Washington, D.C.